A Lynching
in Little Dixie

A Lynching in Little Dixie

The Life and Death of James T. Scott, ca. 1885–1923

Patricia L. Roberts

McFarland & Company, Inc., Publishers
Jefferson, North Carolina

LIBRARY OF CONGRESS CATALOGUING-IN-PUBLICATION DATA

Names: Roberts, Patricia L., author.
Title: A lynching in Little Dixie : the life and death of James T. Scott, ca. 1885–1923 / Patricia L. Roberts.
Description: Jefferson, North Carolina : McFarland & Company, Inc., Publishers, 2018 | Includes bibliographical references and index.
Identifiers: LCCN 2018028649 | ISBN 9781476674926 (softcover : acid free paper) ∞
Subjects: LCSH: Scott, James T., approximately 1885–1923. | Lynching—Missouri—Columbia—Case studies. | African American men—Violence against—Case studies. | Columbia (Mo.)—Race relations—Case studies. | United States—Race relations—Case studies.
Classification: LCC HV6462.M8 R63 2018 | DDC 364.1/34—dc23
LC record available at https://lccn.loc.gov/2018028649

BRITISH LIBRARY CATALOGUING DATA ARE AVAILABLE

ISBN (print) 978-1-4766-7492-6
ISBN (ebook) 978-1-4766-3486-9

© 2018 Lawrence D. Roberts. All rights reserved

No part of this book may be reproduced or transmitted in any form or by any means, electronic or mechanical, including photocopying or recording, or by any information storage and retrieval system, without permission in writing from the publisher.

Front cover image of noose in a tree © 2018 Mshake/iStock

Printed in the United States of America

*McFarland & Company, Inc., Publishers
  Box 611, Jefferson, North Carolina 28640
  www.mcfarlandpub.com*

Table of Contents

Preface by Lawrence D. Roberts   1
Introduction   3

1. The New Mexico Mystery   11
2. The Place   21
3. Columbia and the Civil War   32
4. Reconstruction and Beyond   40
5. Life in Chicago   54
6. What James Scott Was Missing Back in Columbia   71
7. James Scott's Possible Great Adventure   95
8. Whose Side Are We Fighting on Anyway?   117
9. Sweet Land of Liberty   131
10. The Last Week   144
11. The Aftermath   159
12. Still Partially Cloudy   171

Chapter Notes   181
Bibliography   187
Index   191

Preface
by Lawrence D. Roberts

Patricia L. Roberts (Pat) researched and wrote the present book over a period of twelve years. While in the final stages of this process, she had a cerebral hemorrhage, resulting in a coma, and six weeks later, her death. I am her husband. For many months I was too sad to work on her book, but eventually I finished the references, and added this preface. The rest of the book is entirely Pat's work.

Pat was the love of my life, and the superb mother of our two sons. She read widely, including many novels. Her undergraduate studies were diversified, and she ended up with a degree in philosophy from Indiana University, membership in Phi Beta Kappa, and graduate fellowship offers. She received a graduate degree in art from the University of Idaho. She always was an artist (as were her father and a grandfather), and after working in painting, print making, and drawing, she switched to photography. Her art often involved humor, and a keen perception of social issues. The present work came from many years of applying her abilities to historical research.

Pat's artistic sensibilities underlie her vision of James Scott. She gives a picture of the historical conditions and events in which Scott lived, thereby describing what an African American man had to deal with in our culture. Scott lived in New Mexico, Missouri, and Chicago, and also in France. While in Chicago as a young man, Scott joined the 8th Infantry of the Illinois National Guard. The 8th was an all-black organization, and with it Scott trained in Chicago, Texas, and France. Then his regiment, entirely under the control of the French, fought in World War I, playing an important role in defeating the German army.

Two questions are basic to this book: who is James Scott, and how could a place like Columbia (home to the University of Missouri) provide a thousand-member audience for a lynching? In answering these questions, Pat's point of view and sympathies are clear, but she usually lets readers draw

Preface

their own conclusions from the historical and cultural surroundings of Mr. Scott's life.

I wish to thank (as well as I can remember) those who helped Pat in her research and writing: Douglas Hunt, Patrick Huber, David Saap, Saral Waldorf, Susan Wyler, and Robin Green; also in this group are the Rev. Clyde Ruffin and members of the Second Missionary Baptist Church in Columbia, who organized a tribute to James Scott in 2012. For editorial help, I am grateful to John Vernon, friend and author of several historical novels. Finally, I thank family and friends who helped me in dealing with grief, and getting to work on completing Pat's book.

Introduction

In the spring of 2003, my cousin called to tell me I should look at a series of articles that had just appeared in the *Columbia Missourian,* the newspaper the University of Missouri's School of Journalism puts out. "You'll be surprised by what you read," she said. Because the *Columbia Missourian* was one of the first university newspapers to go online, within minutes I was reading the account of an event that had taken place in Columbia 80 years before. Here's a short version of what my cousin thought would surprise me.[1]

On a warm April afternoon in 1923 a black man was standing on a bridge near the university. When a 14-year-old girl came by, he told her there was a baby on the railroad tracks below. The girl climbed down the ravine to rescue the child while the man followed behind. When he grabbed her, she tried to fight him off, smashing at his face and hands so hard with her umbrella that it broke. As the attack was going on, a railroad work crew went by on a pushcart. The girl cried out, but no one heard her. Stuffing a dirty handkerchief into her mouth, he continued his assault. According to newspaper reports the next day, this ended only when the girl tossed out a 50-cent piece from her pocket. Though the man said he didn't want it, he nevertheless went to gather it up. Then ordering her not to move, he scrambled back up the hill as she lay trembling on the ground. Sometime after this, she stood up, climbed the ravine and walked slowly to her house several blocks away, fainting once or twice along the way.[2]

A day later, police picked up a black man named James T. Scott, a 35-year-old janitor at the university. He was paraded in front of the girl's house along with several other black men who sported the "Charlie Chaplin" moustache she had described her assailant as having. The girl, watching from inside, identified Scott as her attacker. On two more occasions she confirmed this identification, saying he had the same voice as her attacker and the same "strange looking" eyes. Six days after he was first identified, James Scott was officially charged and jailed. That night, a mob of white men broke into the

Introduction

jail and dragged Scott down to the same bridge the young girl had been crossing a week before. Two men tried unsuccessfully to stop them, but with the crowd urging him on, a large white man put a rope around Scott's neck, lifted him onto the railing and pushed him over. More than a thousand spectators from the university, the town and the surrounding county gathered to watch this happen. Many of them laughed and clapped when Scott died.

Though I have never lived in Columbia, Missouri, I have visited many times. Each Thanksgiving and Easter when I was a child, we would make the round trip from St. Louis to Columbia to celebrate the holidays with the grandparents. My grandfather taught for over 40 years in the German department at the university before he retired in 1943, and the family lived only a few blocks from where the lynching occurred. But in all those years my grandparents never mentioned that event. Only when I began to read the articles in the *Columbia Missourian* did I understand why.

The 14-year-old girl who had been attacked on that warm April day in 1923 as she walked home from a music lesson was my aunt, Regina Almstedt, and one of the men who had tried to stop the lynching, the one who had walked hurriedly from his house on Garth Avenue to confront the crowd on the bridge, was my grandfather, Hermann B. Almstedt. This was the same man who had declared to a reporter soon after Scott's lynching that the matter would never be spoken of again within his family: "We want to try to forget this trouble as soon as possible and lift the cloud that has been hovering over my house for more than a week." And except for a brief visit by his wife and daughter to a nearby town two and a half months later in connection with the lynching, he and the rest of the family kept my grandfather's pledge.

Mental health professionals tell us that keeping secrets can be harmful to individuals and to family relationships. But that does not seem to have been the case here. My grandparents and their four daughters remained a loving, intact unit until death dissolved their ties. My aunt grew up to marry and have a family. She exhibited no signs of overt racism and, in fact, was a caring employer to an African American woman who worked for her for many years. (This is not, I am quick to acknowledge, the same thing as having black friends whom you treat as equals. But in St. Louis in the 50s and 60s, not many whites in her social circle had black friends.) I will never know if Regina Almstedt Hardy felt remorse for what her identification of James Scott indirectly caused. As my grandfather had hoped, no one ever spoke directly to the subsequent generation about the incident.

When I first read about the attack, I wondered how it had felt to live

Introduction

through what could only have been that first horrendous experience, then realize this was just the beginning of a series of events that would swiftly culminate in the death of the man you had identified, a man whose final words continued to declare his innocence. Innocence may be the operative word here—the innocence of a fourteen-year-old destroyed in an afternoon, the guilt or innocence of a man who was killed without being able to defend himself at trial, and finally, the damaged innocence of a group who had not previously seen themselves as hosts to a lynching. Because to me, that is what the more than one thousand people who stood watching a black man being thrown over a bridge railing with a rope around his neck now were: co-conspirators to a murder.

I knew the story of my aunt, but what of the other participants in this drama? James T. Scott was by all accounts a respected man in the black community and an unlikely rapist (for this is what the charge ended up being; the attacker probably did not stop when money was thrown his way, as earlier newspaper articles had reported.) As a janitor at the university, Scott held a steady job and made more money than many black men who lived around him in a segregated section of Columbia. At the time of the lynching he owned a car, and two years before, he had married a local schoolteacher, the daughter of a well-respected Columbia couple. James Scott, or Scottie, as he was said to be called, was not considered by his neighbors to be the kind of man who would attack a white girl, or any girl for that matter. Yet my aunt had identified him three times, and as a result he had been killed. Could he really have been a rapist? Even more out of character was the fact this lynching took place in a college town, the kind of place with which I am familiar since I've have spent my adult life married to an academic. When I read about the events of that year, I was confused. Didn't most lynching happen in the South, and wasn't Columbia solidly part of the Midwest?

The more I thought about what had happened, the more I felt I wanted to try to learn the answers to two questions: first, who was James Scott, and second, how could a place like Columbia provide a thousand-member audience to a lynching? My aunt lived beyond this tragedy, leaving it so effectively behind that we of the next generation knew nothing of it until 80 years later. It turned out the citizens of Columbia were in a similar position. The May 2003 articles in the *Columbia Missourian* were as much of a surprise to many Columbia residents as they were to my family and me.

James Scott disappeared in the early morning of April 29, 1923, his only memorial until recently a small metal plaque in the black section of a Columbia cemetery. But I knew he could not have existed solely as a victim. He was a man who lived his short life in a changing world. The laws enacted after the Civil War gave African Americans their freedom, but it was a freedom that collided with the customs that resolutely kept them subjugated by the larger white world. In finding out who James Scott was, I would be reversing this disappearance, and in the process, getting a better understanding of how African Americans moved through the world as the century changed. I might also be able to give back to his family some part of what my aunt, with her identifications, took away.

What I offer here is not a document written by a scholar. Nor have I managed to find out a great deal about James Scott's actual life. What I have tried to do instead is place his life in a context, and by doing so, acknowledge how slowly our country moved toward racial equality after the Civil War. That this movement wasn't as strong as it should have been in 1923 is a given. That it continues today in Columbia, Missouri, and elsewhere is another given.

Some Difficulties in What I Propose to Do

Having announced, if only to myself, this plan to write about James Scott's life, I began to think what a good biography might look like. Not surprisingly, I remembered the first biographies I read: the orange-covered books I had loved as a child.

In 1932, Bobbs-Merrill began a series entitled "The Childhood of Famous Americans." Less than 20 years later I was reading titles like *Kit Carson: Boy Trapper*, *Clara Barton: Girl Nurse*, and *Jane Addams: Little Lame Girl* (political correctness had not been invented then.) The series' subjects included *Booker T. Washington: Ambitious Boy*, and *George Carver: Boy Scientist*, though I don't remember seeing either of these volumes on my public library shelves in St. Louis. The "Childhood of Famous Americans" series has now been taken over by Simon & Schuster with 70 titles and growing. The number of black subjects has also grown and includes the childhoods of famous Americans like Frederick Douglass, Sojourner Truth, Harriet Tubman, Langston Hughes, and Jackie Robinson. Even Ray Charles makes an appearance.

What I did not realize as I was reading these stories filled with vivid descriptions and conversations was that their authors—and there were many, my favorite being a school teacher from Indianapolis, Indiana, named

Introduction

Augusta Stevenson—had made up some of this material. So this is why I loved these stories so much—they were fiction rather than fact, though to the man who became president of Bobbs-Merrill in 1935, they were above all an introduction to biography. According to D. Laurence Chambers, the background was to be authentic and the book true to the time and place of the subject.[3]

Arnold Rampersad,[4] a professor at Stanford and biographer of such famous figures as Langston Hughes and Richard Wright, has said biography is the history of an individual, and as such, is a branch of history. His point, like that of Chambers, is that none of us lives in a vacuum. Even when we do not participate directly in the politics and wars, or the economic and social upheavals of our time, as the famous American kids of my childhood grew up to do, we are affected by what is happening around us in our present lives and what has happened in the past. As we live, we live *through* history, not realizing how much of the contours of what we would describe as our life stories are influenced by the pressures from outside.

What this means for me as I try to write a biography of James Scott, a notably *not* famous American, is that most of what I will be describing will happen outside the immediate details of my subject's life. As much as I enjoyed those Bobbs-Merrill biographies, I won't be adding fictionalized details or making up conversations. I won't be writing about what I don't know, and in the end, this may be a lot. Especially in the early days of our country, black lives were either forgotten or erased. Scott's ancestors, for instance, would have been nameless if they had shown up on the slave schedules of 1850 and 1860; there men, women and children were listed only by age, sex and color (black or mulatto as judged by the census takers.) Or consider a more recent example: the entire neighborhood in which Scott lived while he was a resident of Columbia has disappeared, razed during urban renewal in the 1950s. The list of disappearances goes on and on.

Besides not knowing, an even bigger problem in writing about James Scott's life may be not understanding. There are several reasons for this inability on my part. First, the history I read and the history I am going to recount to you was, more often than I would have liked, written by white authors. George Orwell has famously said history is written by the winners, and for African Americans, especially during the time James Scott lived, this situation is largely true. But an even bigger misunderstanding awaited me.

According to Sherley Anne Williams, a poet, novelist and critic, "The chasm between black and white life in this country is such that we have been

Introduction

unable to legitimately disabuse ourselves of the idea no white person can truly see through the eyes of a black person." She made this observation in *The Seductions of Biography*, a collection of essays edited by Mary Riehl and David Suchoff, and she is not alone in believing no white person is capable of experiencing the world as a black person does. In 1903, W.E.B. Du Bois wrote of the veil that separates the black world from the white: "Then it dawned upon me with a certain suddenness that I was different from the others; or like [them perhaps] in heart and life and longing, but shut out from their world by a vast veil."

Whether I take the veil Du Bois writes about in *The Souls of Black Folk* to mean the literal coloration of the skin, or a screen that doesn't permit whites and blacks to see each other with clarity, an obstacle remains. Louis Harlan, Booker T. Washington's biographer, explains this difficulty in another way by suggesting that from childhood on, black people are forced to wear a mask and to act in a deceiving manner when they are present in the white world; thus, there is always a line between performance and self. Whites can only know the performance. For all these writers and others in the past and the present, the gulf between the white and black worlds continues to exist, despite Emancipation, despite ratification of the Thirteenth, Fourteenth and Fifteenth Amendments, and, I would add, that despite the fact a black man was twice elected President of the United States, it would be presumptuous of me to think that I, with all good intent, could somehow bridge this gulf.[5]

The historian and biographer Jonathan Spence has described biography as a search, and ultimately a search for self-understanding. The search I embarked on initially was for the facts that would make up James Scott's life. Where was he born? Who were his parents and their parents? Where did he live growing up? What happened to him during World War I? And finally, did he attack my aunt, as the newspapers of the time stated? As I sought answers to these questions and others, I often veered off into more diffuse fields. I followed paths that led nowhere and others that led me to a better understanding of what was happening just outside James Scott's immediate life as he grew into a man. I will never to be able to tell you how James Scott felt about what was happening around him as he made his way in the world. If he communicated those thoughts and feelings to others, nothing beyond the words he uttered at the end of his life were saved (and those were transcribed with uncertain veracity by white reporters). Nor will I be able to write a narrative based on one event following close upon another, all of them building to an heroic end. This will not be the vivid, fast paced biography like the ones I read as a child.

I cannot tell you what it was like to be black during the years 1884 to 1923, but I can tell you what I have learned, and it is this: to navigate the boundaries of what was permissible and available to a black man in the early part of the 20th century took intelligence, strength and perseverance. For those of us who have never faced the kind of barriers that could pop up as suddenly as a white man's challenge to move off a downtown sidewalk, or an angry mob surrounding the streetcar on which you were riding, we will have to use our imaginations and our empathy to understand how James Scott lived. I hope I can make the reader feel how continually dangerous it was for a man like Scott, who to my knowledge never directly challenged the barriers he faced but instead chose to work around them. The biographies I loved as a child were about all heroes and heroines, and while they were partially made up, they celebrated the bravery of their subjects. This biography is not made up, but otherwise I hope you will see it is not so different. It is about a man who was as much hero as victim, like most black people who lived during this time.

A Note About Terms

In 1808, the Constitution put into effect a prohibition against the slave trade. Before then, the men and women brought from Africa referred to themselves and were referred to as "Africans." (They chose this term only because they were not allowed to keep the separate ethnic and tribal affiliations that were more meaningful designations to them.) In the years after 1808, as more and more slaves were born in the United States, the term "African" lost some of its appeal. Black leaders at the time hoped that by dropping the allusion to Africa they would eliminate the possibility of repatriation. They chose instead the term "Negro" (the Spanish word for black) or "Colored American," a phrase denoting the wish to achieve full citizenship in this new country. A few official hold-outs, like the African Methodist Episcopal Church, remained, but until the late 1960s, most blacks and whites used the terms "Negro" and "colored."

When it is a matter of historical accuracy, such as in the chapter on William Elwang's 1904 dissertation or citations by writers such as W.E.B. Du Bois, I use "negro" or "Negro." This is the term Scott would have heard during

Introduction

his lifetime, and it continued into the early 1960s. In his 1963 "I Have a Dream," speech Martin Luther King uses "Negro" 15 times and "black" only four times, and then as part of a parallel construction with "white." Still, "black" was in usage for many years before civil rights leaders like Stokely Carmichael decided to discard "Negro" with its connotations of legalized discrimination, and instead to emphasize "black" as in "Black Power." Not everyone agreed. Jesse Jackson later promoted the use of the term "African American," because he felt it had a stronger historical and cultural basis.

After Emancipation, slaves often renamed themselves, casting off their slave names for others they chose for themselves. In the same way, I have primarily chosen to use "black" or "African American" rather than "Negro," even though Scott may not have heard these terms in his short lifetime. I have done so to reflect the choices made by those who are choosing today.

1

The New Mexico Mystery

In a small, engaging book called *Talking About Detective Fiction*, mystery writer P.D. James tries to explain the fascination we have with detective stories. They work, she says, by bringing order to disorder and by using human ingenuity instead of relying on luck or divine intervention to reaffirm our hope—often dashed in real life—of living in a world where problems can be solved by rational means.[1] Learning about James Scott's life has turned out to be a kind of detective story, and while I have stuck to rational means, there were moments when I might have wished for divine intervention or at least luck in finding out what was really true. The mystery of where he was born is one such moment. I followed the clues, though at times they led me astray, and in the end, I had to choose the mostly likely solution rather than the certain one. The solutions to other mysteries, like who James Scott's father was, have eluded me entirely. But for now, since most detective stories start with a body, that's where I too will begin.

James Scott's death certificate was filed April 30, 1923, one day after he was lynched. On it he is described as a Colored male, married to one Gertrude Scott and employed at the time of his death as a janitor by the University of Missouri. He is said to be thirty-five years, six months and twenty-three days old when he died, and his birthplace is listed as New Mexico. The name of James Scott's father is also listed. He too is called James Scott, though his birthplace has not been filled in. On the line for maiden name of mother, "Sarah Brown" has been written, and her birthplace recorded as Missouri. The provider of all this information is Gertrude Scott of Columbia, the dead man's wife.

While none of us live solely through the vital statistics of our lives, public documents like birth and death certificates, marriage licenses and census reports do provide clues to our journey through life. They would seem to be the firm reckoning points on our own personal timelines. But as I began my detective work to find out who James Scott was, I discovered some of these official reckoning points are less than firm. Nowhere is that more apparent than in Scott's date of birth, which on his death certificate appears as October 6, 1887. That would be fine, except on the 1900 Federal Census, Scott's birth year is listed as 1885, and ten years later on the next census, he is said to be born in 1886. Then there is Scott's draft card for World War I, where his birthday is registered as October 6, 1884. Most confusing of all are the two appearances Scott makes on the 1920 Federal census. In the first, likely taken at his residence, an unknown informant tells the census taker Scott was born in 1891. A few days later another census taker appears at his work to record his birth year as 1887. Thus we have at least seven pieces of "official" evidence of James Scott's birth date if we include his marriage license to his second wife, which records him as twenty-six in June 1912. This last date means his birth year would have been 1885 if we believe he was born in October, the month that is listed in three of these documents.

So what year did James Scott begin his life? The answer took me another few months, and some luck, to answer and even then the evidence is not conclusive. This detective work is going to be more difficult than I expected. The Missouri Board of Health issued James Scott's death certificate on April 30, 1923. Having realized the birth date on the death certificate may not be accurate, I turned a suspicious eye on the other "facts" recorded there. James Scott's birthplace is listed as New Mexico. Could this be true? Could Scott's parents who, I later learned from the death certificate of Scott's brother Akers, were both born in Missouri, have been living in New Mexico in 1887? (Or 1884 or 1885 or 1886?) They are not listed in New Mexico in the 1880 Federal census. Instead, in 1880 Scott's mother Sarah appears as a sixteen-year-old living in the Columbia, Missouri, household of her parents, Thomas Akers and Ophelia Crockett. The 1890 federal census better matches the 1887 birth date on Scott's death certificate, but unfortunately most of that census was lost in a fire. It would not have placed them in New Mexico, anyway. According to another piece of evidence I found, Akers Scott's death certificate, by June 21,1888, their mother was back in Columbia, giving birth to him. Or was she?

I was still suspicious of Scott's New Mexico birthplace even after I found it listed again, this time on his son Carl's social security application. By this time I have come to realize that official documents can contain mistakes and recorded facts can be disputed. Since Scott's birth date has been officially recorded as anywhere between 1884 and 1891, maybe Scott's place of birth was wrongly recorded too. Carl, who was only eight and a half when his father died, could merely have been repeating what he had heard growing up when he filled out his social security application in 1937.

1. The New Mexico Mystery

Because of these doubts, I felt somewhat confidant and even a little self-congratulatory when I came across a marriage license that says a James T. Scott (the name of Scott's father) had married a Miss Walmoth A. Brown in *Mexico*, Missouri, on December 27, 1886. Mexico, Missouri, is in Audrain County, the country right next to Boone County where Columbia lies. The ages of the couple seemed right too. This James T. Scott is listed as over the age of twenty-one, and Walmoth over the age of eighteen (I knew by then that according to her death certificate Scott's mother had been born in 1865.) In addition, "New Mexico" was the name originally given to Mexico, Missouri, and while the "New" was dropped after the Mexican-American War of 1846–1848, I found it conceivable this first designation continued on in people's everyday usage. So, privately patting myself on the back for being such a good detective, I decided *my* James T. Scott was born in Missouri like the rest of his immediate relatives. Yes, Walmoth was not a name his mother ever used, but many blacks changed their names after Emancipation, and while the "Sallie" that appeared in the 1880 census bore a greater resemblance to the "Sarah" by which Scott's mother was later known than did the name "Walmoth," I decided the latter might be a name anyone would want to get rid of.

Even after seeing Scott's birthplace listed as New Mexico on several census reports (including one where the informant could only have been his mother!) I persisted in thinking the New Mexico designation had been a mistake. Then I began to do more reading about the migratory habits of blacks after the Civil War. Showing up in the state of New Mexico in the 1880s didn't seem all that impossible, I discovered.

African Americans were on the move after 1865, and many did head west. The War had settled the question of slavery, but racial prejudice and discrimination never really disappeared. When federal troops were withdrawn from the South in 1877, many freed slaves realized their rights could now be freely violated. Wary this violation would happen to them or watching as it did, they packed up their belongings to head north and west. Called "exodusters," they came up the Mississippi River to St. Louis, often spending all the money they had on boat fare. The black community in St. Louis arranged jobs and food for these emigrants so they could continue on to Kansas, which had been a free state, and beyond. Did James and Sarah Scott decide to join them as they passed by Columbia? Others certainly had, some leaving even earlier than 1877. In the five years after the Civil War ended, the population of one Missouri county had decreased by more than one thousand. Freedmen in the state were searching for places where they could form their own households instead of 'living in' with white families. They were looking for land to farm that was their own, and as farm machinery replaced workers, even those who had stayed were forced to move to the bigger cities where there were more opportunities for jobs. There were many reasons to leave Missouri at the time Scott's parents would have done so, and once I learned something of its history, New Mexico turned out to be a reasonable destination.

Near the end of the Civil War, black troops, the so-called "Buffalo Soldiers," were sent into the New Mexico Territory to protect settlers from Indian raids. Stationed at Fort Selden, about twenty miles north of Las Cruces, these regiments were in the Territory from 1867 to 1891. After the war had ended, some of the Buffalo Soldiers came home to tell their friends and family about life out West.[2] Black migration to the area began. According the Federal census, in 1860 there were eighty-five blacks in all of the New Mexico Territory. By 1880 that number was more than a thousand, and ten years later, almost two thousand blacks lived there.

There was another reason why James Scott's parents might have gone to New Mexico. During the years after the Civil War, more railroads came into Missouri, arrivals that changed forever how its citizens, both black and white, saw time and distance. Now a trip between towns could be done in hours instead of days. Cities in the East and territories in the West were not merely names but possible destinations. In Columbia, the first attempt to connect the city by rail came in 1867 when the Boone County and Jefferson Railroad, a company formed by several prominent Boone County business men, laid tracks from Columbia to Centralia, Missouri, a city to the north some thirty miles away.[3] Columbia, which had been a stagecoach stop on the Santa Fe Trail, was now connected to a railroad system that by the turn of the century would include one hundred and forty-six railroads operated by fifty-eight separate companies in the state. One of these railroads was the famed Atchison, Topeka and the Santa Fe (later shortened to the Santa Fe) that began carrying passengers into the New Mexico territory in 1879.

Black settlers coming into the territory after the war had sought to take advantage of the Homestead Act of 1862, which offered free Federal land to claimants. By the 1870s, freedmen had established the town of Dora near the eastern edge of the territory below Albuquerque. Later a former slave from Georgia, Frances Boyer, created an all-black town, Blackdom, near Roswell. Initially a community of some twenty black farms, Blackdom's later population grew to five hundred, with many of the residents coming from out of

1. The New Mexico Mystery

state. Blackdom was incorporated in 1911, and when it was abandoned several years later during the Dust Bowl and the Great Depression, Boyer created another city, Vado, below Las Cruces, which survives today though its African American population has been replaced by Hispanics.[4] So New Mexico with its all black towns was certainly a possible destination for Scott's parents. Did they head for one of these?

I discovered the answer to this question when I come across the birth certificate of James Scott's second daughter, Helen, a few months into my search. Here in the space left for father's birthplace someone has written "Lansvagus, New Mexico." Finally, I have the name of the actual town in New Mexico where James Scott was born, a name given by the one person who should know best: the baby's father himself, James Scott.

It turned out there is no Lansvagus, New Mexico, but there is a Las Vegas, New Mexico, and in the 1880s, it was a booming place.[5] Most of us are too young to have seen a Tom Mix movie, but many of the more than a hundred westerns he made for the Selig Polyscope Company in the early 1900s were filmed in Las Vegas, New Mexico, on the banks of the Gallinas River that runs through the Great Plains where they meet the Sangre de Cristo Mountains. Established in 1835 when a group of settlers received a land grant from the Mexican government, Old Town Las Vegas was laid out in the traditional Spanish Colonial style with adobe buildings surrounding a central plaza, a design that could serve as fortifications in case of attack. The city flourished as a stop along the Santa Fe Trail for caravans heading west, and when these same caravans made a return trip to east, they often took with them donkeys from the area to sell in Missouri. News from these caravans may have been how Scott's parents heard about Las Vegas. But it wasn't donkeys that created the biggest boom in Las Vegas after the railroad appeared. It was a hotel.

On July 4, 1879, the first Atchison, Topeka and Santa Fe train pulled into town, or rather into New Town, established about a mile east of the Old Town plaza. A mining engineer visiting Las Vegas at the time described leaving his hotel on the day before the train arrived to see two men hanged from a high windmill in the center of the plaza. They had been lynched as part of a cleanup effort the citizens of Las Vegas decided to engage in before the festivities began. Usually vigilantes left their hanging victims on display until noon to give sufficient warning to potential evil-doers, but in deference to the celebration the next day and because town officials needed to decorate the windmill with appropriate banners, the engineer reported the men were taken down early.[6]

A Lynching in Little Dixie

In the month before the railroad arrived, lots had been laid out in New Town and building begun. By the end of August houses and shanties of all sizes and description were scattered around the depot, and more than a thousand new residents had arrived. The streets had been laid out on a grid like an Eastern city, but with more saloons and dance halls than banks, the place had an appearance of a frontier town. Gambling and prostitution flourished openly, at least at first. The dance halls were filled with accommodating women along with gambling rooms for those customers who didn't want to dance. In 1883, law officers cracked down, with the result that the dance halls were put out of business and prostitution and gambling went underground. As the 1880s continued, bathhouses and hotels were built, and horses or mules pulled streetcars along a track laid down between Old Town and New Town. Two miles north of town, the Santa Fe Railroad built a company hospital in 1884. If James Scott's mother had given birth in a hospital, it would have been here. Unfortunately, no records are left from that time.

While the first buildings in New Town were not impressive, a Romanesque-style Masonic Temple and a neo-Classical bank would later appear. What had been built by time the Scotts were in Las Vegas was the Montezuma Hotel or Castle. Six miles northwest of town, the Montezuma in each of its incarnations—for it burnt down twice—was a magnificent sight. In 1879, the same year the railroad arrived, Jesse James had visited his childhood friend Scott Moore, originally from St. Joseph, Missouri, at Moore's Adobe Hotel at Hot Springs. A few months afterwards, Moore sold his interest in the land around the hot springs to Eastern investors, who built a three story stone hotel and separate stone bathhouse for approximately $75,000. In 1880, the Santa Fe Railroad bought the property, and two years later they laid down a railroad spur to the springs. The first Montezuma Hotel had three hundred rooms, a dining space that seated five hundred, and a casino that could hold a thousand customers. When the hotel caught fire in 1884, it could not be saved because of a lack of water pressure (though volunteer firemen did manage to rescue some of the bottles from the wine cellar.) The railroad company rebuilt nearby in another, even more scenic location, and this time the opulent quarters were heated by steam manufactured from gas on the grounds. Visitors came in droves, and famous guests included Ulysses S. Grant and Rutherford B. Hayes.

I mention the Montezuma because it is one of the likely places James Scott and his wife might have worked after coming to Las Vegas. They could also have been employed by the railroad or in other hotels in Las Vegas like the Plaza. Blacks then did not live in a particular residential area, and if James

1. The New Mexico Mystery

had grown up in Las Vegas, he would have attended the public school open to everyone. Fabiola Cabeza de Baca, who was born into a rich Hispanic family in 1898, describes the Las Vegas of her youth as a very democratic town where there was no discrimination as to race or color.[7] This may be hyperbole, but she does write fondly of one local resident, her neighbor, Montgomery Bell, the son of slaves from Missouri, who was called at one time "the wealthiest Negro in the Southwest."[8] Bell, who was born in 1845, arrived in New Mexico with the Stephen Elkins family sometime before 1864. Elkins, who had fought in Missouri on the Union side while his father and brother were fighting with Sterling Price's Confederate forces, had moved to New Mexico to start a law practice. He subsequently provided financial help to Montgomery Bell, the son of one of his family's slaves, so Bell was able to open a store in Las Vegas. (Bell also worked as a manager at the Montezuma Hotel, and later dealt in real estate and livestock.) According to Cabeza de Baca, members of the Bell family who lived near her grandmother, were among the finest people she knew. Bell had by thrift acquired a huge fortune, and Cabeza de Baca reported he was a friend to poor people by becoming their money lender (one hopes not at usury rates). Montgomery Bell's position as a prominent member of the black community in Las Vegas makes it almost certain James's parents would have known him, especially since he came from their home state.

If James Scott's mother was in Columbia as a sixteen-year-old in 1880, and she was back again to have her second son in 1888 as Akers's death certificate declares, the years in which she and her husband James would have lived in Las Vegas were few. That they had gone out there, presumably by railroad, I now found believable. Columbia had a railroad line that went to Centralia. From there Scott's parents would have taken the Northern Railroad to Moberly and Kansas City, then caught the Atchison, Topeka and Santa Fe line out to Las Vegas. In 1885, the Santa Fe, or "Great Middle Route" passed through Las Vegas, New Mexico, on its way to Albuquerque where, changing to the Atlantic and Pacific line, passengers could travel all the way to San Francisco. The Atchinson, Topeka and Santa Fe brochure[9] grandly describes a trip that traverses a region whose climate is "but a modification of perpetual summer" and possesses "the striking wonders and most remarkable scenes of nature." Besides the adobe towns, Pueblo villages, and the natural wonders of Garden of the Gods and Cheyenne Canyon, the brochure lists in both large and small type, "Las Vegas Hot Springs, with its colossal hotel and unequaled pleasure grounds and baths." A round trip excursion fare to Las Vegas in 1885 is a mere thirty-two dollars, and for six dollars extra, one can purchase a berth.

The brochure also records a diary of travel from Kansas City to Las Vegas and beyond, so if James Scott's parents were aboard, we can easily trace their journey. The train would have pulled out of Kansas City at 10:40 in the morning and arrived shortly after noon in Lawrence, Kansas, a town identified in the brochure as "victim of the greatest tragedy of the late war" (the massacre of 182 Lawrence residents by Quantrill's raiders in August 1863). Less than an hour later, they were in Topeka, Kansas, the actual starting point of the Santa Fe Route. Topeka, with its large yards and machine shops to service the trains, served as the home of the Santa Fe railroad. At this point, dinner would have been offered to James and Sarah in the dining cars. Through that first afternoon, Scott's parents could look out on the fields and orchards of central Kansas as the train stopped first at Emporia, Kansas, around four, then Florence a little after five. Here the Santa Fe Route connected with a line to El Dorado in the south. By 6:25 the train was in Newton, Kansas, in what the brochure describes as the "heart of the now famous Cottonwood Valley, not long since an Indian-haunted wilderness, where even they and the buffaloes were considered bad off." The dining car was open again, beginning to serve supper as the train moved into western Kansas. If James and Sarah had paid six dollars extra, they would have had a berth for the night. If not, they slept all night in their seats.

When they awakened, they were on the eastern edge of Colorado, and at 7:10, the train pulled into in La Junta as breakfast was being served. James and Sarah were now five hundred and seventy miles west of Kansas City. At about 12:30, the train moved into the tunnel at Raton Pass, a narrow passageway between Sangre de Cristo Mountains, the southernmost range of the Rocky Mountains in North America, and the Great Veda Arch. According to the brochure, "This is the ancient gateway of the 'Santa Fé Trail', 7,622 feet high, and, as nearly as it may be located, the crest of the continent." James and Sarah had reached New Mexico. They pulled into Raton at 1:15 when dinner was again about to be served. This second afternoon instead of Kansas's fields and orchards, they looked out at mountain scenery until they entered the wide green meadows the Spanish called 'vegas." At 6:45 that evening, the train pulled into Las Vegas, New Mexico. From here travelers could take the spur up to the Las Vegas Hot Springs, and the "magnificent Montezuma Hotel" or continue west to Albuquerque. It seems unlikely that James and Sarah joined the more affluent travelers who had come to enjoy the "plea-

1. The New Mexico Mystery

sure grounds and medicinal baths." That is, unless they were going to the hotel for employment. But like all those who had purchased tickets on the Atchison, Topeka, and Santa Fe, they had traveled approximately eight hundred and seventy-five miles through three states in matter of thirty-two hours, leaving behind the fields and farms of the Midwest for the open lands of New Mexico.

What they did in Las Vegas and how long they stayed there—it turns out James's brother Akers was probably not born in 1888 as his death certificate states—remain mysteries for which I have no real answers. But because of what I learned later, I can put forward this guess. James Sr., and Sarah certainly could have gone to Las Vegas to get better jobs. The Montezuma was hiring, as were other hotels in the town. But another possibility is that they went west because James Sr., had lung problems, and they felt the drier air would help him. I offer this suggestion, because at one time tuberculosis was one of the leading causes of death in America, and in the 1880s those who suffered from it often moved to mountains and deserts in the hope of a cure. About the time James and Sarah were heading to New Mexico, the territory had just begun to advertise its healing climate in order to gain more residents and move closer to statehood. So, for instance, in an 1882 publication *New Mexico: The Tourists Shrine*[10] the writers make the point that New Mexico has the lowest death rate from tuberculosis. In the same year The Atchinson, Topeka, and Santa Fe Railroad Company, as part of a promotion to get people to travel to the Southwest, opened the Montezuma Hotel as a healing destination. An actual sanatorium, St. Anthony's in East Las Vegas, began to operate in 1897.

Is this enough to prove James Sr., went to New Mexico for his health? Of course not. But then I found one more fact that makes my supposition a little stronger. While Las Vegas continued to grow economically into the 1890s, rivaling towns like Denver and Tucson in size, by the turn of the century, the Scotts no longer lived there. The 1900 census records Sarah's address and that of her son James as Chicago, Illinois. And brother Akers, who turns out to be older rather than younger than James, is, according to that same census, living on a farm about fifty miles away in Indiana. But what of James Sr.? The majority of the 1890 census had been destroyed in a fire, but when I moved to the 1900 census, I could find no direct evidence of him in Illinois, Indiana, Missouri, or New Mexico. Instead, I saw that on June 9, 1900, when Sarah Scott was asked by the census taker what her marital status was, she replied that she was a widow.

There are over thirty cemeteries in and around Las Vegas in San Miguel County. Through the efforts of the New Mexico Genealogical Society, visitors can search each one online to find a name. Many of the cemeteries lie outside Las Vegas and contain only Hispanic names, but I looked through them all. Of special interest was the Masonic Cemetery in Las Vegas, which actually contains three cemeteries—Odd Fellows, Masonic, and Montefiore. There are 2,350 names in the index of the stones in these three places, and from the time the list was first compiled in 1978 and rechecked in 1982, several of the names had become illegible. So not finding James Scott's name in this index would not be definitive proof he isn't buried there. Like most of the research I was doing, only a positive result—i.e. finding him listed—would be conclusive. There were two Scotts listed, but neither Orpha, born in 1879, nor George B. born in 1876, seemed to offer much help. I later found a large New Mexico Death Index, but unfortunately, it begins in 1889, or right after the year I am assuming he might have died. (Just to be sure, I entered his name and got no responses, though again, this is not conclusive evidence.)

My hunt for information on James Senior's death was unsuccessful, but this overall search didn't end in complete failure. After doubting James Junior was born in New Mexico, I became a believer, and in reaching this belief, I followed a path that would occur again and again as I continued my detective work. The actual "facts" of the case turned out to be few in number, and often they contradicted one another. With only this evidence, I wouldn't be able to draw many conclusions about James Scott's life. But when I combined the facts I knew with the pieces of history I was learning, I could at least posit some suppositions about what was possible.

Proceeding this way, I began to understand more about the life James Scott might have lived, a life I now believed started in Las Vegas, New Mexico, and ended in Columbia, Missouri, though whether it was thirty-five years, six months and twenty-three days later as his death certificate says, I still don't know.

2

The Place

    I don't know exactly when we started going to Columbia for our Thanksgiving and Easter holidays, but I remember the long car rides through what seemed to be empty farmland before we finally pulled into the driveway at my grandparents' house. At the time they lived on Westmount, two blocks west of their original home on Garth Avenue, the house to which my aunt returned after the attack and from whose porch she identified James Scott the first time. Often on Thanksgiving Day before the big meal, my brother and I would be taken downtown to see a movie to get us out of the way. Columbia felt like a big city to me then, with a fancy theater and diagonal parking along its main street. It also seemed like a small town, since inevitably my grandmother would meet someone she knew as we walked toward the theater. My grandfather, by then long retired, always stayed home, most often behind a closed door in his small study at the end of the hall. Children were allowed in there only by invitation, and my brother and I spent much of our visit being told to be quiet so my grandfather could work or rest. Occasionally, we would be taken on campus—I remember attending a play there with my grandmother when I was a teenager—but more often we stayed around the neighborhood. I don't remember the railroad tracks or the bridge—by then replaced—that went across Stewart Street. Nor do I remember seeing one black person anywhere, though, of course, many lived in Columbia at the time.
    How do I explain the difference between this pleasant Midwestern college town I visited as a child and the place that produced an audience of more than a thousand for a lynching some thirty years earlier? That is the other mystery I hoped to solve when I began this book, and to do so, I need to know more about the history of Columbia and the surrounding area. Within minutes of starting this investigation, I discover my first mistake: Columbia is not really a part of the Midwest but instead sits in a region of Missouri still known to some as "Little Dixie." Seven counties bordering the Missouri River

received this name because their earliest settlers came from the South bringing with them both the agricultural practices and the societal beliefs of their home states. Slavery had some of its firmest roots in Little Dixie, and racial discrimination died a hard death—if indeed it ever has. Columbia began as an outpost of Southern sentiment. The question for me will be how long and in what manner it stayed that way.

As early as 1803, frontiersmen were trying to move into the part of the Louisiana Territory that would later become the state of Missouri.[1] The territorial governor at the time, Amos Stoddard, regarded settlement as an intrusion on Indian lands, and because he did not have enough troops to protect the settlers he discouraged them from coming. But still they came. After Lewis and Clark reported the appearance of salt springs in what would become parts of three Missouri counties (Howard, Cooper and Saline), two of Daniel Boone's sons set out to establish a salt business at what was thereafter called Boone's Lick. Though the Boone boys didn't stay long, by 1811 several hundred families lived in the area around the salt licks. This homesteading was helped by a treaty the Osage Indians had signed in 1809 allowing settlement on their lands—a goodwill gesture that came back to haunt them. Five years after the treaty was signed, settlers in Boone's Lick petitioned Congress to extinguish Indian title to the land, and in 1815 Congress complied. But the greatest influx of settlers into Little Dixie didn't wait for the Osage to lose claim to their property. They began to arrive after the War of 1812, with the largest number coming from Kentucky, where James Scott's maternal grandparents were born; Virginia; North Carolina and Tennessee. They sought fertile ground along the Missouri River in which to plant their crops, and fertile ground it was, so dark and fine an early resident described it as looking like gunpowder. With these settlers came the slaves needed to clear the land and to provide the prodigious amount of hand labor required to produce tobacco and hemp, two of the area's major crops. Farmers in what would become Boone County also planted rye, hay, wheat and corn, all with the help of indentured servants.

In 1810, there were a little over three thousand slaves in the whole of the Missouri Territory.[2] Ten years later that number had more than tripled. In Boone County, where Columbia is located, the slave population increased each year from 1830 to 1860. In 1830, almost two thousand slaves lived and worked here. This was a little over 21 percent of the county's population. By 1860, the slave population had grown to slightly more than five thousand or almost 26 percent of Boone County's residents. According to James McGet-

2. The Place

tigan in his series on slave transactions in Boone County,[3] the two factors that accounted for this continual increase in slave population were the growing number of slaveholders coming into the area and the size of the birth rate for slaves compared to their death rate. For example, in the year ending 1850, McGettigan reports 141 slaves were born in Boone County while only sixty-one died. In 1860, figures estimated from the slave schedule show 175 slaves born with only sixty-two dying.[4] (Interestingly enough, this same ratio of birth to death numbers will be used later to prove the inherent weakness and ill health of Columbia's black residents.)

The majority of slaves in Little Dixie were employed in agricultural work, but unlike the Deep South, Missouri, did not have many large plantations. So while in states like Georgia, Alabama, and the Carolinas, 12 percent of slave owners owned more than 75 percent of the slaves; in Little Dixie only 4 percent of owners owned more than twenty slaves in the years between 1830 and 1860.[5] A more usual number was much smaller. For instance, in 1860, according to that year's federal agricultural census, approximately 83 percent of slaveholders in Boone County owned nine slaves or less. Almost 50 percent owned from three to nine. On smaller farms, family members usually worked among the slaves without the intercession of an overseer. Because of this daily proximity of farmers and workers, it was said slaves in Little Dixie received better care than their relatives in the Deep South. This may have been true—but only if one ignored the basic tenet on which slavery operated: slaves were property, and as such they could be bought, sold or hired out. In Boone County all three actions happened frequently, but not always in a manner we associate with slavery in the Deep South.

In general the people around Boone County did not appreciate slave traders coming in from outside, feeling these men conducted a necessary but sometimes brutal business without a conscience.[6] This antipathy to outside traders is borne out by the fact that in the years from 1820 to 1845, no advertisements for slaves appeared in the Boone County newspapers publishing at the time.[7] This did not mean there weren't slave traders in in the county, however. In the July 14, 1848, *Missouri Statesman*, William H. Northcutt of Columbia placed an ad announcing the highest cash prices would be paid for "young likely negroes." Thomas Selby, owner of the Columbia Hotel, was another Columbian who tried his hand at buying and selling slaves. His first notice for buying twenty slaves appeared in the *Statesman* in January of 1849 and ran for almost five months. In both cases, the purchase and sale of slaves in Boone County does not seem to have been a particularly vibrant business. Little Dixie's farmers and planters did buy slaves, but more often than not it was done so privately from other planters or farmers. They also purchased slaves, sometimes with only a down payment, at courthouse estate or bankruptcy sales. McGettigan reports that from 1820 to 1864 bills of sale for slightly less than 1,100 slaves show only six slaves were bought by traders.[8] The majority of slave sales were between local owners.

More popular than selling slaves was hiring them out. This was done either as a business or during estate settlements. In the forty years before the Civil War, over 60 percent of the estate settlements in Boone County involved hiring out slaves who, as property, had become part of the probate process until a final disposition could be made.[9] Often the heirs to an estate would buy the slaves themselves, thereby gaining not only a slave but also some of the profits from the sale. While this practice meant slaves frequently passed on to family members, the likelihood slave families would stay together was not much greater than if they had been sold to strangers. In the almost ninety slave owners' wills McGettigan examined, he found only one owner who tried to safeguard the slave family in his possession. Henry M. Clarkson asked in his 1858 will that "all members of the same family of slaves shall, when practicable, be distributed to the same heir."[10]

Slightly more frequent were wills in which a master had made a provision for their slaves to be freed. James Laughlin's will, for instance, stipulated not only that his servant boy Edmund be freed, but that he also be given the gift of Laughlin's colt, bedding and wearing apparel. Robert M. Hayden upped the ante on this generosity by supplying his slave John with a horse, saddle, and bridle, plus one hundred dollars at Hayden's death. Still, a declaration of emancipation by the deceased could subsequently be ignored by the heirs. William H. Northcutt, the fellow who advertised for slaves in Columbia, stated that his servant Lewis should be freed on the death of Northcutt's wife. McGettigan found probate records that showed Lewis was not freed but sold. And when Thomas Ridgway died in 1861, his will gave freedom to all his slaves and left one of them, Nancy, his 112-acre farm and all she needed of his personal estate, which included livestock and household goods. This did not happen. Instead the court hired all Ridgway's slaves out and continued to do so through 1864.[11]

Slaves who were to be traded or lent out in Little Dixie were often kept in fairly good condition and provided with an adequate diet. What they were not provided with was an education. Most slave owners did not want their

2. The Place

slaves to learn to read or write, a desire made law as early as 1825 when masters were relieved of the duty of teaching reading, writing and arithmetic to apprentices (who were often slaves). More definitively, Missouri passed a law in 1847 prohibiting a slave from learning to read or write—a prohibition, however, some owners ignored. As slaves were lent to adjoining or distant farms, they began to extend their community and their knowledge. This increased learning made them more likely to run away and therefore, dangerous to their owners, or such was the perception. To control this danger, slave codes modeled on those of Virginia were established in Little Dixie and elsewhere in the state. Whippings could not be more than thirty-nine lashes, and when done by a county sheriff, they were executed with an instrument shaped like a paddle, the flat portion covered in fiber-backed rubber. The blows from such a device were extremely painful but did not leave lash marks, which might have detracted from the worth of the slave.

Whippings were not the only punishment slaves received. In 1843, for example, five slaves near Columbia were involved in the axe-murder of their master. Two received the thirty-nine lashes and were banished from the state, but two others, one of them a woman, were sentenced to public hanging. What drew my attention to this account was that more than two thousand spectators gathered to witness these executions in a town of eight hundred.[12] Thus, the large crowd that came to see James Scott lynched had an historical precedent eighty years before.

Other rules to control slaves included those regarding assembling by slaves. These were rigorously enforced, so it was only in the presence of a white man that slaves could, for example, conduct church services. In 1833, the state legislature passed an act that prohibited storekeepers or tavern owners from allowing either slaves or freedmen from assembling on the storekeeper or tavern owner's premises unless the slaves had been sent by their owners.

When I began my detective work, it seemed likely James Scott's ancestors were slaves. The 1860 federal census records the number of freedmen in the entire state of Missouri as 3,572 while the total number of slaves was 114,931. In Boone County the number of freedmen was even smaller—fifty-three. I knew from the 1880 census that James Scott's maternal grandparents had been born in Kentucky, Thomas Akers around 1830, and Ophelia Crockett in or around 1838. The approximate nature of these dates is not unusual. Many slaves, especially in the early part of the nineteenth century, when asked the year of their birth, could only give an approximate date or associate their birth with a major event such as the election of a new President or the failure of a crop. Henry Clay Bruce begins his memoir by declaring, "My mother often told me that I was born, March 3rd, of the year that Martin Van Buren was elected President of the United States, and I have therefore always regarded March 3rd, 1836, as the date of my birth."[13] Slave family history was primarily oral with few written records unless they appeared in a family Bible. As for James Scott's paternal grandparents and great-grandparents, I am less certain. Whoever they were, given the ratio of freedmen to slaves in the state, a reasonable assumption would be they had been indentured at some point in their lives.

But reasonable or not, it turned out at least some of James Scott's maternal relatives, while they began their lives as slaves, had freed themselves before Emancipation. These transitions began with James Scott's maternal great-grandfather, a resourceful man named Gilbert Akers. Also known by the surname Robinson, Gilbert Akers was brought to Columbia from Logan County, Kentucky, by his owner in 1842. Seven years later Robinson/Akers was able to purchase his freedom with his savings. His owner appears not to have fared as well financially as his former slave. James R. Boyce worked in merchandizing until 1863, when he left Columbia for Denver, Colorado, a departure that may have been precipitated by having his property seized after he spent the early part of the Civil War in the Quartermaster's Department of the Confederate Army.[14] From information recorded in Deed Book S from the Boone County Recorder's Office, we know Gilbert Robinson/Akers was thirty-seven when he purchased his freedom,. Three years later Akers bought the freedom of his wife Susan, James Scott's maternal great-grandmother. She was also approximately thirty-seven years old at the time of her manumission. As he prospered, Akers purchased his children's emancipation too, though he insisted they pay him back.

Of the fifty-three freedmen in Boone County recorded in the 1860 census, thirty-four are adults. All are self-supporting, but only twelve of them own property. The largest landowner among them at this time is Scott's great-grandfather, Gilbert Akers. Akers (still called Robinson then) is said to own two thousand dollars worth of real estate along with a thousand dollars of personal wealth.[15] In 1854, Akers had purchased six lots in Columbia for a hundred dollars from his former owner, James R. Boyce. This was almost an entire city block at the time. Later Akers bought an additional lot for eighty dollars, which he then sold to another freedman for three hundred dollars. He also owned forty acres outside the city for which he paid almost eight

2. The Place

hundred dollars. Another freedman with real estate holdings in the city was John Lang, who had come to Columbia in 1850, his security posted by James Shannon, the president of the university. A year later Lang opened a butcher shop, the first business of its kind in Columbia.[16]

What kind of city was this, I wondered, where six years before the Civil War, freedmen could own large amounts of property and flourishing businesses in a town situated in the heart of Little Dixie? Did Columbia really share the Southern sentiments of its neighbors or was it different? The answer turns out to be more complicated than I expected. For one thing, feelings of support for freedmen like that shown by President Shannon for John Lang were hardly universal. As early as 1835, a meeting was held in the Presbyterian Church in Columbia to establish a Colonization Society dedicated to assisting freedman in Boone County to emigrate to Africa.[17] This was part of the larger American Colonization Society established in Philadelphia in 1816 to deal with the problem of emancipated blacks who, it was felt, imposed a burden on white society. The Columbia chapter of the Colonization Society continued to operate well into the 1850s, and as emancipation became a possibility, the chapter's desire not to co-exist with blacks was extended to all blacks, not just those already free.

Columbia's history was unusual in that the city evolved from a small rural settlement to a sophisticated college town in a matter of a few years. In 1818, a group of settlers in the area realized the increasing population around them would ultimately result in the establishment of another county. So they formed a company to speculate on where the seat of that new county might be. Choosing fertile acreage midway between what they thought might be the county's eastern and western boundaries, Smithton Company investors bought about two thousand acres during a government land sale in November 1818. They divided their purchase into eleven and forty acre plots and platted a town named after the company. When early Smithton residents were unable to get usable water from the wells they dug, company trustees decided to move the town east to a spot along the bank of Flat Branch Creek. The new site was called Columbia, a popular name at the time. When the state legislature passed an act to establish the new county in 1820, the citizens of Columbia were ready. A donation to the state by the city of fifty acres, two public squares, $2000 and two wells sealed the deal. Columbia was now the county seat of the newly created Boone County. The rather primitive log cabins that had been erected at Smithton were hauled over to Columbia, and in the spring of 1821 the new city was laid out. The first house was said to be a log cabin that stood on the corner of what became 5th Street and Broadway. A hotel and the first brick house were built in 1821, and the first business, a grocery, stood on another corner of 5th Street and Broadway. As William F. Switzler describes it in his *History of Boone County*, in 1821, Columbia did not attain a greater growth than fifteen or twenty houses, all of them were mud-daubed log building of the smaller size, and but one story high. They were situated in a 'clearing' in the midst of stumps and brush, while all around stretched a dense and trackless wilderness.[18]

The author of this somewhat grim description was originally a resident of Kentucky who had come to Columbia in 1841 at the age of twenty-one to use the law library of James S. Rollins, a well-known lawyer and legislator in the city. By the time Switzler passed the bar in 1842, he had assumed the post of editor of the *Patriot*, a Whig paper in Columbia. When two years later he was offered the chance to buy a half interest in the paper, he accepted and changing its name to the *Missouri Statesman*, he continued on as editor for the next thirty-two years. Colonel Switzler, as he was later called, became a force in Missouri politics after the war, and his name appears in this account of Columbia's history more than once.

In the years between the incorporation of Columbia in 1826 and James Scott's great grandfather's arrival with his owner James Boyce in 1842, not only were more businesses created and expanded, but two colleges were established. The first of these was Columbia College, chartered by the legislature in 1833, with classes starting in 1834. But an even bigger prize for Columbia was winning the bid to establish the state university there in 1839. Nine hundred citizens in Boone County pledged a total of $117,921 in cash and land to beat out five other counties to build what would be the first public institution of higher learning west of the Mississippi. More schools followed. In 1851, Christian Female College was chartered, and in 1855, Baptist Female College was established. Both schools continue to this day, albeit with new names (Columbia and Stephens). Of course, none of these schools allowed black students (the University of Missouri at Columbia did not admit African American undergraduates until 1950 when ordered to do so by the courts), but they did provide employment opportunities for black men and women in town. Both Christian College and the University of Missouri hired enslaved women and girls as domestics and laundresses, and enslaved men and boys to do janitorial work and odd jobs. When James Scott began to work as a janitor at the University of Missouri medical school in 1920, he was following a long tradition of employment for black men and women on campus.

2. The Place

Slavery continued to be the underpinning of agricultural practice in Little Dixie, and it also functioned as an integral part of Columbia's economy. Black women and older girls worked as domestics in town, doing laundry, cooking, and sewing for white families and businesses. Male slaves who worked in skilled professions like carpentry and blacksmithing saw their worth increase when they were offered for sale or hire. The April 12, 1845, *Missouri Statesman* contained a notice of sale for a Negro who was a hatter by trade. Other owners sought to sell a shoemaker and a teamster. Hiring out skilled slaves was a valuable business, and losing one meant less income for the owner. Here is Mrs. Walter Lenoir in 1852 writing to her sister back in North Carolina about her misfortune: "I was so unfortunate to loose [*sic*] Anthony with Cholera in August. he was hired in Town at $25.00 a month, it is a great loss to me, he generally made me $1.00 every day he worked."[19] Skilled slaves could on occasion even earn income of their own. Under state law slaves were not to possess money, but local practice sometimes allowed slaves to work for themselves during the "Long Sabbath," from Friday sunset to Monday dawn. In the April 24, 1854, issue of the *Statesman*, a runaway slave is described as having "the best clothing," and "a fine gold watch and plenty of money," all acquired because he was a blacksmith by trade.

As Columbia grew, it became more cosmopolitan. The first theater in the state started there in 1832, and two years later the well-known artist George Caleb Bingham opened an art studio. But this apparent sophistication did not dispel the city's belief in and dependence on slavery. In 1854, the Kansas-Nebraska Act was passed. Originally meant to open the area for a transcontinental railroad, the final bill did a lot more. It repealed the 1820 Missouri Compromise, which had forbidden slavery in the Louisiana Territory above the 36'30" parallel, except for Missouri, and it allowed settlers within the territories of Kansas and Nebraska to determine the issue of slavery for themselves. In Kansas pro-slavery settlers and abolitionists poured in from outside to influence the vote. In adjacent Missouri, those who believed in the institution began to get worried.

On Saturday, June 2, 1855, William Switzler reports a public meeting was held in Columbia. The location had originally been the courthouse, but the crowd who assembled was too large to fit into the building so they moved east of the city to the fairgrounds. The topic to be taken up was the recent activities of abolitionists in Kansas, but the bigger concern was states' rights and the ability of the Union to hold together. Switzler was one of the main participants, and his account in the *History of Boone County* paints a vivid, if perhaps biased, picture of the feelings elicited as the important men in the county attempted to put forward a series of resolutions that all could agree upon.[20] The group broke up into two factions: the Whigs and the Democrats. After they reconvened, Switzler read out the eleven resolutions of the Whig contingent, which he later characterizes as "national, conservative, loyal to the South and to the Federal Union." These resolutions clearly assert the rights of the slave States and severely condemn the heresies of "Abolitionism, Freesoilism, and Nullification."

Now it was the Democrats' turn. Among their resolutions was a call for domestic slavery to be regulated only by the municipal policy of the states. Any interference in the institution of slavery in the States and the Territories would be an unpatriotic destruction of "our domestic peace," and an insult to "the sovereignty of the slave States." But the Democratic resolutions, unlike those of the Whigs, went even further in their protection of slavery. Arguing that human government exists in accordance with the will of God and the consent of the governed "if they are morally and intellectually qualified for self-government," the Democratic preamble asserted that if a government failed to protect its citizens, it was the inalienable right of those citizens to take matters in their own hands using extra-legal means if necessary. In the case of Abolitionists, who seek "to render our slave property insecure, and to excite the evil passions of those slaves to insubordination," the Democrats asserted citizens were justified in abating this through means "peaceable if we can, forcible if we must." In other words, Democrats were ready to fight to retain their justly held property. They went on to warn the Free States that if the Abolitionists were not controlled, the Union was in peril. Resolution 8 is especially direct in its opinion:

> 8. That the whole State is identified in interest and sympathy with the citizens on our western border; and we will co-operate with them in all proper measures to prevent the foul demon of Abolitionism from planting a colony of negro thieves on our frontier, to harass our citizens and steal their property, it matters not whether that colony be imported from European poor-houses and prisons, or from the pestilential hotbeds of New England fanaticism.

According to Switzler, what happened next was "considerable excitement and disorder." Someone called for both sets of resolutions to be adopted while another voice countered that the sets needed to be voted on separately since he had found several resolutions in the second, Democratic, set "very obnoxious." A third man suggested they vote on every resolution separately. At this point, "noise and confusion bore sway." Finally, someone took charge, and

2. The Place

the first set of resolutions, those of Switzler and his group of Whigs, were put up for a vote and passed with a majority. When the chairman held a second vote on whether to consider the second set of resolutions, the response was unclear. Sterling Price, Jr., an adjunct professor at the university and the son of a man who will figure prominently in the Civil War, attempted to bring the second set of resolutions to a vote. He was joined by James Shannon, president of the university, who said that he had opposed the first set of resolutions because it contained, in his words, "a lurking treason to the South." When this attempt at consensus failed, those who favored the Democratic resolutions withdrew from the meeting and at some distance away reconvened to pass their own set unanimously.

What this debate tells us is that while all the powerful men in Columbia and Boone County were united in seeking the protection of the institution of slavery, there were some who would do so even if it meant the dissolution of the Union. And they were not alone. Missouri's residents, as the Civil War began, may have been divided in their desire to remain part of the Union, but they were not divided in their belief in the institution of slavery. The Abolitionists who existed in the state were the minority, and almost none of them lived in Columbia.

As I read Switler's account of this 1855 meeting, what struck me was the Democrats' assertion that under certain circumstances (in this case the government's failure to protect their property) it was the *inalienable right* of citizens to take matters in their own hands. Is this the same right the men who took matters in their own hands to lynch James Scott felt they had sixty-eight years later? Certainly, the idea that popular sentiment supercedes governmental law has a long history in our country, and in 1855 popular sentiment about the status of slavery was strong in Columbia and the rest of Little Dixie. Slaves were property, and as such, no government had the right to take them away from their owners.

However, how to defend this proposition soon became a more difficult question to answer.

3

Columbia and the Civil War

Before 1860, most white residents of Columbia were united on two propositions: that Missouri should not withdraw from the Union and that slavery must continue. When Lincoln was elected in November and in the next month South Carolina seceded, these two propositions started to come apart. By the time the President took office in March, six more states had followed South Carolina's lead. Lincoln gave his first inaugural address on March 4, after which the *Missouri Statesman* reassured Columbians the President had provided adequate guarantees slavery would not be interfered with in the states where it now occurred and fugitive slave laws would be faithfully enforced. The writer of the editorial, the newspaper's editor, William Switzler, told his readers Lincoln was "for conciliation not coercion."[1] But when the Confederates fired on Fort Sumter April 4 and Lincoln responded by calling for federal troops to move in, the balancing act between protecting slavery and staying in the Union became more difficult.

On Saturday, April 20, 1861 a meeting of those interested in Southern rights was held in Columbia at the courthouse. Once again, William Switzler was there and as he notes in his *History of Boone County*, "Something of the temper and sentiments of a portion of the people may be gathered from the proceedings."[2] After the meeting was called to order, the speaker declared a committee of two representatives from each township be formed to prepare a set of resolutions reflecting the position of those present. Just as the committee was retiring to do its job, a group of men entered the courthouse, carrying a Confederate flag. A cheer went up for Jefferson Davis and the Confederacy. Then someone stepped up to list in "an eloquent and patriotic manner the many insults and injuries which have been heaped upon the South by the fanatics of the North." The committee resolutions that followed were full of condemnations of President Lincoln, beginning with the accusation he provoked war by sending an armed fleet into Charleston Bay forcing the Border States to choose

3. Columbia and the Civil War

either with the fanatical Abolition and negro-worshipping States of the North, in the subjugation of their brethren of the South ... or of uniting their destinies with their sister Southern States and resisting to the death the tide of Northern fanaticism and aggression which threatens to overwhelm and annihilate the dearest rights and liberties of a free and independent people.

The twelve resolutions that followed were affirmed with deafening applause.

Sixteen days later an even larger group of men from Boone County gathered in the same courthouse to offer their support of the Union. Again a committee was formed to draft resolutions expressing the opinions of those present. The document that came out of this committee begins in the following way:

> WHEREAS, Civil war has been inaugurated in the United States, brought about by the extreme men of the North and the extreme men of the South; and whereas the State of Missouri occupies a position central between the two extremes, and has hitherto earnestly opposed all hostile demonstrations on the part of either; therefore, Resolved, 1. That the true policy of Missouri, at present, is to maintain an independent position within the Union—holding her soil and institutions sacred against invasion or hostile interference from any quarter whatever. 2. That we approve and indorse the reply of the Governor of the State of Missouri to the Secretary of War, in refusing to furnish troops for the purpose of coercing our Southern brethren. 3. That patriotism and policy, and the preservation of the public peace, alike require on the part of the Federal Administration a prompt and immediate recognition of the Southern Confederacy, as a government de facto, and forming an alliance, offensive and defensive, with it, for mutual protection. 4. That in our opinion Secession is a remedy for no evil, real or imaginary, but an aggravation and complication of existing difficulties; but if we are reduced to the necessity of engaging in the present war and strife, that then we will stand by and co-operate with the South...[3]

Three additional amendments were added, but unlike the earlier Southern Rights meeting, when the resolutions began to be offered up for a vote, the group could not reach consensus. Odon Guitar, a lawyer in Columbia who had served in the Missouri House of Representatives and who owned slaves, stood to say he did not want to influence anyone else, but he could not endorse either the third or fourth resolution that called for a recognition by the Federal Government of the Confederacy and a willingness to co-operate with the Confederacy. This was, he said, the time to answer a single question: "Are we for our country or against it?"[4] Guitar did not believe in the right of secession and even less in the concept that had been put forward of "peaceable secession." When another prominent Columbian, F.T. Russell, who later became a colonel in the Union Army, responded that he saw the choice as one between recognition of the Confederate states or war, and he

A Lynching in Little Dixie

preferred recognition, an amendment that explicitly repudiated the constitutional right of secession was offered. The resolutions were voted on again and passed with Mr. Guitar as the only negative vote and several others abstaining. Elder T.M. Allen, a preacher and slave owner, spoke last, making what was described by Switzler as "an eloquent appeal to people to maintain an armed neutrality with the Union, and not be driven away by passion and prejudice into the dangerous experiment of revolution and anarchy."[5] While Elder Allen's plea to continue on a middle course found favor with many present, it would turn out to be an impossible path to follow.

By early summer, people in Boone County were finding neutrality, armed or otherwise, difficult to maintain. On June 7, two Boone County men requested the county court make an appropriation to arm the local militia in accordance with a bill passed by the pro-secessionist state legislature in May.[6] Odon Guitar, the lawyer who had spoken out at the earlier meeting and would later fight in the Union Army, strongly opposed this request, pointing out such an appropriation would put Boone County at war with the U.S. government. The court turned down the two men's request, but it did so by citing financial concerns rather than inflame those residents of the county who were perfectly willing to engage in battle with the federal government now that it had, in their view, attacked the South. Ten days later, the first skirmish of the Civil War in Missouri took place approximately 25 miles west of Columbia. Grandly titled "the Battle of Boonville," its participants included one Boone County sheriff who had organized a company to join the pro-Confederacy State Guard. After a Union victory that took less than an hour, the commander of the Union forces, General Lyon, offered amnesty to those State Guards who would return to their homes and not fight against the United States government. The sheriff and some of the recently formed company took the offer. Others in the county, however, went off to join Sterling Price's Confederate Army, now located in the Southwest part of the state. By October, there were almost enough soldiers from Boone County joining Price's troops to form a thousand-man-regiment. Support for the Confederacy in Little Dixie continued to be high.

In the first year of the war, while Union troops were stationed in almost twenty county seats north of the Missouri River, Columbia was temporarily exempt, possibly because of the very visible loyalty to the Union shown by some of its leading citizens. Still, local pro-Confederacy feeling was strong enough that on Sept 4 a colonel in the Union Army along with six to seven hundred infantrymen and a hundred cavalry paid a visit to the city. They stayed overnight at the university and left the next morning, an apparent show of force to those—and there were many—who continued to have Southern sympathies.

While relations between Union and Confederate sympathizers still appeared to be amicable, elsewhere in Boone County rebel sympathizers were active enough that in the middle of November 1861, General Benjamin Prentiss, commander of the Union forces in central Missouri arrived in Columbia with a large contingent of infantry and cavalry. Calling a mass meeting a day after his arrival, Prentiss warned that although important Union citizens had tried to maintain the peace and protect the rights of all in the county, if rebels and secessionist troops in the area continued to steal property and harass and threaten residents favoring the Union, he would have no recourse but to put a regiment of troops on the university campus. A month and a half later, that's just what he did. On January 2, 1862, a large part of the Second Cavalry Regiment, Missouri, volunteers, known then as "Merrill's Horse," arrived in Columbia to set up operations on the campus. They stayed until July, when another militia unit replaced them. From then until the end of the war, Union troops were stationed in Columbia.

Colonel Merrill turned out to be a strict enforcer of the loyalty oath, demanding that certain groups of citizens—county and town officials as well as university professors—affirm their loyalty to the Union. If a citizen, prominent or not, was suspected of Southern sympathies, he was made to sign an even stronger oath than usual, guaranteed by a personal bond and an amount in securities ranging from $1000 to $10,000. In addition, any soldier who returned from Price's Confederate Army was arrested then made to post a bond. Colonel Merrill held court martial sessions daily on campus, and in March 1862, a military commission convened to arraign the proprietor and editor of the *Columbia Standard*, charging that he had given information for the benefit of the enemy and encouraged resistance to the government and laws of the United States. The commission found him guilty of violating the laws of war and seized and sold off his printing equipment before banishing him from the state. The same military commission found three men guilty of burning a bridge on the North Missouri Railroad and sentenced them to be shot dead. However, the sentence was to be commuted if they took an oath of allegiance and gave a bond for $2000 each to insure future loyalty to the federal government.[7] This sort of harsh punishment on local citizens by outsiders had its own reverberations. Ben M. Anderson, who was a small boy when Merrill's troops were stationed on the university campus, later described "the air of silence and mystery that sometimes hung over Columbia" and how guards would rush to the block house that stood on Eighth and Broadway if sentinels saw clouds of dust in the distance because this meant rebels were coming in on a gallop. Anderson also remembered the time Merrill's men brought in Confederate prisoners and marched them up Broadway only to have one shot after he called out a hurray for Jeff Davis.[8]

Even with Federal troops stationed in town, Columbia residents were not always protected from rebel guerrilla attacks. On August 13, 1862, two hundred guerrillas swooped down from the north, picketing the major cross streets and the roads leading out of the city, allowing no one to pass and catching by surprise a small contingent of Federal soldiers who were walking about. Most of the guerrillas headed for the jail, where they demanded the keys from the jailer then released the three Confederate prisoners they had come for. While all this activity was happening, some of the more rowdy guerrillas who were apparently intoxicated went up and down the main streets yelling and swearing. One man tore down a Union flag and dragged it through the dirt while singing songs and shouting for Jeff Davis. Another group of guerrillas assembled outside the offices of the *Missouri Statesmen*, preparing to demolish it. This action was thwarted when a Confederate lieutenant and some of the less rambunctious Southern troops intervened.[9]

As the war continued in its second year, normal activities in and around Columbia slowed down or disappeared. Currency was depreciating, businesses had fewer customers and farms were planting less and less. The district schools had closed, an action that left hundreds of teenage boys available to fight on either side. Where they went depended in some cases on how strongly their parents felt about slavery. Initially many in Boone County stood with the Constitutional Party and the Union because they believed their property rights were legally guaranteed by the Constitution, and slaves were property. But when General Frémont and President Lincoln began to speak of emancipation, local slave owners and their sons took note. If their property and inheritances were taken away, life as they knew it would be irrevocably changed. Added to this possible loss, Union authorities had begun to assess what seemed harsh levies on those they judged to be disloyal. Union field commanders could and did requisition forage and supplies from the farms of secessionists. Resentment and hostility in those who had tried to stay neutral built up, and guerrilla activity increased.

Up to 1864, no actual battles had been fought in Columbia, but when General Price and his men started a march north from Arkansas into Missouri

3. Columbia and the Civil War

in the fall of that year, Unionists in the city realized they might be in danger. After Price and his men were turned away from St. Louis, they headed west, reaching Jefferson City by October 7. Eleven days earlier Bill Anderson's guerrillas had killed a hundred Federal troops twenty-three miles north of Columbia in Centralia. Anderson, also known as "Bloody Bill," was one of the more infamous of the guerrilla leaders in the Civil War. Initially a member of a group of anti-slavery guerrillas, he switched sides and sometimes rode with another notorious guerrilla leader, William Quantrill. In response to the Centralia slaughter, the men of Columbia had quickly formed a home guard company, The Columbia Tigers, and erected a massive log blockhouse at 8th and Broadway in the middle of downtown. Now with Confederate forces on either side of them, Columbia merchants were boarding up their storefronts and preparing to send their goods out of town. R.B. Price, cashier at First National Bank of Columbia, published a notice telling creditors to present their claims against the bank as soon as possible because First National was closing out its affairs. Then Price took the remaining notes out of town and buried them, so worried was he that Anderson's gang would rob the bank. Pickets from the Columbia Tigers were sent out to watch for the approach of both Anderson's guerrillas from the north and Price's army from the south while the rest of the Tigers waited behind the blockhouse on Broadway or behind barricades around the courthouse and the university building. In the end, neither group appeared in the city, though Price's army did move as close as Boonville twenty-two miles away. There the small home guard didn't put up much of a fight, and soon Boonville residents were warmly greeting those Confederate soldiers who had grown up in the area. Confederate flags appeared, as storekeepers accepted Confederate scrip for supplies the soldiers had not seen in a long time. General Price met with guerrilla leaders and ordered them to destroy railroad and telegraph lines to the west, the direction he had decided to go. Columbia to the east was spared.[10]

While white men in Columbia were free to choose on which side to fight, black men there initially had no choice at all. In the first years of the war, blacks in the North and Border States were not even considered for service in the Union Army. But as Lincoln began to understand the war would not be ending anytime soon, he consulted with Edwin Stanton, his Secretary of War, who in turn corresponded with governors of the northern states. The Militia Act of 1862 was meant to raise three hundred thousand men for nine months of service. If a state failed to meet its quota through volunteers, a draft would take place in that state. What made the Militia Act of 1862 important for northern blacks was that it allowed their use in the war "for the purpose of constructing intrenchments, or performing camp service or any other labor, or any military or naval service for which they may be found competent." Blacks who served under this act would be paid "ten dollars per month and one ration, three dollars of which monthly pay may be in clothing" or approximately half of what a white soldier was getting. (Congress vacated that portion of the Militia Act in June 1864 and granted equal pay for all black soldiers.) Emancipation would follow for those who served and their families, but this freedom applied only to those slaves who "shall owe service or labor to any person who, during the present rebellion, has levied war or has borne arms against the United States, or adhered to their enemies by giving them aid and comfort." In other words, black men were being allowed to come into the Union Army primarily as laborers for which they would be paid less than white enrollees, and they would be freed afterwards only if they had been owned by Confederate rebels. In Missouri and other states, those slaves who had been released to work for military employers, as the Militia Act of 1862 allowed, could be reclaimed by their owners. Slaves who worked for the military in other states might receive wages and rations, but this situation did not always happen in Missouri. There Federal officials usually argued that because bondage was still legal in the state, it was the slave owners who needed to support the slaves—even those slaves who had fled their masters to work for the Union Army.

During this same period General Schofield, Senator John Henderson of Missouri, and Secretary of War Stanton were trying to encourage the President to order the recruitment of all slaves, not just those of disloyal owners. Lincoln partially succumbed in October 1863, when he approved Stanton's suggestion to recruit slaves in Maryland. Two days later, he gave his approval to General Orders 392, a secret—it would not be published—plan to recruit slaves not only in Maryland, but also in Tennessee and Missouri. But when the President realized that judicial elections were coming up in Missouri and that this act could have an adverse effect on the outcome, he eliminated Missouri from the order. A subsequent strong electoral showing by Union candidates allowed Lincoln to add Missouri back in. On November 14, 1863, Schofield issued General Orders 135 authorizing the state provost marshals to recruit all black men, both free and slave in Missouri. All loyal owners would be given three hundred dollars once they filed a deed of manumission and also signed an oath of allegiance. A board appointed by the President would determine a claim's validity.

3. Columbia and the Civil War

In May 1864, the report from the provost marshal of the Ninth District, which included Columbia, showed that 386 blacks had been enrolled in the Union Army, with eighty-one coming from Columbia (a number second only to Jefferson City, which had 203). Six months later another draft was held in the St. Charles headquarters of the Provost Marshal. Of the 144 white men from Boone County whose numbers were called, thirty-nine offered substitutes, and eighty-six did not report (many because they had already enlisted in the Confederate Army). There were an additional twenty black draftees, none of whom hired replacements. In the end, a total of 8344 colored troops were recruited or drafted from Missouri. Of these 665 were substitutes for white men.[11] It should be noted, though, that of 2500 black soldiers raised in Kansas and Iowa, a majority came from Missouri. About one in five black Missourians served in the Union Army, approximately the same percentage as white Missourians.

Does this mean Thomas Akers, Scott's grandfather served in the Union Army? He would have been thirty-one when the war began and thirty-four when he became liable for the draft. His father, Gilbert, had paid for his freedom sometime before 1861, so he was a free man during the war. Thomas Aker's name does not appear in the Missouri records for Civil War soldiers, nor is he anywhere in the Kansas and Iowa records. We do know he was living in Tipton, Missouri, some fifty miles southwest of Columbia when the war ended, because his daughter Sarah, who became James Scott's mother, was born there in October of 1865.

Whether Scott's relatives served in the Union Army or not, Columbia after the war was not the same place it had been before for either its black or white residents. The men of power in Columbia had held divergent views about fighting against their Southern neighbors, but few if any felt slavery was wrong. The beliefs of those who supported the Confederacy didn't change after 1865. They merely went underground. The Civil War didn't erase racism, nor did it foster a greater sense of unity within the Union. In states like Missouri, it merely meant blacks could no longer be considered property. But they certainly would never be considered equal to whites. As for the black residents of Columbia, the initial pleasure they must have felt as the war ended and they were freed soon dissipated as the realities of their lives during Reconstruction and afterward became apparent.

4

Reconstruction and Beyond

One of the first accounts I found of how Columbia treated its black residents after the war was a book published in 1987 under the auspices of the Boone County Historical Society. Its author, John C. Crighton, devotes a chapter of *A History of Columbia and Boone County* to the city's transition from slavery to freedom, and as I read it, I realized what he was *not* saying was as interesting as what he was.[1]

Crighton begins by noting the black exodus from country to town began as far back as the summer of 1863, when black men working on farms in Boone County started to join the Union Army, leaving behind wives and children who were forced to move into town. Unfortunately, Crighton reports, there were no provisions or facilities for providing for these slaves and former slaves even after Emancipation. He could find no evidence that white churches, the Freedmen's Bureau or the town government offered any help. Thus, we are not surprised to learn that during the harsh winter of 1864–65 a total of thirty black men and women died of exposure and starvation on Columbia's streets.

Fortunately, some in the black community were able to respond to this exodus, including a man we have read about before—James Scott's great grandfather, Gilbert Akers. Crighton lists Akers along with John Lang, Sr., and Beverly Chapman as those black men who stepped forward to provide housing and food to black families who had been forced to move into Columbia from Boone County. How these men handled the refugee problem remains unclear to Crighton, but he does say some black families who owned houses opened their doors to their relatives, friends, and even strangers. He knows this information, because the Columbia Board of Trustees in a December 1865 meeting responded to this hospitality by telling the town marshal to forcibly evict more than one family or more than five single persons living in a single room within the corporate limits. Crighton goes on to say shanty

4. Reconstruction and Beyond

settlements were built on the north and west borders of the city—Akers and Lang owned property there—and he suggests a community garden or a community woodpile might have been set up for those freed blacks who had come off the farms.

What blacks deserved, Crighton intones, was the opportunity to operate for themselves: to establish and teach in their own schools rather than to attend white ones, and to worship in their own churches so they could sit on the front rather than the backbenches. What he neglects to mention is that most of the white community in Columbia wanted no part of freed blacks in their schools or churches. Even when the Missouri legislature passed a law in 1865 that briefly made school segregation optional, there was no question in Columbia of accepting black students into the few white schools that existed then. Integration would not happen until Brown vs. The Board of Education in 1954, at which time Missouri was one of seventeen states still *requiring* segregation. Here is Crighton's description of the transition period in Columbia after the war:

> Relations between blacks and whites were generally friendly and cooperative. The excesses of the reconstruction period found elsewhere were lacking in Columbia. Many of the blacks in town had been household servants and had adopted the conventions, values and family names of their white masters. So it was easy for them to adjust to the dominant culture.[2]

But as I looked closer, I found that as much as Crighton might have wished it, relations between the races in Columbia and Boone County were not quite as friendly and cooperative as he described them. A different opinion is given by General Clinton Fisk, the commander of the District of North Missouri, as he traveled throughout the state in March 1865:

> Slavery dies hard. I hear its expiring agonies and witness its contortions in death in every quarter of my district. In Boone, Howard, Randolph and Callaway the emancipation ordinance has caused disruption of society equal to anything I saw in Arkansas or Mississippi in the year 1863.[3]

Guerrilla warfare had increased during the last year of the war, and proponents of the Confederacy didn't just disappear from rural Missouri once the war was over. White supremacist newspapers like the *Lexington Weekly Caucasian* and even some factions of the Radical Republicans were encouraging blacks to leave the state and country if they wanted equal rights. If they remained, the writers suggested, they would "deteriorate and finally disappear." To an extent, blacks took their advice. While white Missourians had lost a great deal during the war including family members, property, and a sense of community challenged by divergent allegiances, their overall population in the state increased in the ten years from 1860 to 1870. During this same period, Missouri's black population decreased from 9.8 to 6.8 percent of the total population. Rural blacks who lived on farms in 1865 found themselves pushed out, or in danger from guerrillas, if they remained. Many left for the free states on either side of Missouri or moved into garrisoned towns, though they did not always find jobs there.

In the years immediately after the war ended, some of the more intransigent former slave owners hired bushwhackers to hang or shoot any slaves who had abandoned their plantations, and in some places obsolete slave codes continued to be enforced. Even where the need for farm workers was great, farmers who had previously owned slaves often refused to hire emancipated workers. Other farmers who would have hired them or rented out their land to them were intimidated enough not to try. In the end, General Fisk came up with a solution to the problem of newly freed slaves who sought work: he had them transported from overcrowded towns in Boone and other Little Dixie counties to the border areas of Kansas, Iowa, and Illinois. Fisk, an early Abolitionist and later a supporter of black education (he endowed Fisk University), chose this action while believing the state should not be deporting manual labor but importing it. But when he saw what these newly freed men faced, he understood their opportunities might lay elsewhere.

Lincoln's Emancipation Proclamation of 1863 had freed the slaves in the Confederate states, but it said nothing about the freedom of slaves in Missouri and the Border States. A year later, John B. Henderson, a Missouri Democrat, submitted a joint resolution with two other senators for a constitutional amendment to abolish the institution of slavery. Before this time, it had been Republicans who usually offered these amendments, but Henderson was one of the War Democrats, a group who sought a more aggressive stance toward the Confederacy. Though he represented a slave state, Henderson may have been influenced by his own history when he submitted his resolution. Born in Virginia, he had come to Missouri with his parents as a toddler. When both his mother and father died prematurely, ten-year-old John was "bound out" or indentured to a farmer until the age of eighteen. This early apprenticeship was one supposition put forward as to why he would offer an amendment to abolish slavery even though many in his state still favored it. The Senate passed Henderson's amendment in April of 1864, but it didn't get an affirmative vote in the House until January 31, 1865, and then only because President Lincoln worked behind the scenes to get enough votes. It would

4. Reconstruction and Beyond

take another three hundred and nine days for the Thirteenth Amendment to the United States Constitution to be ratified by the states.

Missouri, however, didn't wait that long to abolish slavery. Radical Republicans in the state had come to power during the fall elections of 1864. In addition to winning the governorship, they won two-thirds of the delegate seats to a new state constitutional convention. When the convention met in January, they had the votes to put through several key amendments. To begin with, they passed an ordinance abolishing slavery or involuntary servitude. The newly elected Radical Republican governor, Thomas C. Fletcher, ratified this ordinance on January 11, 1865. Then they turned their attention to the civil rights of those freed slaves. Article 1, section three of the new state constitution guaranteed the following:

> That no person can, on account of color, be disqualified as a witness; or be disabled to contract, otherwise than as others are disabled; or be prevented from acquiring, holding, and transmitting property; or be liable to any other punishment for any offense, than that imposed upon others for a like offense; or be restricted in the exercise of religious worship; or be hindered in acquiring education; or be subjected, in law, to any other restraints or disqualifications, in regard to any personal rights, than such as are laid upon others like circumstances.[4]

In other words, rights that before now had only been afforded to white residents of the state were now extended to blacks, with one notable exception: the right to vote. This issue wouldn't be dealt with until five years later. The new constitution also provided a means to education for Missouri's black residents. Section one of Article IX of the new constitution stated that free schools would be established for all persons in the state between the ages five and twenty-one. Section two went on to say separate schools would be established for children of African descent, and the funds provided for public schools would be appropriated in proportion to the number of children without regard to color.

While this sounds like an equitable arrangement, a lot depended on the men supervising it. For the most part, Superintendents of Schools in the state in the period right after the War were dedicated to following the law. Blacks, when they were supported within a district, also worked hard to establish and maintain their schools, as we shall see in Columbia. But in those parts of Missouri where sympathies had been firmly with the South, few schools for blacks were established. In 1868, the State Superintendent received the power to establish schools for black students in those towns, cities or villages where the school board had neglected to do so. At the same time the number of black students necessary to establish a school was lowered to fifteen. The separate but equal doctrine the Radical Republicans tried to put into place was not always visible. The average length of the school term in black schools in the state was twenty-eight weeks as opposed to the average of thirty-four weeks in white schools. The average expense per day for a black student was 7.8 cents vs. 8.1 cents for a white student.[5] The 1873 "Annual Report of the Superintendent of Schools" reported an average monthly salary for male teachers in white schools of $87.72 as compared to an average monthly salary for male teachers in the African American schools of $46.70. Women teachers of both races made even less.

By the mid–1870s, the black public school system in Missouri was up and running. The goal of giving black children the same educational advantages as white children had been helped along by the legislation put forward by the Radical Republicans when they were in power. But after the 1874 fall elections politicians from the Democratic Party took control, and the new state constitution, ratified in 1875, made each school district independent with the decision to levy money or extend or shorten the school term going to the voters of that district. Legislation in 1875 also made it clear separate schools would be established for colored students in the state. (When a court case came up later involving a black student who because of an insufficiency of other black students in his town had attended a white school, the state passed a law in 1889 making segregation mandatory.)

In Columbia, public schools, which by law had served only white students before 1860, suspended operation during the Civil War. When they began again, they continued to serve only whites. Black Columbians, therefore, needed to establish their own schools, and in the summer of 1865, they set out to do. Members of the black Methodist and Baptist churches called a meeting to raise money to buy land on which to erect a building to be used both as a school and a church. The combined congregations raised one hundred and forty-nine dollars, twenty dollars of which went to James Scott's great-grandfather, Gilbert Akers for a lot he owned at Third and Ash. But this plan did not proceed smoothly. After dissention erupted between the two congregations, the Baptists pulled out of the agreement and brought in a white man from Ohio to teach about fifty students in a private home. Around the same time, the trustees of another black church, St. Paul's AME Church, started a school for black children in their church building, and they appealed to the state legislature for money to fund this venture. The Columbia school board gave the school seventy-five dollars promising more in the

4. Reconstruction and Beyond

future. The school board later went back on that promise and gave the additional funds to the school run by the Baptists, which had by then moved from the Lang house into a building erected on the original lot purchased from Akers. So when the new school year began in 1867, there were not one but two black schools in Columbia—a private school in a black church and what was now recognized as the city's public school for blacks on the southeast corner of Third and Ash. A year later, after many dinners, festivals, and picnics, a July 4th fundraiser was held by Gilbert Akers and the rest of the committee of the Colored People's Temperance Society. To this was invited "Everyone, white and colored,"[6] and enough money was raised by the black community of Columbia to complete the construction of a two-story public school. They had a thousand dollars, and an additional eight hundred was contributed by the Freedmen's Bureau and our friend William F. Switzler. This kind of support, however, was not universal. In 1867, whites fired on a Christmas Eve service at St. Paul's AME Church in Columbia, killing one black and wounding another. Between 1866 and 1869 at least three black schools in the state were set on fire.

The new school was named Cummings Academy in honor of its first principal, Charles E. Cummings. Born in New York in 1840, Cummings had grown up in New Haven, Connecticut, before attending the Toronto Grammar Institute, one of the oldest secondary schools in the city. After teaching in St. Louis for two and a half years, he came to Columbia, where he spent the next nine years as principal at Cummings Academy. During this time, he made the acquaintance of James S. Rollins, the lawyer who had helped William F. Switzler get a law degree, and subsequently had served both in the U.S. Congress and in the Missouri State Legislature. Rollins received several letters from Charles Cummings in which the latter sought help in procuring a government job. When Rollins wrote back to say that because of a change in power at the state level, appointments would no longer be made in accordance with party affiliation, Cummings responded by asking for permission to use Rollins' earlier endorsement and "well-known name" as he continued to seek a government position. He ended by saying, "I am assured of the honesty of my aim, and not without hope that the claims of the colored man of Mo. may be recognized through *me*."[7] However, the "colored man of Mo." did not have the same educational opportunities Cummings had as a free man beginning his life in the East. Think of Thomas Akers, James Scott's grandfather, who was born in approximately the same time as Cummings yet had no opportunity to go to school until he was a grown man.

Enrollment in Cummings Academy grew. In 1867, there were sixty-three students; two years later they numbered about a hundred. The school was crowded almost from inception due primarily to the enrollment of non-residents and those either underage, or in the beginning, over the regular school age. (Many adult former slaves used this opportunity to become literate.) In 1883, members of the black community in Columbia petitioned the school board for a loan of five thousand dollars to purchase a new site and to build a school adequate for the black school population. Columbia residents voted this levy down because they had just finished paying for a white public school. The arguments supporting this request—Flat Branch creek had washed away half the school lot so that there was no playground, students had to carry drinking water to school since there was none there, and the building itself was poorly heated, lighted and ventilated—fell on deaf ears. Two years later however, another petition was presented, and this time the levy passed.

It was around this same time a short notice appeared in the *Missouri Statesman*: "The colored public school (Cummings Academy,) was burnt to the ground early last Saturday morning. It is thought to be the work of an incendiary."[8] Did someone from the black community burn down the school so it would have to be replaced? Or, as is more likely, was this the work of someone who had no use for black education? *The Statesman* had published a very similar notice five months earlier: "On the last Sunday night fire was discovered in the colored public school building—Cummings Academy—and as the building had not been used for ten days there is the smell of an incendiary being around."[9] In neither instance was there any follow-up in the paper. The two-story brick building with six rooms built along the Flat Branch after the levy was passed was soon overcrowded. It took eleven more years for Columbia voters to approve another loan so additional rooms could be added. In 1898, with Cummings long departed, the school was renamed to honor Frederick Douglass, the great American social reformer and abolitionist.

As much support as black education had gotten from state overseers, it was often predicated on some seriously racist notions. Consider the explanation about how black students progress through the grades by the State Superintendent of Public Schools W.E. Coleman in 1889:

> ...the African characteristics drop out and the Caucasian predominate, thereby showing conclusively that the African is not capable of receiving and utilizing the school advantages afforded him, with the readiness and to the extent of the Caucasian.[10]

4. Reconstruction and Beyond

Despite the inequities, blacks in Missouri were not dissuaded from seeking an education. At the time of Emancipation the majority of slaves in Boone County were illiterate; thirty-five years later over 70 percent of those between the ages of twenty-one and thirty were literate, and in the thirty-one to forty-year-old group it was 50 percent. In the 1880 census, all the members of the Akers family indicate they can read and write, and James Scott's mother, Sallie, along with his aunt and uncle, Lulu and Thomas, are all said to have attended school within the census year. This school would have been the Cummings Academy.

After the war, the more affluent blacks bought land in the northwest part of the city:

> Even the colored people have caught the spirit of progress, and having bought lots in the suburbs, are engaged in building small residences according to their means, and a new frame church 36 × 60.[11]

There were no zoning restrictions, so lot owners could build small frame houses, using the local abundance of wood available at that time. John Lang, Sr., had already begun this tradition of real estate purchase by buying up lots downtown. In 1851, Lang had opened a butcher shop at Fourth and Cherry, and for many years afterward, he had the only store of the kind in the city. When the war came, he kept his stock up by going out into the countryside to buy animals, a sometimes risky trip that paid off when a local militia group, the Columbia Tigers awarded him the contract to supply their beef.

In 1869, Lang moved his shop to Broadway and extended the store's offering to fresh vegetables, another first for Columbia shoppers. Two years later he admitted Thomas Akers, Scott's grandfather, into partnership with him. Continuing as an innovator, Lang began a dairy business that delivered milk and butter to its customers twice a day. John Lang's son, John Lang, Jr., had by this time begun work as a contractor, and in 1871, he was awarded a contract by the county to complete five miles of the Columbia-Blackfoot turnpike. During the next ten years, the junior Lang's contracting company performed many of the construction jobs on Columbia's streets. But it was his father who remained the city's largest black landowner. By the time he was finished, John Lang, Sr., owned most of the area in a square block bound by Fifth Street, Broadway, Fourth Street and Walnut. He also continued to own the land at Fourth and Cherry, the original location of his store, and on Ash Street just east of the courthouse.

James Scott's great grandfather, Gilbert Akers also flourished economically after the war. As earlier noted, he was able to offer land to the coalition of black churches so they could build a school, and later in conjunction with another businessman he purchased an eighty-acre tract in the county. His son Thomas became a landowner too when he bought a home site on the southwest edge of town along Flat Branch Creek.

When the rail line from Columbia to Centralia was finished in 1867, a building boom arose around it. In the northeast part of town white suburbs, including the homes of some of Columbia's wealthier citizens, were built. By 1869, Price Avenue, named for Robert Beverly Price, president of the Boone County National Bank, had been widened to fifty feet and macadamized. A year earlier an advertisement in the July 31, 1868, *Missouri Statesman* called for a hundred laborers to work on the Columbia to Rocheport turnpike. This call for workers meant some of those jobs would go to black men, since, according to John Crighton, the city at the time had no sizable class of white manual or skilled workers, nor did they have unions with restrictive policies. Columbia was a wealthy town then, which meant black men could work at manual or unskilled jobs while black women could serve as cooks, maids, laundresses, and nursemaids to white families.[12]

After Emancipation most blacks who had attended churches like First Baptist and Methodist Episcopal left to form their own congregations. In 1866, black Baptists and Methodists came together to form their own church to be called African Union Church. When this arrangement dissolved and the Methodists left, those remaining changed the name to Second Missionary Baptist Church. For several years this congregation met at the Cummings Academy at Third and Ash, but in March 1873, they began to build a small one-room church on Fifth Street between Locust and Cherry. The structure was dedicated six years later, and for the next twenty years services were held there. In 1884, the Reverend Amos Johnson proposed a plan to build a new sanctuary. John Lange, Jr., donated land at Fourth and Broadway, and when the building fund wasn't growing enough, Columbia's most renowned black musician, John William "Blind" Boone loaned the church $3,000. Judge John A. Stewart, a white man who had a livery stable on a corner across from the church, added another loan of $4,000. (Stewart, a prosperous farmer and stock trader, later platted and developed the land southwest of town. Stewart Road, which passed over the bridge from which Scott was lynched, was named for him.) In 1894, the sanctuary of Second Missionary Baptist Church was completed in a Gothic and Romanesque style with beautiful stained glass windows and arched doors. The Methodists who had left went on to create

4. Reconstruction and Beyond

St. Paul African Methodist Church in 1880. The cornerstone for their building was laid in 1891 at Park and Fifth.

The support given to black churches by some of Columbia's more prosperous white residents didn't stop with loans. If invited, the white elite would often come to the picnics and other festivities the black churches put on to raise funds, though always sitting at the separate tables church members happily provided. But these visits sometimes included judgments. Suzanna Maria Grenz cites one such assessment made after a reporter from the *Missouri Statesman* attended a black revival meeting:

> As yet the negro has a primitive idea of the complex institution called religion. But believing as we do that everything connected with humanity possesses an inherent dignity, we recognize the usefulness of religion, even though it may find expression in crude form.[13]

As useful as black religion might have been to whites, it was of even greater value to blacks. The church was one of the few places where newly freed citizens could feel empowered and validated. The black church in Columbia continued to be an occasional object of derision into the twentieth century, but for its congregants, it remained a source of support and intense pride.

In 1872, this small notice appeared in the *Missouri Statesman*:

> A Double Sorrow.— "Uncle Gilbert Akers" (as he is familiarly known,) a well known and very respectable colored man and long resident of this place, recently met with a double sorrow in the death of two sons, Abner and Gilbert, the former near Linden, Alabama, on Monday, the 16th, and the latter in St. Louis on Friday, the 20th, both of smallpox. Two deaths of the same disease, in the same family, in the same week, and a thousand miles apart, are rare afflictions indeed.[14]

While two smallpox deaths in the same family within the same weeks but miles apart may have been rare, the threat of the disease at the time was everywhere in the state, including Columbia. During the 1870s and 1880s there were outbreaks of smallpox serious enough that the city's Board of Trustees appointed the president of the university and another member of the board to draft a health ordinance in May 1879. The trustees also created a Board of Health composed of a physician and a chemist. The physician accompanied by the town marshal was instructed to make a monthly inspection of all those places in which filth, offal and stagnant water could accumulate. The chemist, a professor at the university, was charged with conducting tests on public and private wells and ponds. In addition, the Board of Trustees passed an ordinance that required offal from the pork-packing factory, the distillery and the slaughterhouses in town to be hauled away once a day and dumped outside the city limits. Before this ordinance was passed, offal would have been dumped into the natural drainage system around town because there were no sewers. This method of disposal didn't always stop after the ordinance was passed. The town had no landfill area, so the men who hauled away the offal and other waste sometimes saved themselves the long trip into the country by dumping their loads in Flat Branch creek, which flowed just within the western city limits. The creek was also the place many black residents disposed of their waste since it ran right by their houses.

Within two months of the Board of Health being created, the physician sent out to inspect for health hazards had detected so many violations that he was unsure what to report. Three months later, the chemist quit after he became discouraged by the lack of action on the part of the public and the local government to clean up the various water supplies he had tested and found polluted. The physician followed the chemist's lead soon after. The Board of Trustees, ignoring the official reports, responded to the resentment of white Columbians at being asked to clean up their property by passing a much milder version of the ordinance. They also made sure the new Board of Health contained no academics.

Columbia in 1880 was not quite ready to establish municipal services like sewers and fire hydrants. Many residents, white and black, still kept farm animals within city limits, and almost all residents used outhouses. It wasn't until twelve years later, when a fire burned down the administration building on the university campus because there was no professional fire department or water main, that the city turned its attention to improving municipal services. A threat by the Missouri legislature to move the university elsewhere brought about first a private and later a public municipal water plant.

When the new administrative building on campus was completed in 1895, new faculty was brought in, and because they needed a place to live, another housing boom like the one that had surrounded the railroad spur occurred. This time neighborhoods developed to the south and west of campus on the other side of Flat Branch creek. City streets began to be paved, including a section of Broadway that despite earlier macadam at times became a sea of mud. Hamilton-Brown, a shoe company from St. Louis, was encouraged to establish a branch in northeast Columbia by a bonus of sixty thousand dollars raised by popular subscription. The population of Columbia grew from 2,236 residents in 1870, to 5,561 in 1900. Ten years later, almost ten thousand people lived in this city that Crighton declared "modernized," with its

4. Reconstruction and Beyond

paved roads, sewer system, and municipal fire department. What had not become modernized, however, were the areas in which most of Columbia's black community, including some of James Scott's ancestors, lived.

As we have seen, Gilbert Akers, Scott's great-grandfather, continued to prosper after the war. He was able to provide help to those newly emancipated slaves who came into Columbia, and he sold one of his lots so a black school could be established at the corner of Third and Ash. Gilbert Akers does not appear on the 1870 census, but in 1880 he is, at sixty-eight, still working as a laborer, while his wife Susan, who is sixty-five, continues to keep house. On the same page, a Bart Akers is listed. He is a middle-aged man of forty-one who works as a teamster while his wife Irena, who is thirty, is at home raising their children—Mattie, thirteen and William, eleven. We will hear more about Mattie later. Gilbert Akers also appears several times in the local papers after the war including a notice in 1867 when he was part of the committee putting together a dinner for the Negro Temperance Society.

From the 1880 census we know James's mother Sarah (originally called Sallie) was born in 1865 in Tipton, Missouri, some fifty miles southwest of Columbia. We also know six years later she and her parents are back in Columbia because in 1871 her father, Thomas Akers, went into the grocery business with John Lang, Sr. Though Thomas and his wife Ophelia lived the rest of their lives in the city, Sarah's parents were not Columbia natives. Thomas, son of Gilbert Robinson/Akers, had been brought from Kentucky, and it is likely his wife began her life there too. Ophelia Crockett was probably owned by a man by the name of Caswell G. Crockett. The 1850 slave census lists Caswell Crockett as having four slaves including a nine-year-old girl—the math isn't exact, but close enough given the inaccuracy of birth dates for slaves—and like a lot of Boone County inhabitants, he came from Kentucky, the same state where Ophelia was born around 1838. Of Thomas and Ophelia's children, all were born in Missouri. Getting evidence from the federal census becomes more difficult in 1890. Because of a fire, little of that year's census is available. Because of a newspaper article reporting on a lawsuit with the Gilbert Akers's executor,[15] I know that Gilbert, James's great-grandfather, died in October 1885. Thomas Akers, Gilbert's son and James's grandfather, passed away two years later. Both were still living in Columbia at the time.

Slave schedules possessed no black names, but fortunately the Boone County Marriage Book does; otherwise, I would have found no direct official evidence of James Scott's father's existence. I could find no birth record for him or any death certificate either. Nor does he appear in any census. But on July 6, 1882, James Scott Senior, over the age of twenty-one, and "Miss Sallie Akers," over the age of eighteen, both of Boone County, Missouri, and "both colored persons" are recorded as receiving a license and being married by the Minister of the Gospel Amos Johnson.[16] Because the Reverend Johnson was the spiritual leader of the Second Baptist Church, we can assume the ceremony took place there. This is the same church Sarah will attend when she again lives in Columbia, and it is the same church where her son James will be married for a third time. But none of this has happened yet.

Who was this man who named one of his sons after himself? Without any official confirmation, I can only put together the clues myself and others have found.[17] The 1870 census lists a Stephen and Sallie Scott, both of whom are black and live in Cole County, Missouri, approximately thirty-one miles south of Columbia on the Missouri River. Stephen, a farm laborer and Sallie, a housekeeper, have three children: James, who is eight, George, who is three, and John W, who was born the year of the census. Could this be the James Scott I am looking for? Ten years later according to the new census, Stephen and Sallie's family has grown. There are now five children, but the oldest, James, is nowhere to be seen. Instead, the census records a male son, Caswell, who is now twenty (James would have been eighteen). Records are not always exact, so it is hard to draw a conclusion from this discrepancy. The only piece of evidence I could find that Caswell Scott and James Scott Senior are two different people is a record of a "Coswell" Scott marrying a young black woman named Ellen Howard in Cole County, Missouri, in 1885. Neither Caswell nor Coswell Scott appears on later federal censuses. James Scott, Sr., does appear, but only indirectly as we shall see.

The physical size of Columbia grew in the years after the Civil War, and it continued to grow well into the twentieth century. Large parcels of land were added to city and platted for residential use to the north and west, and developers like John A. Stewart, who earlier lent money for a new building to the Second Missionary Baptist Church, made sure they included paved roads, sidewalks and sewers—features that did not appear in black neighborhoods until many years later. As one of the city's biggest fans, William Switzler, boasted in his 1882 history that, "those who came to the place, as a rule, were wealthy, cultured and refined people, attracted by the educational and kindred advantages."[18] And while this boast may have been true to some extent, it was true only for the white residents who came. Blacks who resided in Columbia had not for the most part chosen this city.

4. Reconstruction and Beyond

They were brought here as slaves, and when Reconstruction came, they were left to their own devices. As time went on, when the economy in Columbia did not grow as Switzler and others had hoped, these devices became fewer. In the Columbia of the years before the turn of the century, black residents went from being slaves to being a problem, or at least that's how the descendants of those wealthy, cultured and refined people Switzer refers to viewed them.

5

Life in Chicago

Timidly, we get off the train. We hug our suitcases, fearful of pickpockets, looking with unrestrained curiosity at the great big brick buildings. We are very reserved, for we have been warned not to act "green," that the city people can spot a "sucker" a mile away. Then we board our first Yankee street car to go to a cousin's home, a brother's home, a sister's home, a friend's home, an uncle's home, or an aunt's home. We pay the conductor our fare and look about apprehensively for a seat. We have been told we can sit where we please, but we are still scared. We cannot shake off three hundred years of fear in three hours.[1]

These are not the words of Sarah and her son James when they first arrived in Chicago, but they could be. They were written by Richard Wright to accompany the photographs in a remarkable book about the Great Migration called *Twelve Million Black Voices*. Wright, who was born in Mississippi in 1908, had himself escaped to Chicago in 1927, and though the people he is describing here came to the city later than James and his mother, their feelings must have been similar.

Sometime after James's birth in New Mexico around 1884 and before the 1900 census was taken, Sarah and her son moved to Chicago. They probably did this by train, climbing aboard one of the Chicago and Alton passenger cars that passed through Centralia, twenty miles north of Columbia before heading east and north on an almost three hundred and forty mile journey that took about thirteen hours to reach Chicago's original Union Depot, where the terminal stretched out an entire city block just west of the Loop. From there, James and Sarah headed downtown to catch a streetcar to their new home. But unlike most of the later migrants, they didn't go south but north to the section of the city where they would live for the rest of their time in Chicago.

From the Great Fire in 1871 to 1900, the black population of Chicago had almost doubled every decade. This increase was the result of several fac-

5. Life in Chicago

tors including crop failures in the South and the withdrawal of federal troops there in 1877. With the soldiers gone, white southerners who had opposed emancipation felt freer to act. They passed Jim Crow laws—named for a nineteenth century minstrel act—that were meant to enforce the pre-war codes of behavior for blacks. Because blacks in the South were no longer bound to the land, when the indignities of living under these racist laws became too great, they left to find better employment opportunities and safer lives for themselves and their children. In 1900, Chicago's black population was around 30,000 out of a total of more than 1,698,000. During the approximately twenty years James Scott lived there, the city added one million black residents. With this increase in population came an increase in racial tension. Competition for housing and jobs grew stronger, and animosity between black and white workers increased after companies used black strike breakers to fight the unions (unions that would not accept black members) in 1904 and again in 1917. But all this came later. In 1900 there was relatively little enmity between the races. Blacks lived in all thirty-five of the wards, and in eight of those, there were enough residents to form a community.[2]

I do not know exactly why James's mother chose to move away from her family in Columbia, but her status as a widow in 1900 might be one reason. She was the sole support of herself and her family by then, and we don't know how long she'd shouldered this responsibility. When Sarah and James got on that streetcar heading north, they were traveling to a town adjoining Lake Michigan, called Lake View, which had an interesting history. Originally used by Native American tribes like the Miami, the Winnebago and the Ottawa as a camp and trail, Lake View's first white resident was a man from Switzerland who immigrated in 1837. He was followed by farming families from Germany, Luxembourg, and Sweden so that in its beginning Lake View was primarily farmland known for its celery production. By the mid-nineteenth century, it had also become a summer vacation spot for city dwellers, many of whom came there during the summers 1848 and 1855 when cholera was especially virulent in Chicago. By the time James and his mother arrived, the town had a steady year-round population of well above 45,000 and had been absorbed into Chicago itself. However, very few of those 45,000 residents were black. According to the 1900 census, one hundred and seventy-eight blacks lived in the 25th ward that ran along the lake and comprised much of Lakeview. (Contrast this to Chicago's 3rd ward, which had 7,618 black residents in 1900.)

Why, I wondered, had Sarah chosen a place like this to live when most blacks arriving in Chicago headed south. I discovered the answer to this question when I happened to see a familiar name in *The Professional World*, a black newspaper published in Columbia at the beginning of the twentieth century. In a column called "Local and Personal," I noticed the following: "Mrs. Bart Akers and little grandson Master W.B. Akers returned last Thursday from a month's visit to Chicago and St. Louis."[3] Recognizing the Bart Akers' name from the 1880 census, I went back to see to whom he was married. This turned out to be a woman named Irena with whom he had had two children: Mattie, then 13 and W.B. who was 11. Twenty years later (a year before the notice in *The Professional World*), the 1900 census shows a Mattie Akers employed as a teacher in Chicago. In fact, Mattie Akers Marshall, for she had married by then, lived in Lake View. I also learned from 1900 census Mattie Marshall was a widow whose husband and two children had all predeceased her. The "Mrs. Bart Akers," who was visiting Chicago, must be Mattie's mother, Irena, and Mattie herself was Sarah Scott's cousin. Like Mattie, Sarah was also a widow in 1900, so who better to go to for help than her cousin, who not only had steady employment as a teacher but owned her own house in Lake View? Sarah does not appear to have trained for a professional career like teaching—remember, she married at just eighteen and had two sons soon after—but perhaps through her cousin, she was hoping to find a nice place to live not too far from Mattie's house.

Checking the census again, I saw this was true. In 1900, Mattie lived at 1969 Marshfield Avenue, while Sarah and James had rented an apartment at 1534 Addison, approximately two minutes away by foot. Because of this same census, we know Sarah's husband was no longer alive, but where was Akers, her other son? Only James and Sarah are recorded as living in Lake View. It turns out that at the end of June 1900, Akers, or "Acres" as his name was spelled in that year's census, was a farm worker in West Creek, Indiana, some fifty-four miles south of Chicago. He lived with the farm's owners, William and Nellie Hayes and was said to be fifteen years old at the time. This information seems to confirm the fact Akers was James's older brother rather than his younger one as I had originally thought when I only had Akers's death certificate as evidence. But nothing is conclusive. Like James, we have our choice of birthdates for Akers. In the end, I found two documents—the 1900 census and Akers' draft notice in 1918—listing his birth year as 1884. The 1910 census, which seems mistaken in several parts, has him born in 1885. His death notice, as I have mentioned, records his birth as 1888. Finally, the 1940 census records his age as fifty-seven in April of that year, which would

5. Life in Chicago

mean he was born in 1882 if we believe his birthday was June 21, the day that appears several times on official documents. If we go on the assumption—a fragile one at best—that the truest date is the one most likely to be self-reported, we might conclude Akers was born in 1884. As for his relationship to William and Nellie Hayes, I was unable to find one. William's parents came from Virginia and Nellie's from North Carolina. William was also born in Virgina March 1852 while his wife Nellie was an Illinois native born in September 1873. They seemed to have no relationship to anywhere or anyone in Missouri, so while we might expect fifteen-year-old Akers to be lodging with someone he knew, I could not prove this was the case.

James was lodging with someone he knew, and when Rebecca Schnederman, the 1900 Lake View census taker, visited their house on June 9, she found nine people in three apartments. In the first apartment, W. Lane resides with his wife Mary, his brother-in-law John Hill, and another woman, a widow by the name of Thornton. The first three come from Maryland, while Mrs. Thornton is a Canadian by birth. Mr. Lane works as a dishwasher, while his wife and Mrs. Thornton are laundresses, and John Hill is a porter. Sarah and James occupied the second apartment, with Sarah's occupation listed as maid, while James in 1900 works as a laborer in an unidentified club. With a birth date of October 1885, James is said to be fourteen and presumably not in school—nothing in that column is filled in. Both James and Sarah were unemployed in previous months—eight for Sarah and two for James—so possibly James was finishing school during that time. In the third apartment are Alonzo Turner, his wife Sallie and his mother-in-law, Cassie Burris. Mr. Turner, who is from North Carolina, is, like John Hill in the first apartment, employed as a porter, while Sallie, who was born in Kentucky, works as a laundress. All the residents of this two-story house a few blocks from the lake are black.

The occupations of those living at 1534 Addison reflect a pattern common in Chicago at the time. In 1900 over 80 percent of black women and 65 percent of black men worked as domestics and personal servants. Even ten years later, 45 percent of black men were confined to just four job categories—porters, servants, waiters and janitors. And 63 percent of black women were domestic servants like Sarah or laundresses like several of the women living at the same address.[4] Rebecca Schnederman didn't find any other blacks living in this section of Addison or on Halstead, the cross street she surveyed that day in June. But the people at 1534 were not stranded in their essentially white world. The one reliable factor that integrated Chicago from the beginning was the public transportation system. When the Chicago Commission on Race Relations was convened after the 1919 riots, they queried black residents about freedom and independence in the city compared to what happened in the South. One respondent said that he had come to Chicago not only for higher wages, but because he could go anywhere he wanted on the streetcars there. Another pointed out he could sit anywhere he wanted on those cars.[5]

The first elevated lines in Chicago had been built from downtown south to Jackson Park in 1893, the year the Columbian Exposition was set up there. (This was the same year Ida B. Wells encouraged all blacks to boycott the Exposition after authorities refused proposals for exhibits showing black progress.[6]) The next two elevated lines went west from downtown, and finally around 1900 a fourth line traveled north to Howard Street passing a few blocks from where Sarah and James lived. But even earlier horse-drawn streetcars had appeared, and then gave way to cable and electrified cars. Anyone with five cents could ride the elevated train or the streetcar, and because cars were often crowded, white and black passengers had to share a seat. This cohabiting didn't mean white Chicagoans gladly occupied seats with blacks; nor did it mean they refrained from complaining about the conduct or smell of their fellow black passengers. But there was no such thing as an official black streetcar or L train. Whites in Chicago may not have liked sitting with blacks, but they most often suffered quietly, at least until the Great Migration made the presence of the growing number of blacks in Chicago even more obvious. The black community knew they were not always welcomed on public transportation. An article in the Chicago *Defender* spelled out their civic duties for them:

> On street cars, buses and in public places you come in contact with others who pay the same price and have the same rights as you. You have a right there the same as they, but you also owe a duty as a citizen to the public and the individual to be neat and clean and not make yourself a nuisance and objectionable. One seat on a street car is all any individual is entitled to. To sprawl all over a car or engage in loud talking, eating and sleeping shows very bad manners.[7]

What this advice makes clear is prejudice in Chicago often had as much to do with class as race.

Writing about James Scott's life in Chicago after that first appearance in the 1900 census has turned out to be a sort of hit and miss affair. Not only did he not live on the South Side, the area most documented by historians and sociologists, but the actual details of his life turn out to rest on a very

5. Life in Chicago

few official documents and what I could extrapolate from them. So here is the best version of how James Scott grew up in Chicago, gathered from the facts the documents contained, though sometimes even these facts seemed to be supplied by less-than-reliable narrators.

The 1910 census is a good example. Having discovered where James was living in 1900 by using that year's census, I decided to check the next census to see where he was and what he was doing ten years later. A lot can happen in a decade (and it turned out it did). FamilySearch, the website created by the Church of Jesus Christ of Latter Day Saints, has the 1910 census online, so I began my search with the information I knew—name, gender, and race. When asked to "Search by Life Events," I chose birthplace and entered New Mexico, and at "Search by Relationships," I decided to stay with the one I knew most about. I filled in his mother Sarah's name and birthplace. Then I clicked on the blue Search button.

Nothing. Or more exactly, two hits, one for "Jim Scott" and the other for "Scott," both with birthdays not even close to that of my James Scott, and living in Louisiana and Georgia. I went back and deleted the New Mexico birthplace. I also guessed James would be married by 1910, which turned out to be true. This time when I clicked on "Search" the first entry was a hit, although some of the information it contained was mistaken. Poor Akers, who in the 1900 census had been listed as "Acres" was now ten years later "Akaas." Whoever had been questioned on that April day in 1910 also told the census taker that James had been born in Texas and that his older daughter's name was Emma. This last piece of information may have been true, but every piece of evidence I found referred to her as Anna. (I also looked at the actual census sheet to see if perhaps a slightly illegible hand had made Anna look like Emma. It had not.)

Still, from the census I learned a lot. James had indeed married in the intervening ten years and had also become a father. His mother (Sarah) had married too, and it was with her and her husband, Charles Clemens, that James and his family were living. According to the 1910 census, James Scott and his wife Grace had been married for five years, which means they tied the knot around 1905. I searched in vain for a copy of their marriage certificate for a wedding which I assumed—perhaps erroneously—occurred in Chicago. (Later I discovered additional information that told me Grace's maiden name was Williams, and that she was born in Pennsylvania. So I searched, again in vain, for a copy of the marriage license there. Finally I tried Indiana, an adjacent state, and Missouri, where James and Sarah had family. I came up empty both times.) Charles Clemens, the head of the household, was employed as an elevator operator in a shoe store, and his wife Sarah was working as a milliner out of their home. They all lived in an apartment at 316 W. Chicago Avenue northwest of the Loop, about fourteen blocks from the lake and four miles south of James and Sarah's apartment on Addison.

So between his first appearance in the 1900 census and the 1910 document, James had wed a woman who would have been around nineteen at the time of their marriage if—and it is a big if—her age was correct in the census. Grace's parents are said to come from from Virginia and Maryland, but because Williams is such a common name, I had no luck in tracing her birth. A year or so after their marriage, Grace and James had a child, recorded in the 1910 census as Emma, but whose name was more likely to be Anna. (This was the daughter James referred to later when he denied attacking my aunt because he has a daughter around the same age.) In January 1909, Grace and James had a second daughter, Virginia. She was born in Evanston, Illinois, just north of the city, information I later learned from another document.

As with James and Sarah's earlier home in Lake View, their neighbors on W. Chicago Avenue, this time including those in the same apartment building, were all recorded as white, while everyone in the Clemens's household was said to be mulatto. I initially found this description of James and his mother as black in one census and mulatto in the next confusing. Then I read that census takers in 1910 were told to choose between these two categories based on skin color. So while James and Sarah appeared to Rebecca Schnederman to be black in 1900—in fact, there was no "mulatto" category then—Fred G. Lando, the enumerator in 1910, felt that everyone in the Clemens household was light enough to be mulatto. We can assume both census takers were white themselves, since sending a black enumerator into a white neighborhood would have been asking for trouble. But just to be sure, I checked Schnederman and Lando's own census records to confirm this assumption.

Charles Clemens, James Scott's step-father, was forty-six years old in 1910. He was from Kansas City, Kansas, though he has lived in Chicago for twenty-six years. His marriage to James's mother was his first. For Sarah, whose age is listed as forty-five here (which would accord with dates given in the 1880 and 1900 censuses), this was her second marriage. She had been employed as a milliner, or hat maker, during the four months of 1910 covered by the census but was unemployed for twenty weeks in 1909. Whether this period of unemployment came at the beginning or end of 1909, we don't

5. Life in Chicago

know, nor do we know whether she was out of work continuously or in an intermittent fashion.

The rate of unemployment for blacks in Chicago was always higher than that of whites, which was understandable since a majority of black migrants coming to Chicago during the years after 1900 were originally farm workers from the South. Even if some of the migrant men were skilled craftsmen, they were unwelcome in most Chicago unions. The main industries that employed black workers arriving in the city were meat packing factories and the steel mills. James Grossman in *The Land of Hope* quotes a black railroad porter who recalled that during the years of the Great Migration a black man could always get a job in the stockyards.[8] As it turned out, James Scott and his brother Akers never had to work in the stockyards or the steel mills. While Akers was listed as a farm worker in Indiana in the 1900 census, by the 1910 census he was employed as a canvasser for a wholesale grocery business in Chicago. Later, he would become a chauffeur and mechanic for a transfer company, and subsequently a chauffeur and servant in a private home north of the city. James too changed jobs during the twenty years he lived in Chicago. Beginning as a worker in a club when he was only fourteen, he is recorded ten years later as being a laborer in the street. A few years after this another document lists his occupation as fireman, and when he fills in his draft card for World War I, he says he is a janitor employed by J. Frost, though whether this was an individual or a business I was unable to trace.

How did Akers and James get these jobs? Probably, like many of the people who came to Chicago later during the height of the Great Migration years, they were told of positions by others they knew. Not many employers advertised in a black newspaper like the *Defender* until 1919. If they had no friends or relations to help, black job seekers coming to Chicago could use private agencies and public employment services as well as help from their ministers.[9] The jobs open to young men like James and Akers were often in the service industry where few chances to move up existed because employers hired blacks in no positions higher than janitor or workman. James and his brother were gainfully employed throughout their time in Chicago, and while they never held high paying jobs, James was able to support a growing family while Akers moved from farmhand to mechanic and chauffeur. But at no time was Chicago a land of equal opportunity for blacks. Even when the law demanded equal access as it did in civil service positions, those in charge found ways to control the hiring and advancement of blacks. Alan Spear in *Black Chicago: The Making of a Ghetto 1890-1920* describes how officials charged with appointments circumvented legal requirements for hiring by holding examinations infrequently, filling vacancies with temporary appointments they renewed repeatedly, and showing favoritism in the examining process. And if blacks were appointed, they faced segregation in their working conditions and discrimination in promotion. One of the more notorious examples was the Chicago Fire Department, which had what Spear calls "Jim Crow units" until the 1930s.[10]

Three months after their appearance in the 1910 census, James and Grace had another daughter born on September 10, 1910. Unfortunately, it was not a birth certificate that gave me this information, but a death certificate. The baby's name was Ida, and she only lived for six months and twenty days, dying on the afternoon of March 30, 1911, at the Evanston Hospital after a four day stay. At the time of her death James and Grace were living at 1621 McDaniels Avenue in Evanston, where they presumably moved after their family increased in size. According to the doctor who signed the death certificate, Ida had died from "maramus," or a protein and calorie deficiency that can occur shortly after weaning if a baby does not get enough to eat. She had—again according to the death certificate—had this condition for six weeks. Because Grace and James already had two children who had not starved to death after weaning, which is what maramus essentially is, I wonder if this diagnosis was merely an attempt to provide an explanation for an outcome without a known cause or explanation. "Failure to thrive" is a diagnosis that describes a set of conditions rather than causes, and in all likelihood, this is the more appropriate description of what happened to the infant Ida.

Whatever the cause of Ida's death, it appeared to have put a strain on the marriage. James and Grace divorced sometime after (though once again, I could find no official document) because on June 24, 1912, almost a year and three months after Ida's death, James married a young woman named Lucille Smith. The marriage license was issued by the Cook County clerk, and on it James is referred to as "James T. Scott Jr.," a personal suffix that does not appear elsewhere on official documents. James and Lucille were married by the Reverend H.E. Stuart, whose church address is listed as 2252 N. Clark Street, which turns out to be a narrow, three story brick building that today has a store on the first floor. At the time of James and Lucille's marriage, the Reverend Stuart's church was probably one of many located in a Chicago storefront, though unlike most of them, it was not located on the South Side but on the North Side approximately five miles from where James and Lucille would live.

5. Life in Chicago

Whether large or small, refined in its practices or extravagant in its emotional displays, churches were important institutions for blacks in the city, supplying not only spiritual care but also social, economic, and cultural support. The Chicago *Defender*, in encouraging black migration from the South, listed the addresses of churches people could write to for help. Larger churches like Olivet and Bethel AME, which many of Chicago's black elite attended, provided assistance with housing, schooling, and childcare to those who had just arrived. Olivet even sent members of its congregation to the Chicago Terminal to meet incoming trains. There they would greet the migrants and direct them to places of assistance. So successful were they in providing social services that as Milton Sernett writes in *Bound for the Promised Land*, the church quickly gained a reputation throughout the South "as an oasis of mercy in the urban desert."[11]

One would assume the social good these black churches did would be favorably commented on in the local press, and to a degree it was. But like the articles about blacks in the Columbia papers around the same time, praise could be mixed with criticism. In 1916 Junius B. Wood, a reporter at *The Chicago Daily News*, wrote a series of articles for the paper later reprinted in a small publication called *The Negro in Chicago* with the rather lengthy subtitle: *How He and His Race Kindred Came to Dwell in Great Numbers in a Northern City; How He Lives and Works; His Successes and Failures; His Political Outlook*. One of Wood's subjects was the black church in Chicago at the time. "Churches probably wield more power among colored people than among any other single class in the United States...." Wood begins, adding, "The churches are an influence for good citizenship and an educational factor second only to the public schools."[12] According to a survey taken by the paper, 42.5 percent of Chicago's black residents belonged to a church, whether it was one of the large ones like Olivet Baptist with thirty-five hundred members or "the private ventures where a 'brother' or 'sister' with a can of paint and a brush has converted a vacant store into a mission."[13] In tallying up the numbers in 1916, Wood says Baptists lead the various denominations with thirty-six churches and 12,230 members followed by the African Methodist Episcopal with fourteen churches and 10,390 members. But with all this power and influence, he takes pains to note their clergy could sometimes be bought off. Wood quotes an unnamed black man fighting to keep saloons at some distance from churches and out of residential neighborhoods.

> Too many of our clergymen do not have the courage of their convictions and will not lead a determined fight against evil influences and institutions which encroach on their neighborhoods, usually conducted by white men.... A campaign contribution to the church from this or that politician has in some instances silenced criticism.[14]

This pattern of extoling then condemning in the same piece is one that appears repeatedly in white newspaper articles, as if the reporter or the editor wants to reassure his readers that he hasn't been fooled completely by the good works being done by blacks.

The question of how newspapers treated race in Chicago was one of the issues taken up by the Commission on Race Relations after the 1919 riot. Along with describing what could be construed as incendiary headlines about the riots in several papers, the Commission made a list of articles on racial matters between 1916-1917 in the three white newspapers in the city with the largest circulation: the *Chicago Tribune*, the *Chicago Daily News* and the *Chicago Herald-Examiner*. They found 1,551 articles, editorials and letters to the press, with the largest numbers having to do with riots and clashes (309), followed by crime and vice (297). Only when the category was soldiers—this was during World War 1—did a large number of articles (199) reflect a positive note on blacks in the city. To quote from the Commission's report,

> Generally these articles indicated hastily acquired and partial information, giving high lights and picturing hysteria. Frequently they showed gross exaggeration. The less sensational articles, permitting a glimpse of the stabler side of Negro life, were less than seventy-five.[15]

During those years that James Scott and his family were living on the North Side of Chicago economic and political growth of the black community increasingly focused on the South Side. As blacks began to face more discrimination with an increasing population, their leaders decided to build a series of community enterprises and institutions on the South Side. In doing so, they would not fight this discrimination by trying to integrate, but instead create a city within the city.[16] The large black churches were already there, along with the boys and girls clubs, literary societies, and even a church-sponsored kindergarten. African Americans had begun the century residing in various parts of the city, but by 1910, 78 percent lived in a chain of neighborhoods called the Black Belt. In the beginning. this section, which was then never more than seven blocks wide, ran along State Street from 22nd to 31st Streets. As more and more African Americans came north, the Black Belt expanded, but it could only do so in certain directions. To the west, were the Irish and other ethnic groups who had no desire to share their

5. Life in Chicago

neighborhoods. To the east, were railroad tracks and the meatpacking and brewery businesses. The only direction to go was south. Population density increased, and housing that had been adequate or better at the turn of the century turned into slums as several families often filled a small apartment. A street like Cottage Grove Avenue, which had been home to prosperous Jewish families at the turn of the century, now changed. As blacks moved in around them, Jewish homeowners moved out. But in many cases, the former residents kept their businesses in black neighborhoods going. Whites may not have wanted to live among blacks, but many had little problem doing business with them.

This open attitude about doing business with blacks was not, however, universal. Illinois had passed strong civil rights laws after the Civil War, including a prohibition against segregated schools in 1874 and a law to provide public accommodation for all in 1886. Yet black men and women never really knew how they would be treated once they left their own safe South Side neighborhoods. Segregation may not have been officially condoned, but law usually gave way to custom. Some businesses outside the Black Belt had signs in their windows restricting their clientele to whites, and when a large theater opened on the edge of one South Side neighborhood, blacks were seated only in the balcony. In city hospitals, no black nurses were employed to care for white patients, and while the Chicago public school system was officially desegregated, white students who found themselves in overwhelmingly black schools usually transferred out. In fact, in the first fifteen years of the twentieth century, proposals to segregate Chicago schools were repeatedly introduced at school board meetings.

Because James Scott lived at various addresses all on the north side, we can assume his children went to schools with white students during the time they were in Chicago. Adams Elementary was only a few blocks from the 316 W. Chicago Avenue address where Grace and Anna were living in 1909. So by the time her father married again, Anna would have been of school age. In fact, James's new wife was not much beyond it. The marriage license James and Lucille Smith signed on June 25, 1912, records his age as twenty-six and hers as sixteen, with Lucille marrying with the permission of her mother. A little more than nine months later, James became a father again, and again the child was a girl, Helen Elizabeth Scott. Helen was born at St. Elizabeth Hospital in the 1400 block of Claremont Avenue, five miles south of where James and Lucille live at 4509 N. Ashland. On the birth certificate, James's occupation is listed as janitor, and somehow both he and his wife have stayed the same ages they were when they married in June. (If we assume James's birth month is October, which appears on several documents, this information wouldn't have been accurate.)

But this was not a time of unalloyed happiness for the new father. At almost the same moment Lucille was giving birth to Helen at St. Elizabeth's Hospital, Virginia, James's four-year-old daughter with his first wife Grace, was being treated for meningitis twenty minutes away at St. Joseph's Hospital on North Lakeshore Drive. Grace brought Virginia to the hospital on March 28, and five days later she was dead, succumbing to the disease early in the morning on April 3. Thus within two days, James Scott gained a daughter and lost one. Death from meningitis was not unusual in 1913. An infection of the protective membranes that cover the brain and spinal cord and often goes into the blood, meningitis then killed approximately 75 to 80 percent of those afflicted with the disease. (It was also in 1913, but too late for Virginia, that an American physician, Simon Flexner developed a serum shown to decrease mortality in meningococcal meningitis patients.) Virginia was buried in Rosehill Cemetery, the same place her sister Ida lay in rest. Chartered in 1859, Rosehill on Chicago's North Side is the oldest and the largest cemetery in the city and like most cemeteries in the Chicago area, it has a black section. We can only imagine the devastation this death caused both James and his former wife who, according to Virginia's death certificate, was still living with James's step-father and mother when the tragedy happened. For both Grace and James, it was the loss of a second child within two years; only Anna now remained from their marriage.

More than a year later, on October 14, 1914, a happier event occurred. James and Lucille had another child, this time a boy they named Carl Earl. 1914 was also the year Sarah's second husband, Charles Clemens, died suddenly on April 21 at his home. At this time he was not living at the 316 W. Chicago Avenue address that appeared on the 1910 census but had moved to 4447 N. Paulina, about five and a half miles north. The informant on the death certificate is listed as Mrs. B.A. Clemens at the same Paulina address. I think we can assume that sometime between April 1910 when the census shows Sarah and Charles living together and Charles's death in April 1914, the couple separated and divorced. They may still have been together in April 1913 when James and Grace's daughter Virginia died, but sometime after that Sarah left Charles and moved back to Columbia. James and Lucille remained in Chicago with their two children, Helen and Carl, while Anna, James's first daughter with Grace Williams, also stayed there with her mother. (The evi-

5. Life in Chicago

dence for Anna continuing to live in Chicago with her mother came when her father was lynched in 1923. Newspapers reported Anna, but not Grace, came down from Chicago for the funeral. James Scott's oldest daughter would have been around seventeen then.)

After discovering the important clue as to why James and Sarah lived on the North Side of the city from a newspaper article, I began to wonder what newspapers Scott himself might have read during the time he lived in the city. I knew local papers like the *Sun-Times* (originally the *Evening Journal*), the *Tribune,* and the *Daily News* had started before Scott arrived in Chicago, and the *Examiner* began soon afterwards. But these papers were directed primarily at white readers. What about newspapers intended for a black readership? It turns out Scott would have had his choice of several papers that began publication in the late 1800s or early 1900s. The most successful of these was the Chicago *Defender*, whose reports of employment opportunities in the city helped encourage the Great Migration and which continues publishing today. The *Defender* started in 1905, when Robert S. Abbott, who had studied printing at Hampton Institute in Virginia and received a law degree from Kent College of Law in Chicago, decided to publish a newspaper. With an investment, it is said, of twenty-five cents and a plan formulated in his landlord's kitchen, Abbott began *The Defender* as a four page, six-column handbill. Soon it had turned into one of the most widely circulated weekly black newspapers in the country, with two thirds of its copies distributed outside Chicago.[17]

The *Defender* would not have been James Scott's only choice of a paper intended for blacks, nor was it the first one to be established in the city. That honor belongs to the Chicago *Conservator,* founded in 1878 by another lawyer, Ferdinand Barnett, who sold the paper to his wife, the journalist and crusader, Ida B. Wells in 1895 before they married. Wells had already made an illustrious career as a militant journalist and crusader against the practice of lynching. When she took over the *Conservator,* she focused on stories about the local black community and on occasion berated her readers for not voting for the black candidate in a field of whites. The *Conservator* ceased publication in 1914, after losing its fight for readership.

Another newspaper whose readership extended beyond Chicago's city limits was the *Appeal*, originally called the *Western Appeal.* Begun in 1885 in Minneapolis, at one time the paper was published not only in Chicago, but also in Washington, D.C., Dallas, Louisville, and St. Louis. While the *Appeal* was the most-read black newspaper in Chicago in 1888, its popularity had declined by the time James Scott arrived in the city. Like the *Appeal*, the *Broad-Ax* started publication elsewhere, then in 1899, the paper moved from Salt Lake City to Chicago with its publisher, Julius Taylor. Taylor was a Democrat at a time when most blacks were Republican, and while he was a strong advocate for his race, he abhorred the popular "cake walks" and "coon songs," which he felt degraded blacks. He began by printing editorials calling Booker T. Washington, whom he disliked, "the greatest white man's 'Nigger' in the world," though when Washington began to focus more on education and less on politics, Taylor relented. Finally, there was the *Chicago Whip*, started in 1919 by yet another lawyer, Joseph Bibb. Second only to the *Defender* until its demise in 1939, the *Whip* was a racially militant paper known for a campaign to encourage blacks not to spend their money where they couldn't work. This campaign helped place 15,000 black Chicagoans in jobs.[18]

Whether James Scott read any or all of these papers, I don't know. But thousands of other black Chicagoans did, looking forward each week to news that was relevant to their concerns. (The 1912 sinking of the Titanic, for instance, received very little coverage in the *Defender* and none in the *Broad Ax*.) Black newspapers reported on a world parallel to the white one from which their readers were so often excluded. They gave legitimacy to the interests and concerns of Chicago's black residents, and when employment for blacks opened up in the city in the years leading up to and into the First World War, it was a paper like *The Defender* that brought this news to its out-of-town readers. Advertisements too were directed at the black consumer. In the May 2, 1914, *Broad Ax*, for instance, ads for several black lawyers appear in one column, including a name I recognized, Franklin A. Denison, whose office was then downtown at 36 W. Randolph. He fought four years later alongside James Scott in France during World War I. The second page of the January 8, 1910, *Appeal* listed colleges and schools available for black students to attend and included Atlanta University, Howard, and Tuskegee, along with trade schools and seminaries like Tillotson College in Texas and Gammon Seminary in Georgia. What black newspapers reported on were the successes and possibilities of its readers, not just the problems they might cause.

In the years James Scott lived in Chicago, the black population more than tripled, from approximately 30,000 in 1900 to over 100,000 twenty years later. The largest increase came between 1916 and 1920 when European immigration halted and the able-bodied white men already here went off to war, a turn of events that gave black men and women the opportunity to fill their jobs, as these letters indicate:

5. Life in Chicago

Mobile, Ala., June 11, 1917

Dear Sir: Will you please send me the name of the society in Chicago that cares for colored emigrants who come north seeking employment sometime ago I saw the name of this society in the defender but of late it does not appear in the paper so I kindly as you please try and get the name of this society and the same to me at this city.

St. Petersburg, Fla., May 31, 1917

Dear Sir: pleas inform me of the best place in the north for the colored people of the South, I am coming north and I want to know of a good town to stop in. I enclose stamp for reply.

Atlanta, Ga., April 17, 1917

Dear Sir: I am a reader of you paper and we are all crazy about it and take it every Saturday and we raise a great howl when we don't get it. Now since I see and feel that your are for the race and are willing to assist any one so I will ask you to please assist me in getting imployment and some place to stop with some good quiet people or with a family that would take some one to live with them. I will do any kind of work. I am a hair dresser but I will do any kind of work I can get to do I am a widow and have one child a little girl six years old I don't know any body there so if you can assist me in any way will be greatly appreciated now this letter is personal please don't print it in your paper. I hope to hear from you soon.[19]

These are a few of many letters written by African Americans who wanted to leave the South to find a better life in the years leading up to the First World War. Collected and published in 1919 by Emmett J. Scott, the private secretary of Booker T. Washington, and later special advisor to the Secretary of War, they show the determination of people who are ready to leave behind all that is familiar for a chance to make a better life for themselves and for their children. In this way, they are the successors to Sarah, James, and Akers Scott, who had made the same decision a decade or so earlier.

James Scott grew from a teenager to an adult in Chicago. He married twice, and he fathered five children, three of whom lived. He worked hard to support his family, and when the time came, he volunteered to defend his country. We have no record of how he felt about living in a city in which the opportunities were so different from those in Columbia, but we can read how other black men and women felt after they arrived. From the same *Journal of Negro History*, here are two letters written home by men who made the journey north:

Whats the news generally around H'burg? I should have been here 20 years ago. I just begin to feel like a man. It's a great deal of pleasure in knowing that you have got some privilege. My children are going to the same school with the whites and I dont have to umble to no one. I have registered—Will vote the next election and there isnt any "yes sir" and "no sir"—its all yes and no and Sam and Bill.

> Well Dr. with the aid of God I am making very good I make $75 per month. I am carrying enough insurance to pay me $20 per week if I am not able to be on duty. I don't have to work hard. dont have to mister every little white boy comes along I havent heard a white man call a colored a nigger you no now—since I been in the state of Pa. I can ride in the electric street and steam cars any where I get a seat. I dont care to mix with white what I mean I am not crazy about being with white folks, but if I have to pay the same fare I have learn to want the same acomidation. and if you are first in a place here shoping you dont have to wait until the white folks get thro tradeing yet amid all this I shall ever love the good old South and I am praying that God may give every well wisher a chance to be a man regardless of his color, and if my going to the front would bring about such conditions I am ready any day.[20]

By 1917, when these letters were sent, James may have become used to the liberties and freedoms that Chicago offered. He had lived there more than seventeen years, though he had chosen to go north instead of south on arrival. He traveled in a city that did not deny him any seat on its public transportation, and he never had to step off the sidewalk when approached by a white man or woman as his cousins had to do in Columbia. In Chicago, James Scott did not have to "umble to no one." And as it turned out, he too was willing to fight for these conditions on the front.

6

What James Scott Was Missing Back in Columbia

As the twentieth century began, Columbia, like Chicago, was considering how to relate to its black population. In both cities, articles about "negroes as a problem" appeared in the local press, but in Columbia, this problem was also being addressed in the products of higher learning. The same educational institutions I assumed would have had an ameliorating effect on small town racial prejudice turned out, in one case at least, to be responsible for affirming racism. But before I turn to what educated white Columbians saw when they looked at the blacks around them, let me describe a happier situation: what one black Columbian saw when he looked at his own race in those early years of the century.

Robert Abbott in Chicago wasn't the only black man starting a newspaper at the beginning of the twentieth century. On Friday, November 1, 1901, in Columbia, Rufus Logan put out the first issue of *The Professional World*, a newspaper devoted to what was going on the black community in Columbia and beyond. At a cost of one dollar and fifty cents a year, the paper's subscription list crossed the color line, which meant that every Friday, Richard Jesse, the president of the university, and George Swallow, the dean of the agricultural college, as well as prominent members of the black community could unfold their *Professional Worlds* to read about Booker T. Washington's enthusiasm for equality through segregation or such local achievements as the appointment of a local black doctor to the Republican Party convention. Rufus Logan's editorials pushed for the establishment of a black-owned grocery store that would return profits to the black community (apparently John Lang, Sr.'s store was no more by then) and reported on the success of a local black transfer company. In the pages of *The Professional World*, Columbia's blacks did not appear as a problem to be solved but rather as a group ready for greater success.[1]

Among the news in that first issue were the names of the colleges the children of black Columbians would be attending after graduation. George Caldwell, for instance, was going to Fisk College in Nashville, Tennessee, while Virgie Muse was headed to George R. Smith College, a black school founded in Sedalia, Missouri, in 1894 with the assistance of Freedman's Aid and the Southern Education Society of the Methodist Church. The second page of the inaugural issue of the *Professional World* also contained state and national news, including a report on our harbor defenses and a column listing the market prices for cattle, cotton, and other commodities in New York, St. Louis, Chicago, Kansas City, and New Orleans. Advertisements included one for syrup of figs, "an Excellent Family Laxative," and another showed the latest fashion men's shoes, union made, offered by W.L. Douglas Company of Brockton, Massachusetts. With the ads, editor Logan added the following warning: "Readers of this paper desiring to buy anything advertised in its columns should insist upon having what they ask for, refusing all substitutes or imitations." (In later editions, Logan strikes a less cautionary note, suggesting repeatedly that his subscribers buy the products advertised.) The final page of Columbia's first black newspaper continued with a mix of the local— the editor's appreciation to those who have subscribed, listing some of their names—and state and national news, like the request of a delegation of Negroes to have their own building in the upcoming Louisiana Purchase Exposition to be held in St. Louis in 1904. This page was also filled with articles one can only call educational, with such titles as "The Diet of Crustaceans," and "Cicero's Wit." (As odd as these subjects may appear to the contemporary reader, they were a staple in many papers, white and black, in the early 1900s.)

In "No. I, No. 1" of his paper, Rufus Logan declares, "The columns of the Professional World will be open to all for the discussion of subjects pertaining to the education and elevation of the negro." And from the beginning that is what happened. Later editions included a regular farm column plus announcements that Hetzler Bros. of Columbia was buying hogs for packing purposes and that "Grocerymen are getting all the rabbits the trade demands." There were advertisements for medicines and cures, including Lydia Pinkham's Vegetable Compound, and more dismayingly, a big spread on Face Bleach with before and after pictures and a mention of hair straightener and face powder. In 1902, Logan added a column called "General Happenings Throughout The State Prepared for Perusal by Busy Readers." "Trigg's Farm Notes," written by J.S. Tripp of Rockford, Iowa, was also a regular feature, as

6. What James Scott Was Missing Back in Columbia

was a listing of lodge and church times and their leaders. Nothing was specifically designated as "colored," including the names of those who appeared in "City Notes." Occasionally, Logan made it clear the subject of an article was black, but usually only when it was someone who was not local, for instance a young woman in Philadelphia who had won a scholarship to Bryn Mawr, or a local man who had been murdered and was referred to as "a well known Columbia negro." While Logan was very happy to get subscriptions from white readers and regularly listed them along with new black subscribers, this was a paper by and for blacks in the state. The importance of *The Professional World*, which unfortunately only lasted three years—the final issue was December 25, 1903, and included letters to Santa along with its usual fare—can be seen when contrasted to what was later being written in white Columbia newspapers about the city's black residents.

Logan's paper disappeared at almost the same time the sociology department at the University of Missouri began to pay attention to Columbia's black community. Unlike *The Professional World's* emphasis on "the education and the elevation of the negro," the sociology department's scholarly writing appeared to be predicated on the belief that local blacks were a problem and placed an unavoidable burden on the community. The theses produced by the department's graduate students in the early 1900s possess a degree of racism that would take the present day reader's breath away. In this display they are not unusual. But because they are based on surveys done at the time, they also possess data about the black community we would otherwise not have, so for this reason alone they are valuable.

With one exception, the theses referred to here were written under the supervision of Charles Ellwood, an academic who had come to Columbia in 1900 to set up the sociology department at the university. Born in upstate New York in 1873, Ellwood attended Cornell University as an undergraduate. There he was persuaded to study the newly formed science of sociology rather than law. He continued his graduate studies at the University of Chicago and in 1899 received his PhD magna cum laude. Because the field of sociology was in its infancy, Ellwood did not immediately get a full-time teaching job. Instead he became secretary at a charitable organization in Nebraska and taught part-time at the university until he got the call from Missouri. (In this way, interestingly enough, he followed a career path similar to that of my grandfather, Hermann Almstedt, who also got his PhD at Chicago then took on an administrative position until he too was called to teach in the German Department at the University of Missouri in 1901.)

Professor Ellwood, who was a proponent of Social Darwinism, began his career believing racial heredity was a factor in social problems. In Chapter X of his bestselling textbook, *Sociology and Modern Social Problems*, he notes that the African environment, whose tropical heat punished those who worked hard and whose bountiful vegetation supplied food without much labor naturally resulted in a failure by the Negro to develop any instinct for work and "favored the survival of those naturally shiftless and lazy." To explain what Ellwood described as the "strong sexual propensities" in the Negro, he points to the extremely high death rate in Africa, which of necessity leads to an extremely high birth rate:

> It is not claimed that the shiftlessness and sensuality of the masses of the American negroes to-day can be wholly attributed to hereditary influences, but it would be a great mistake to suppose that the African environment did not have something to do with these two dominant characteristics of the present American negro.[2]

As false as a statement about the dominant characteristics of an entire racial group may sound to contemporary readers, Charles Ellwood, like other early sociologists, saw sociology as a means to an end, a way of making the world better. The purpose of the theses he directed in those first years of the department's existence was to provide the information needed to make improvements in the world. That we now read these works as racist might come as a shock to him, especially if we look at his subsequent actions and statements. In 1925, as the 14th President of the American Sociological Society Association, Charles Ellwood gave a presentation entitled "The Menace of Racial and Religious Intolerance," in which he encouraged social workers to address this rising intolerance in our nation by not permitting religious differences to separate us, and "that in particular we will not allow any prejudice of race or color to injure our just and kindly and happy relations with our fellowmen, regardless of race or color...."[3]

That Ellwood acted on this prescription is evident from what happened shortly after James Scott was lynched. A person Ellwood thought was a student but turned out to be a reporter from the *St. Louis Star* had followed Professor Ellwood into his office to ask if a community in which a lynching takes place, like Columbia, had lower moral ideals than the rest of the country? Ellwood apparently considered his answer, but then said yes. The subsequent article in the St. Louis paper brought him notoriety and condemnation from Columbia's town paper, but he did not back down.[4]

However, in his early years of teaching at the university, the students Professor Ellwood supervised did not always display quite so clear in a sense

6. What James Scott Was Missing Back in Columbia

of toleration. The most prominent thesis produced under the professor's supervision was a socio-economic census of the Columbia black community presented in 1903 by William Elwang. Entitled *The Negroes of Columbia; A Concrete Study of Race Problems*, this document was later sold at the 1903 St. Louis World's fair for fifty cents a copy. When I first read Elwang's thesis, I was struck by how much its author disliked his subjects. What I didn't understand at the time was how fervently Elwang believed in the tenets of Social Darwinism, a theory that applied, or perhaps misapplied, Darwin's laws of natural selection in the world of plants and animals to the evolution of human beings in society. Social Darwinism was a concept used to explain the success and failure of certain social groups, and while Professor Ellwood had a more nuanced view of its uses, his student Elwang, a member of the Columbia Charitable Aid Society, employed it bluntly to discover why a disproportionate amount of the Charitable Aid Society's funds and effort were used for the black residents of Columbia.

The Negroes of Columbia; A Concrete Study of Race Problems begins with a preface by William Elwang's thesis advisor. Arguing that the conditions for Negroes in Columbia are typical of those in a great many Southern towns, Professor Ellwood goes on to suggest that while the author of this monograph "is a gentleman of Southern antecedents and education" his opinions "seem to me remarkably free from personal or sectional bias." (Most contemporary readers would not agree with this.) He then offers his own personal statement of perspective:

> I must confess that, after three years of residence in a community where thirty per cent of the population are negroes, I have been compelled to revise to some extent my opinions on the race question. How totally out of adjustment the average negro is to the society in which he lives, has been impressed on me as never before.[5]

As I noted earlier, Charles Ellwood was a man, one of few, who in 1923 actively spoke out against James Scott's lynching. But twenty years earlier he said he revised his feelings about race after three years of living in Columbia, and does not discern any regional prejudice in the author of *The Negroes of Columbia*.

In the ten chapters that comprise this publication of his thesis, Elwang discusses the economic conditions, religious views and politics of the almost two thousand black residents of Columbia in 1900. He draws much of his data from house-to-house canvassing done by a sociology class from the university, though he warns, "The negro, like the Chinaman, has both an esoteric and an exoteric standard of living."[6] In other words, appearances can be misleading. What is not misleading is the historical background for present day problems. Slavery, Elwang says, had inevitably bred "moral debasement" in slaves, and when they were set adrift as freedmen, they were completely incapable of self-direction:

> It is, in a word, the same old and seemingly so hopelessly complex problem of the childish race in competition with the manly. Left to themselves no peoples of the black race have ever risen much above the primordial stage. None has ever created an institution or given birth to a social organization above the plane of barbarism. No division of it has ever had a written language, or developed an architecture.[7]

Drawing our attention to the comparable rates of growth, black and white, in both Boone County and Columbia populations, Elwang concludes that while the percentage of increase of the two populations remained similar, Negroes show what he calls "a strong and deplorable tendency to congest at the centers of population."[8] Examining the Columbia tax lists, he finds that only 4.09 percent of the black population owns any taxable property and that nearly half of all Negro property is the hands of thirty-one individuals. From this finding he concludes that only 31 of the 434 Negro taxpayers have shown an ability to make and hold on to their money. Elwang then offers this almost reasonable explanation for the failure of blacks in Columbia to prosper financially, though he cannot contain himself in the end:

> The very low rate of wages obtained for such labor as the negro can do, together with the steadily rising price of real estate, even in the localities by rigid class distinction set aside for him, have something to do with the failure. But laziness, misdirected energy, lack of foresight, pleasure seeking, immorality, have all been much more potent factors in keeping him in poverty. These traits lie at the root of his economic failure.[9]

Moving to the occupations and wages of his study group, Elwang begins with a complaint:

> Here is a large group of persons, most of them crassly ignorant, inefficient, and often dishonest, in competition with a much larger group of well-trained, steady and masterful persons of a different race, upon whom it devolves in some wise, to solve the pressing problem of economic survival, the everlasting question of "bread."[10]

Listing the occupations of the eight hundred and fifty-nine people about whom he has obtained reliable information, he notes twenty-five are in the learned professions and have become teachers, doctors, engineers and clergy, sixty are in skilled trades, such as bricklaying, carpentry, plastering, and tailoring; twenty-four independent proprietors "in more or less responsible positions"; one hundred and sixty-three in a superior class of laborers, one hundred and thirty-three are cooks, two hundred and thirteen are laun-

6. What James Scott Was Missing Back in Columbia

dresses, and two hundred and forty-one are common labors. The large number of common laborers in proportion to the skilled category discourages him. Then he adds, "The women are mostly cooks and laundresses, and very indifferent ones at that." He reaches this last conclusion by interviewing thirty-three white families of wealth to discover from their housekeepers that Columbia's colored help is in nine times out of ten utterly incompetent and furthermore, ignorant, shiftless, lazy, impudent, and dishonest. Wages of Negro workers range from one to four dollars a week up to ten dollars and over a week. By dividing the number of workers into the total amount of wages, Elwang comes up with an average weekly salary for the male worker of $5.69 and an average weekly salary for the female worker of $3.75. Further calculation shows him that the white population of Columbia must "gratuitously support, from their larders" a large portion of the black population of the town.[11]

Chapter four includes the description of the benevolent, insurance and social societies open to the Negro in Columbia. Dividing those societies formed by and controlled by the Negroes themselves and those organized and managed for them by the whites, Elwang finds there are at least eight secret societies organized by Negroes. They include the Masons, the Odd Fellows, and the Knights of Pythias, all of whom collect dues and have burial benefits. Some also have sick benefits. In societies controlled by whites for blacks, there are two: Metropolitan Insurance Company of New York, which has between eight and nine hundred policies in the county, and the Co-Operative Mystic League, which collects an average monthly payment of fifty cents from each of its 341 members. From the manager of the Mystic League, Elwang learns more than a third of its members never made a second payment, and almost three quarters of the group lapsed during the first year. Elwang writes:

> Comment upon these figures is unnecessary. Every reader can draw his conclusions about the negro's inability to persevere long in a course of action looking to a future good if it involves a present self-denial.... Lamentable improvidence and wastefulness seem to be inherent traits of the negro character.[12]

Disappointed by their participation in insurance societies, Elwang moves on to discuss church attendance. He finds there are four churches in Columbia who offer a religious life to the Negro in the early twentieth century: the Second Baptist Church, the African Methodist Episcopal Church, the Methodist Episcopal Church, and the Christian Campbellite Church. The two Methodist Churches have the majority of members with 396, followed by the Baptists with 251. The Christian Campbellites come in last at 58. Elwang notes the value of the church property in each case, and then makes the point that when he attended church, "the Columbia negro is in surroundings not at all commensurate with his financial abilities." He also comments on the paucity of support for foreign missions or even local charities. In fact, the whole of this chapter is a denigration of the black church, which Elwang describes as primarily a social center around which the lives of its members revolve. The ministers of black churches do no more than point out certain well-known moral precepts such as "Do right and you will go to heaven" and, according to Elwang, "there is very little in the service that bears directly upon the lives of an humble, ignorant and helpless people." The explanation for their continued misbehavior is simple: "a long and dark heredity has made it almost impossible for them rightly to adjust the relation between morality and religion."[13]

As for education, Elwang declares that although the statutes of Missouri never directly prohibited the education of slaves (ignoring the Ordinance of 1847), the slaveholders here as elsewhere felt that educating a slave made it more likely he would be dissatisfied and rebel. After the Civil War, "self-appointed educational missionaries from the North" along with the Federal Government in the form of the Freedmen's Bureau came in to offer the former slaves an education. To Elwang, these efforts were ill-advised and caused "almost irreparable injury to the race."

> Happily for the negroes of Columbia, their mental improvement was left entirely to their own care and that of those who understood them best—the white people of their own immediate neighborhood, their former masters.[14]

Statistics tracing the early progress of Negro education are few, but Elwang does provide a table noting the number of black school children in the district compared to the number attending. In 1867, sixty-three or 16.09 percent attended. By 1894, the percentage had risen to almost 70 percent (a year that might have included both James Scott and his brother Akers, were they living in Columbia at the time). This percentage fell off later; in 1902, only 55 percent of school age black children were attending. These are, in Elwang's view, discouraging figures, though he notes that some decrease in attendance in the later years can be accounted for by a bitter opposition to the school's principal on the part of the Negro community. He then offers a further possible explanation for the decline: that a kind of shifting process was going on in which some of the Negro population were sinking back into

6. What James Scott Was Missing Back in Columbia

"confirmed ignorance" while those with better blood persevered toward the goals that freedom allowed them to have. In other words, what was occurring was the survival of the fittest.[15]

In the chapter on Health and Morals the author begins by noting that according to 1900 federal census the average age of death for whites is 35.8 years. For blacks it is 28.0 years. From these figures, Elwang concludes the Negro has "much less power of resistance in the struggle for life than his Caucasian competitor."[16] Unfortunately, because births and deaths are not recorded in small towns like Columbia, Elwang cautions us that the local data he can offer will be meager and the generalizations therefore vague—though, as we will see, they don't appear vague.

In Columbia in the year closing in October of 1901, Elwang tells us there were forty-eight Negro deaths, thirty-four of them adults and fourteen children. Typhoid, pneumonia and tuberculosis accounted for the most deaths with other causes being accidents, bronchitis, whooping cough, and unknown in the case of seven infants. From this death count plus a list of the diseases Columbia's *only* [emphasis mine] black doctor was treating during the first three months of 1902, Elwang points out many Negroes were ill and dying from lung diseases, and a large number (fourteen) were under treatment for sexual diseases. Explanations for the high death rate among Negroes in Columbia were easily discerned, he said. A large proportion, especially of the children, did not receive adequate medical attention. In addition, the sanitary conditions in the black section of town are, in his words, "simply appalling." The houses—one, two or three room shacks—have no indoor plumbing and are usually not connected to the city sewer system even though it is within easy reach. Water is generally drawn from unwholesome wells or cisterns, and garbage is usually thrown in the yard for chickens and hogs or left there to rot.

> But after all that can be said about hygienic and sanitary conditions existing among the negroes and operating as causes for the high death rate among them, it remains to be stated that the most potent cause of all is the negro's constitutional weakness and defect. Whether such weakness and defect be an inheritance from his forebears in Africa, or result of climate, or of debauchery and vice since his transplantation to America, the fact of its existence seems to be unquestioned.[17]

According to William Elwang, almost the entire black population in Columbia is more or less afflicted by syphilitic poisoning and because of this affliction they are particularly liable to tubercular diseases. Therefore, no effective remedy for the high death rate can be instituted until the deplorable "race traits and tendencies" are eliminated.[18]

Elwang spends the last part of this chapter suggesting the low birth rate among blacks in Columbia is due to what he calls *"pre-natal murder,"* i.e., abortions. His proof for this practice is sketchy and need not be mentioned. Nor do I need to dwell on his descriptions of promiscuity among the Negroes of Columbia. Again, his data was based on repeated verbal inquiries and served by his premise that "negroes are still controlled by animal impulses.... Physical stimulation is their chief craving and highest achievement."[19]

The chapter on crime is short, in part because Elwang can find no official statistics on the subject. He does manage to make charts for convictions of whites and Negroes in City Police Court and Boone County Circuit Court in 1901. The former shows many more whites than Negroes are convicted of drunkenness, but "the negro's characteristic traits appear conspicuously in the very high proportion of convictions he furnishes for disturbing the peace, lewdness, gaming, assault." The fact that there were five cases of vagrancy among the whites and none for the Negroes, Elwang explains by suggesting that if the police arrested the Negro population for vagrancy, 25 percent would be behind bars. He is even quicker to explain away the dichotomy between the number of white convictions in the Circuit Court (seventy) compared to Negro convictions (twelve.) The higher number of white convictions has to do with the special efforts made at that time to control the illegal sale of liquor in the county. Elwang does note that the police are more likely to arrest Negroes than whites in Columbia, and he also mentions what he calls the "tacit assumption" that a black man once arrested is certainly guilty of something. Thus white juries almost always voted to convict.[20]

The chapter on politics is also brief, because its author believes the Negro of today is no more capable of casting a ballot than he was when he received his freedom and "was as incapable as a Hottentot of rightly understanding and performing the high duties which the chances of war had thrust on him." Despite this, at the time Elwang is writing, there are 1,125 Negroes of voting age in Boone County and 6,690 whites. In the city of Columbia, 445 Negroes can vote along with 1,098 whites. Angry that his vote can be countered by that of a black man, Elwang takes pleasure, it seems, in noting that because there are so many more Democrats than Republicans in Boone County, (4,840 to 1,679) and because most Negroes vote Republican, they never share in the political "spoils." Not even the janitor at the Columbia post office is Negro, he says. And of course, where their votes would be important, as in school elections, Elwang says they can be bought.[21]

The final chapter of Elwang's work begins posting this question:

6. What James Scott Was Missing Back in Columbia

Two alien races cannot occupy the same territory indefinitely on terms of perfect equality. All sentimentalists to the contrary withstanding, race consciousness, with its resulting affinities and repulsions, exists and operates. What, therefore, will be the final destiny of the American negroes?[22]

One answer, the euphemistic "Forcible application of mechanical means by the stronger race" is, according to Elwang, impractical. Deporting eight or nine million Negroes to an independent territory would not work, not only in terms of logistics but also because agriculture and manufacturing in the South would be paralyzed for generations. The South needs the Negro, and according to Elwang, the Negro needs the white man's supervision and control. Nor can education provide the sole answer. A few years of schooling could easily remedy the Negro's ignorance, but it would not touch the difficulty that "lies embedded in the racial character." The Negro race, as Elwang has said more than once, lacks the strength that enabled the Caucasian to hold its own. Sending Negroes off to institutions of higher learning would not transform a man morally. What he needs most is "the inculcation of the work habit.... Labor, foresight, self-control—these are the lessons that the negro must learn. And it will take more than one generation to drill them into him."[23]

Placing a Negro on a level beyond his abilities is the Negro problem in a nutshell: "He is out of place in America. Nature never intended that this country should be his habitat."[24] (We can almost hear Professor Ellwood's comment about the deleterious effect of hot weather on the black man.) The simple fact is that no matter how well one educates a Negro, he cannot compete with the white man. Elwang closes with a short discourse on "the social question" in Columbia, where the Negro is as segregated as he can be while remaining a part of the population and serving his white neighbors in "various humble capacities." Among the whites, the general desire is to be helpful "to a helpless people." Yet, for some reason that eludes Elwang, the attitude of the Negroes in Columbia, especially the young, is one of "distrust or latent animosity."[25]

Later Elwang writes, "Wherever the two groups touch, the white man commands, the black man obeys. Of inter-racial social life, there is not the slightest trace. The 'color line' is distinct. It is also ineradicable."[26] In the meantime, he suggests the Negroes in Columbia ought to be treated as wards of the nation as the red man was. Nothing is more idiotic than the Missouri constitutional provision that calls for separate but equal schools for the Negro. They do not need an education that would fit them for an ideal condition, i.e., equality with whites. Nor should they have the same police force and courts as the white man. Because the lack of a wholesome home lies behind much of the crime committed by Negroes, punishment should be less punitive and more reformatory. Politically, they should be disfranchised. Elwang is clear:

> They are "political idiots" and it is sheer madness to permit them to misuse and prostitute a privilege which the Anglo-Saxons won for themselves only through a thousand years of painful history. This would, certainly, work an immediate hardship upon a worthy few, but in a complex race question such as this, the individual can have no rights.[27]

As for their religious understanding, Elwang asks why we are sending well-educated and trained missionaries to die of fever among the savages of Africa, when we are turning over the religious education of the Negroes here to the guidance of ignorant, self-conceited and often immoral Negro preachers? The small number of Negro clergy with education and character has little real influence over the mass of their constituents. Elwang concludes by declaring, "We have taken hold of this entire negro problem at the wrong end. It is high time to admit the error and begin aright."[28]

The man who wrote these words was at the time a Presbyterian minister in Columbia. William Wilson Elwang was born in St. Louis in 1865 (the same year as Scott's mother) and after receiving his bachelor's degree at Southwestern University in Tennessee and his divinity degree at Columbia Theological Seminary in Columbia, South Carolina, he became pastor of a Presbyterian church in New Orleans and later one in Orlando, Florida. Pastor Elwang arrived in Columbia in 1899, a year before Charles Ellwood, and he served as a minister there until 1920, when he left to become a teacher of English in the Philippines and China. He returned to Columbia in 1926 and died in 1938. He got both a Master's and a Ph.D. at the university, his 1919 dissertation entitled "The Social Function of Religion," which was perhaps a more congenial topic for him since it involved a subject close to his own experience.

It is easy to dismiss some of Elwang's more outrageous statements in *The Negroes of Columbia; A Concrete Study of Race Problems*, but the fact is this was a piece of scholarship not only accepted by the faculty at a well regarded university in fulfillment of requirement for an advanced degree, but also promoted at the 1904 World's Fair. What William Elwang assumed about the black race is what most whites, educated or not, assumed at that time. For my investigation, the real question is, how prevalent were those assumptions by 1920 when James Scott came back to live in Columbia?

6. What James Scott Was Missing Back in Columbia

In 1906, another of Professor Ellwood's students, Charles Harvey McCord used his professor's theories on the racial characteristics of the Negro to divide Negro society into four groups in his master's thesis, *Negro Criminality*. Like the Nazi's later use of Social Darwinism, McCord's statements about the black man who is near in physique to the ape[29] and who while becoming civilized under slavery now shows signs of reverting, would be outlandish—if so many people did not believe as their author does. In 1914 McCord expanded the material from his thesis to produce *The American Negro as a Defendant, Defective and Delinquent*, a book that has been reprinted several times since then. From the title, I initially believed McCord had merely amplified his seriously defective theories. Then I came upon a section of the book in which he analyzes criminal cases against blacks. In Chapter Three, The Criminal Negro, McCord describes a case in which a fourteen-year-old girl returns home late one evening and explains her tardiness by saying she was raped and gives a description of her assailant. A few days later a Negro who matches the girl's description is arrested, tried and sentenced to be hanged. Because of a technicality, there is a retrial, and McCord, who has read about the case, decides to investigate. Here are five of the arguments he presents to the governor to prove the accused's innocence:

1. He had a good reputation, so far as he was known, as to sobriety and industry.
2. He had no unsavory history as to former crime, bad morals, or degenerate habits.
3. He did not try to escape, evade, or resist arrest.
4. He consistently and persistently asserted his innocence of the crime charged.
5. The girl's evidence was the only evidence against him, though he failed to prove an alibi.[30]

It is difficult not to think of James Scott when reading these statements. And it is difficult to consider Charles McCord as a thoroughgoing racist when he puts them forward. Yet the book he publishes in 1914 is filled with statements about the inherent nature of the Negro that would lead him to commit criminal acts.

During the same period Columbia's black residents were being studied by university students, they were also being studied and reported on in the local newspaper. The *University Missourian*, the same paper whose 2003 series on James Scott's lynching started me on this quest, published a three-column piece in 1911, describing "The Negro in Columbia" to its readers. The article begins on a positive note:

> If the negroes as a race were up to the standard of the negroes of Columbia they might well be intrusted (sic) to work out their own salvation. The negro population of Columbia stands above the level of the race in several ways. They own more property in proportion to their numbers, and they have the advantage of educated leaders. They live under better conditions, and have a better general religious and educational atmosphere.[31]

By the start of the second paragraph, however, the report changes tone:

> The old rule, that there is always some mischief for idle hands to do, is true of every race. But the negro, particularly, ought to be kept busy with his hands. He ought to be given every opportunity to make money, then restricted in spending it.[32]

This opinion doesn't just belong to the reporter, he tells us: the "best informed negroes in Columbia" agree. These same best informed Negroes also agree that white civilization is far too advanced for their "relatively primitive race," and Negroes may have received the right to vote too early because they are not always "adjusted to the conditions of self-government," a failing that makes them easy targets for corrupt politicians. On the whole, however, thoughtful Negroes in Columbia are optimistic about local conditions.

One of these conditions involves education, and in this regard commendations again flow. The head of the Frederick Douglass School has graduated from Howard College, and other teachers, many of them graduates of Lincoln Institute, are competent. At this time, four hundred and fifteen students out of six hundred black school-age children attend the ten grades at Douglass including forty in the three grades of high school. In the lower grades the work is exactly the same as that found in the white public schools. In the high school, German, Latin, and algebra are offered along with carpentry for the boys and sewing and cooking for the girls. There are also courses in music, penmanship, and drawing. But while the curriculum is good, the physical plant isn't. The building itself possesses only ten rooms in the main section and two more in the annex. They were poorly arranged and badly heated, and noise from one area carried over into another. These conditions, along with the absence of many mothers in the home during the day, accounted for the truancy problems at Frederick Douglass. On a more positive note, while teachers at the school do not receive salaries comparable to those of their white counterparts, they do spend time, and often their own money, to keep up with educational reforms. For instance, when J.B. Coleman was prin-

6. What James Scott Was Missing Back in Columbia

cipal, he purchased one of the first sets of the Century Dictionary sold in Missouri, spending one hundred dollars to do so.

Moving from education to religion, the reporter puts forward a critique about black churches similar to one made by Elwang in 1903, though this time the problem is quantity rather than quality: Why? Because the white population of the city, which outnumbers the black by three to one, has seven churches, while the blacks have four, and these "have become almost a burden on the negroes, for they are not as able to support them as are the whites." Although the four black churches are fairly well equipped with an average seating capacity of three hundred and a large membership, according to the reporter, their pastors have become "actuated too much by pecuniary interests, for they must keep urging in order to get their salaries." The section, however, ends on a positive note. When the reporter goes to a service at one, he discovers not only is the worship of the "old-fashioned, demonstrative kind," with songs, prayers, and scripture reading, incorporating a simplicity white churches have almost abandoned, but everyone has an opportunity to participate.

A discussion of black economics in Columbia begins with the denial of what is apparently a common assumption among the paper's white readers—that all Negroes in Columbia are common laborers. In fact, among the population are graduates of the University of Kansas, the University of Iowa, Fisk University, and the University of Michigan. (Noticeable is the absence of the University of Missouri, an omission that will not have the possibility of being rectified until 1950.) The reporter says that "probably" no fewer than three quarters of Columbia's black residents own their own homes (this may be an exaggeration), and several have accumulated large amounts of property and wealth. One man is worth more than $25,000, and two or three others have assets of more than $10,000. Negro barbers make as much as their white counterparts, and there are black grocers who carry the same stock as white grocers, though in smaller quantities. Two Negro doctors and a black pharmacist serve the black community, and all these people, according to the article, are trying to serve as examples to their race.

The problems come, according to the reporter, with housing and sanitation. An average-size black family numbers six, and an average-size black house is about three rooms. Some of these houses, says the reporter, are no more than sheds with rag-filled windows and walls and roofs with holes. There are no sidewalks, and dirt and filth is everywhere. It is no surprise then that the death rate is higher for people living under these circumstances, especially when many of them are ignorant of the laws of health. Tuberculosis conditions are especially bad. In 1910, there were twelve deaths from tuberculosis among Negroes and thirteen among whites at a time when whites outnumbered blacks three to one. These same bad living conditions along with the ignorance of the parents as to how to care for their young play a large part in the high black infant mortality in Columbia.

Having described these rather bleak conditions, the reporter then declares that according to Negroes themselves, one of their greatest needs is recreation facilities for their young men similar to those the Y.M.C.A. provides for white young men: "They have no uplifting places of amusement; they have no reading and game rooms; they have no places where they can get together in an atmosphere that is socializing and humanizing." At one time, the Negroes in Columbia did have a movie theater of their own, the reporter tells us, but it failed because they were unwilling to go up an alley to attend it. Instead, they went to the opera house where they flocked to the shows popular with white audiences.

Negroes in Columbia may not have their own theater, but they did have their own newspaper. The *Professional World*, which in 1911 had briefly restarted after its earlier demise, is the only black newspaper in Missouri north of the Missouri River, and at the time of this article, the paper had six hundred subscribers in the city and the rural routes leading into town and twelve hundred subscribers outside this area. R.L. Logan, a conservative Republican, was the publisher, and his aim was to "promote the best interests of the negro." As the reporter happily notes, "Nothing is even printed that would tend to arouse enmity and strife between the races."

The article goes on to discuss crime among members of the black population in Columbia, and again it presents a more balanced picture than readers are initially led to expect. Citing a city judge of the police court, the reporter states that while there are three times as many arrests for drunkenness and petty offenses among Negroes as whites, this situation may not be entirely the fault of the Negro population since "a negro stands a greater chance of being arrested for a petty offense than a white man." When arrested, the black man is placed in a dark, ten-by-twelve-foot cell meant to hold four men without regard to their offenses. Thus on a Sunday in March, twelve black men and five white men were in jail including a cell that held a twelve-year-old Negro boy, a fourteen-year-old Negro boy and two Negro men. The twelve-year-old had been accused of stealing a pocketbook containing $8.50 while one of the Negro men was charged with first-degree murder.

6. What James Scott Was Missing Back in Columbia

The final paragraph of this 1911 article reads:

> Under the conditions even as good as these existing in Columbia, the negro still presents a problem. This problem is big enough to call for the most serious thoughts of the most serious men. It doesn't seem that the negro was created to be always under the white man's foot. The race is now trying to go forward. It has a dark past behind it, but its more advanced members think there is light ahead. The solution to this problem is probably as much a matter of time as civilization is a matter of time. Conditions are gradually improving, but the result cannot be foreseen. Co-operation between the races for the advancement of the negro seems to be one of the greatest needs at the present time.[33]

As provisional as these statements sometimes read ("It doesn't seem that the negro was created to be always under the white man's foot.") whoever wrote this article—there is no byline—appears to be making an earnest attempt to "explain" the Negro in Columbia to the paper's white readers. The problem the Negro presents is never explicitly stated but a possible solution mentions both time and civilization. I thought of both words when I paused to wonder how many of the *University Missourian's* white readers in 1911 were standing on either side of the bridge twelve years later, watching one of the most uncivilized acts a society can commit.

Two years after the first article on "The Negro in Columbia," the *University Missourian* revisits the topic. This time the subtitle of the report spells out at least one concrete problem: "Black Population Is at a Standstill, the Death Rate Being Two and a Half Times That of White People." The 1913 article begins this way:

> A visitor at Boone County Fair, judging from the complexion of the noisy crowd, especially at night, would think that about seven-eights of the population of Columbia is black. If he happened to walk north of the city hall or for a few blocks and saw the number of negroes that live in one small house, he would feel sure of it. But as a matter of fact the negro population of Columbia has not increased at all in late years, while the white population has made a rapid increase.[34]

It turns out in 1913, the estimated population of Columbia not counting the students is 10,000. Of these, 7,500 are white and 2,500 are black. Thirteen years earlier, the population of Columbia was one third black, not one quarter as it is now. The death rate for Negroes in the city is two and a half times that of whites. In 1912, the white population had seventy-six deaths and one hundred and ninety-two births. The black population had sixty deaths and only twenty-nine births. The death rate for Negroes is 24 per thousand while for whites the death rate is 10.1 per thousand. The conclusion: "This shows that the vitality of white people in Columbia is much greater than that of negroes." Sound familiar?

The article goes on to say that while half of white laborers are skilled, only 7.8 percent of black laborers are. This statistic suggests that 602 black men and 323 black women are unskilled in 1913. They earn an average minimum wage of $7 a week, and "few get any more than that because they are only casual workers and only work when it is absolutely necessary." (Remember Ellwood's theory that the black Africans who survived were those who did not expend much energy in tropical climates?) As in the 1911 article, housing for a majority of Negroes is described as very poor with no water or sewer connection and bad ventilation and lighting. A large number of people often reside in each house. And while this area is responsible for most of Columbia's crime, the reporter does add that not all Negroes are shiftless or criminal. "There are in Columbia several educated, intelligent negroes who have made a success in life that many white people could not make under similar circumstances." The *Professional World* is again cited as the newspaper for blacks in the city.

The same four black churches exist in 1913 as 1911, and their total membership is now 775. This time the problem is not the salaries of the ministers, but the fact that neither of the black Methodist churches has a young people's society, similar to the one the white Methodist Church has. One of the black Methodist churches does have a Young People's Entertainment Club, which provides musical entertainment enjoyed by approximately a hundred people every Friday night. The reporter says that when a class of university students studied "the negro problem" during the previous year, they visited this club. They found the main attraction was singing, although there were also recitations "that sounded a little like Shakespeare" and a quotation from some other author. According to the students, "The service was rushed through, for refreshments were served afterwards and then all enjoyed a taffy pull. This program probably accounts for the large attendance at the services."

In 1912, enrollment in the Frederick Douglass School is 430. Average attendance is 91.6 percent as compared with 95.6 percent for white students. (Given that truancy was listed as a problem in the 1911 article, this figure seems high for black attendance, especially since it can be assumed the same problematic large percentage of black mothers were still not at home but working to support their families.) Frederick Douglass High School has two football teams by this time, and is planning a tennis club for the girls. At 1911 commencement, the students performed three plays at the Airdome. As if he were painting too rosy a picture, the reporter then adds,

6. What James Scott Was Missing Back in Columbia

> The problem of the negro in Columbia is to get him to do something for himself, to learn some trade and to keep at it. The school is training along the right line, but many of the negro children are reared in such surroundings and under such influences that they cannot break away from the shiftlessness and carelessness of their parents.[35]

The article concludes by reporting that the Charity Organization Society, a group in which Charles Ellwood and William Elwang had participated, receives many calls for help from Negroes. But the group does not actually help as many Negro families as it does white families because in the case of the former, "so many of the requests are from families who do not really need help." To illustrate this point, the reporter relates the story of a Charity representative who attempts to visit a black man allegedly too sick to work. When the representative does not find the man at home and inquires where he is, his wife says he has just stepped out but cannot work due to his rheumatism:

> The Charity man looked around the room—he said he was afraid to touch anything—and saw a black foot sticking out from a tangled mass of bedclothes on the bed. When a pointed question was asked, a wooly, black head emerged from under the pillow.
> "I'se sick boss," it said.
> "What's the matter?"
> "I'se got the rheumatiz, I has."
> "Well, we have to have a doctor's report before we can help you. Have you had a doctor?"
> "No, boss, I aint got no money to buy a doctor."
> "Well, we will have to send one."
> "All right, boss, I'll use any doctor you send."
> But the charity man believed that one deception was pretty sure proof of more duplicity and marked that family down as unworthy of aid.[36]

If this were not indictment enough, "The Negro in Columbia" ends by recounting the story of the Charity Society representative who was led to believe by one man that he had tuberculosis when, in fact, it was the man's downstairs neighbor. In this case, assistance was given but to the wrong man.

This is the information about blacks that white Columbians were reading seven years before James Scott returned to live here. At the heart of each of these documents, whether they were meant for a select academic audience or a more general one, is the belief something must be done to help blacks, either because they cannot help themselves or because they are too lazy or ignorant to do so. But people cannot single-handedly put in a sewer system or sidewalks. They cannot earn enough money to live well when the jobs they are offered pay little. Being helped because you are a victim of circumstances, whether of your own making or from powers not under your control, is far different from being a problem to be solved just because you are black and therefore inherently unable to cope. And unlike the growing black population in Chicago, the percentage of black residents in Columbia declined as the century progressed. The degree of racism, however, did not. It just went underground a little more. Reading these theses and articles, I feel I am getting closer to solving the mystery of how more than a thousand people could watch a lynching in 1923 without intervening.

To conclude this chapter, I offer the 1915 editorial cited by James Jindrich[37] as part of the title for his 2002 thesis, *Our Black Children: The Evolution of Black Space in Columbia, Missouri*. The editorial writer acknowledges the many inadequacies with which blacks had to cope:

> Our Black Children
>
> In Columbia there are a lot of Negroes—not four times more Negroes than Whites, as the disseminator of false information is fond of telling you, not anywhere near that many, but enough to make them a very large factor in the community. Now Columbia, all sob stories to the contrary, does not treat her Black children shamefully. Of course conditions exist in their quarters which should be remedied. An open sewer draining through part of the district is unsanitary and uncivilized, and for the good of the Blacks and the Whites, should not exist. The Negro school is crowded. So are many of the other schools. Some of the streets in the low section should be paved or drained, and in other places granitoid walks would lend much to the joy of life. Some few shacks should be torn down, and, of course, if it were possible to supply everywhere sewage connections and modernly equipped houses, it would be highly desirable. But since such a thing is manifestly impossible, the hue and cry that is being continuously raised about Negro housing conditions is both unfair and foolish.
>
> Perhaps the greatest need, on the whole of the Negroes of Columbia, is the one touched upon the seldomest—the need of harmless places of amusement. No theaters, no picture shows, no soda fountains-where would you go if such conditions existed for you? Don't be too sure you would not resort to the old, old weakness supposed to be a particularly darky characteristic—craps.[38]

What made these improvements in Columbia's black neighborhoods "manifestly impossible" had more to do with white opinion than with physical impossibility. Just four years after the editorial above, a student at the University of Missouri, August Larson, surveyed access to basic city services in six different sections of Columbia including Sharp End and Railroad Row. He reports in his 1919 thesis, "*A Housing Survey of Columbia, Missouri*,"[39] on appalling conditions in Sharp End and Railroad Row, but instead of blaming the victims, he decided that everyone deserves adequate living conditions made possible by equal access to city services. For instance, when city sewers were finally extended into black neighborhoods, he discovered landlords (both black and

6. What James Scott Was Missing Back in Columbia

white) made almost no effort to connect their properties to the sewer lines. Of the seventy-five houses he visits along Walnut Street, forty-five had potential access to the city sewer, but only nineteen were connected. In Railroad Row, the possibilities for black residents were even worse. Of the eighty houses he surveyed, forty-five were on streets without potential sewer access, and blacks occupied forty-four of those. In the whole city, then, only 5 percent of black houses were connected to a sewer while 80 percent of white houses were. More than half of the black households Larson surveyed used city water, but only ten hydrants were inside a dwelling. The rest were outside which meant that some residents had to haul their water a full block to get back home. Those who did not use city water drew from wells, none of which, Larson found, met a reasonable standard of sanitation. And since there was no city garbage removal, most blacks disposed of their rubbish, ash, and sludge by dumping it in their backyards or on their streets. This lack of access to city services together with poverty led to increased health hazards, which in turn reinforced the idea among whites that blacks were the inherently weaker and dirtier race.

James Jindrich had noted these and other reasons in his explanation of how the segregated neighborhoods in Columbia came to be. "*Our Black Children: The Evolution of Black Space in Columbia, Missouri*" is a masterful history of Columbia's neighborhoods. I owe much to Jindrich's work. Below I have encapsulated what he says about how the physical space of black Columbia evolved.

Drawing on the work of Thomas Woofter and John Kellogg, Jindrich describes how Columbia fell into the settlement type first described by Woofter in 1928. Here cities in border states often created strictly defined neighborhoods where a high concentration of Negroes were tolerated. These "colored" areas became home to many ex-slaves driven off farms after Emancipation, and in this way a city's racial population could increase suddenly. In the case of Columbia, Jindrich notes that in the forty years between 1860 and 1900 the black population increased by 350 percent (541 to 1,916), while the white population increased only by 140 percent (873 to 3,735.) What Woofter doesn't explain are the processes by which a particular "colored area" was chosen. For this, Jindrich turns to John Kellogg's articles on post bellum Lexington, Kentucky. Kellogg describes four basic patterns in which blacks inhabited Southern cities before the war. The first two, which involved the establishment of hidden black neighborhoods within white areas as ex-slaves became domestic servants, do not appear in Columbia. But Kellogg's third and fourth patterns did.

In the third pattern, skilled freemen, like John Lang, settled in a relatively affluent area within a city in order to market their goods to the larger white customer base. (Remember Lang's butcher shop?) At the same time, these freedmen were creating a community with black churches, stores, and homes independent of their white customers. Because the white population of the city needed these services, this black settlement, which occurred prior to Reconstruction, was welcomed and made part of the city economy.

Kellogg's fourth pattern of black development is the shantytown, which first arose on the fringes of Southern cities in the 1850s and continued as the result of the uncertain place of blacks after the war combined with white landowning power within the city. These shantytowns usually had two characteristics in common: they occurred on bottomlands or near railroad tracks, city dumps, or cemeteries, and they were often situated on steep slopes or other places where residential development was unlikely to occur. One reason that the original white marketplace in Columbia moved from the corner of Cherry and Fifth may have had to do with dampness, and certainly the part of West Broadway where it crossed Flat Branch in what became the black section of town was often so wet that dray horses had to be kept nearby to pull wagons out of the mud. So while the black neighborhoods of Columbia can be seen to fit Kellogg's descriptions at least in part—consider where Columbia Cemetery is—they differ in that the owners of what would become Sharp End, like James Scott's great grandfather Gilbert Akers, were initially black not white. By the turn of the century, land ownership in the black neighborhoods was biracial, but the nucleus remained in black hands.

As Jindrich notes, segregation may have begun with freedmen wanting to live apart from white control, but the division between the black and white communities in Columbia was reinforced as the nineteenth century ended and the twentieth began. At the turn of the century, the frontiers between the white and black areas often involved a street's name change, so that, for instance, Fifth Street became Washington as it entered a white area; and Walnut, a racially identified street, ended abruptly when it entered the more affluent West Broadway neighborhood. A less obvious distinction, Jindrich notes, was to term any street that entered a black area as "West." By 1900, the axis of the Flat Branch was the defining marker for black space in Columbia. The creek was used as a sewer by the local slaughterhouse and by many residents. In fact, in some late nineteenth century maps, a tributary that ran between Ash and Park Streets is explicitly labeled as a sewer. The only other area occupied by blacks was another poorly draining, undesirable spot north of down-

6. What James Scott Was Missing Back in Columbia

town by the Wabash railroad tracks. In the Flat Branch area, the more well to do blacks lived higher up, nearer the white neighborhoods. But lower-down roads were not paved. Pigs and other animals were kept in back yards, and the resultant feces put into the creek. As we have seen, the physical ugliness of Sharp End became unfairly associated with the qualities of its inhabitants. Because the black community contained mud in the bottomlands along with some dirty industries, it was associated with disease in white citizens' minds. So prevalent was this connection that Columbia public schools for a long time did not provide books to students for fear of causing an intermingling between black and white students.

Between 1905 and 1915, two transient populations became important to the city and the spaces it had to allocate. Investments in the railroad and the university resulted in doubling the population between 1900 and 1910. Areas to the north and the south of the city center were annexed. The student population at the university kept growing, especially after the Journalism School was established in 1908. A year earlier, the Hamilton-Brown Shoe Company began operation north of the city. Well-to-do neighborhoods built up around the university, with Broadway becoming a dividing line in social standing and wealth. In the early 1900s the most affluent part of the city was in the east end surrounding Stephens College. Parallel to that on the west end was the area where the most prosperous blacks lived. By 1915, wealth had shifted to the south and the southwest by the university, leaving the black areas isolated from this prosperity. When white workers who lived north of Broadway in the west section wanted to go downtown, they had to go through the black area. But in the south, a bridge was built across the MKT tracks below the black section (the same bridge under which my aunt was attacked and from which James Scott met his death), and a private park was created along a tributary of the Flat Branch in this section. In the black neighborhood, there was no park until much later when urban renewal came in. Instead houses were built up to and sometimes over the creek.

As older residents of Columbia lost influence and wealth to those employed by the university, family connections became less available to blacks seeking work; there were also fewer black public figures in city affairs. The white working population increased, and often they won the low-end jobs available. Blacks were forced to lower the wages they asked in order to compete with the larger number of whites available for jobs, and the number of black workers employed in skilled occupations decreased during this time. Property values on the whole increased, though not in the black neighborhoods. Black businesses declined, and access to city services did too. By 1919, when Larsen made his survey, all the white areas of the city had sewage, water, and garbage removal. Streets were paved, except in the area where the shoe factory workers lived. The black community did not receive these same services. Blacks after 1900 were trapped in substandard housing and low wage jobs, and then told by Elwang and others it was their fault. The black population peaked at 1,800 in 1915. This was also the year the percentage of black citizens in Columbia fell below 20 percent.

Almost forty years later, in 1954, an urban renewal project began in Columbia. By the time it was over, most of the homes and businesses within the black community around Sharp End were razed. The two creeks that ran through the neighborhood disappeared as they were deepened and forced underground to become sewers. Public housing replaced what were described as "shanties," and roads in the area were drained and paved, often for the first time. What urban renewal brought to the black neighborhoods of Columbia was generally considered progress, but it was progress with a cost. Were James Scott's relatives to return to where they grew up, or even where Scott died, they would find little evidence of what had been there. What was part—but only part—of the "Negro Problem" for Elwang, McCord and the others had been bulldozed away. And with it went a history that no one, black or white, was inclined to talk about.

7

James Scott's Possible Great Adventure

Up to now, the evidence I have presented about James Scott's life has come from official documents like the census and marriage and birth certificates: places where his name has appeared. To augment this, I have tried to describe what was happening in the larger world around him during this time. But whether or how these events affected him, I cannot be sure. Now I come to the part of James Scott's life where what is happening in the larger world around him has a very direct effect on his life, or so I assumed when I began my research. Whether I was correct in making this assumption turns out to be a small mystery itself. The time James Scott spends fighting in France will end up being the biggest adventure of his life, as it was for many men who became soldiers during World War 1. The only difference will turn out to be if you are a white soldier or a black one.

In the years leading up to the First World War, America was hardly a comfortable place for blacks to be. Racial conflicts including lynching were increasing. In 1910 a local chapter of the National Association for the Advancement of Colored People, or NAACP, was founded in Chicago. The genesis for this organization had begun a year earlier in New York City when a group of white liberals angry about the growing number of lynchings in the South called a meeting to discuss racial justice.[1] Sixty people attended including W.E.B. Du Bois and Ida B. Wells-Barnett. Together the group set as its goal securing the rights provided by the 13th, 14th and 15th Amendments to the Constitution for all. By 1912 there were fifteen local chapters, and by 1920 four hundred chapters of the NAACP existed from coast to coast. Much of the credit for this increase goes to one of the NAACP's most enthusiastic supporters, Joel E. Spingarn, a white college professor from New York City who will indirectly play a small part in James Scott's life. Independently wealthy, Spingarn was elected chairman of the executive board in 1914, and soon after he made two separate trips west at his own expense to promote the NAACP.

On one of these he stopped in St. Louis, where he was invited by some liberal white businessmen to speak at a luncheon at the City Club. His speech was entitled, "The Colored Citizen and His Future," and as Spingarn later recalled, as he began to talk, first one person then another got up to leave. By the time he finished his speech almost three-fourths of the audience had disappeared. That night he spoke to a black audience at a local church. He told them what had happened earlier and encouraged them to form an NAACP chapter in St. Louis, which they did the very same evening. Within a year the chapter had grown to a thousand members, in part because J.E. Mitchell, the editor of the local black newspaper, *The Argus*,[2] was a strong supporter who devoted large sections of the paper's front pages to membership drives. When, nine years after Spingarn's first visit, James Scott was held in jail in Columbia, it was a representative from the St. Louis chapter of the NAACP, a lawyer by the name of George Vaughn, who took the train up to Columbia to help with Scott's trial. Later he would write an account of what happened for the NAACP.

Even if he had known the role the NAACP would play in his life, James Scott would probably not have joined. By all appearances, he was one of those men who believed, as Booker T. Washington did, that what the black man must do is lead an industrious and exemplary life, and his opportunities would come. But in 1910 James Scott did join a local organization; he enlisted in the 8th Infantry of the Illinois National Guard. We know he was part of the 8th beginning in this year, because on May 29, 1915, the weekend edition of the *Chicago Defender* published an article about a large reception held for 8th Regiment at the new armory on 35th and Forest Avenue. After a dress parade and before the grand march and dance, there was a medal presentation where Colonel E.R. Romberg of the governor's staff presented awards to those who had served in the 8th Regiment for five to fifteen years. Among those the medal recipients was Private James T. Scott of Company D, who at that time had served for five years.

I never did find a copy of that first volunteer form James filled out, but on 21st day in July 1913 Captain Benjamin E. Pinkney swears him in to Company D of the 8th Infantry of the Illinois National Guard for a second time.[3] On this second form I finally see a physical description of the man whose life I have been investigating: James Scott is listed as five foot seven inches tall with black hair, brown eyes and complexion. He is said to be a fireman and lives at 4509 N. Ashland, the same address he occupied when his daughter Helen was born a few months earlier. On this date in 1913 James Scott is said to be 26 years old. This means he will have slightly less than ten years to live.

7. James Scott's Possible Great Adventure

In joining the 8th Infantry, James chose an organization with a long and determined history.[4] First formed in 1878 as the 16th Battalion in the Illinois State Militia, the state legislature decided after four years it was no longer able to maintain a "colored unit," so they dropped the 16th Battalion from the military register. Undeterred, the 16th reorganized as the Chicago Light Infantry, which in 1884 had 75 members. When this group disbanded after three years, several of the men came together to form the Illinois State Militia at Chicago. Known first as the 9th Infantry Battalion, they were subsequently to form the nucleus of the 8th Illinois Volunteer Regiment. As enrollment in the 9th increased, the battalion applied to Illinois Governor Joe Fifer for admission into the state guard. Fifer refused, saying there was not enough money in the state treasury to support them. The men of the 9th, suspecting this decision had been made on the basis of race rather than finance, placed one of their own officers, Major J.C. Buckner,[5] in nomination for state representative. Buckner was elected, and he subsequently framed a resolution that became law creating a vacancy in the state militia and making appropriations for it. The 9th renewed their application to join the National Guard, and on November 4, 1895, they were welcomed in.

During the next three years the 9th expanded and was re-designated as the 8th Illinois Voluntary Infantry Regiment with twelve letter companies drawing their personnel from throughout the state. The 8th was called up for the Spanish American War and served in Cuba during 1898 and 1899. Here is the beginning of a laudatory article about their homecoming after Cuba:

> 'Twas a right royal welcome, but fully deserved, which was given to the Eighth Illinois Volunteers on its arrival in Chicago last Saturday. The men were tired from travel but they made a fine parade and were cheered continuously by the thousands which lined the streets in their route from Twelfth street station to the Second Regiment armory. Fully twelve hundred stalwart men were in line under the command of Col. John R. Marshall, the first Afro-American upon whom that title was ever bestowed in the volunteer army of the United States.[6]

Could a young James Scott have been among them? After returning from Cuba, the 8th engaged in regular peacetime duties with two large-scale maneuvers at Fort Benjamin Harrison in 1908 and in Peoria in 1910. The regiment was again federalized in June of 1916 to serve for several months in the Mexican Border War in Texas. But their biggest call to duty was yet to come.

While the 8th Infantry was composed entirely of African Americans from the top down, it was also a part of the larger Illinois National Guard.

How important this was for Scott and the other black men in the 8th is the subject of a paper by Eleanor Hannah called "Soldiers Under the Skin."[7] In it she argues that in the nineteenth and early twentieth century, the Illinois National Guard was one of the few places that united men across social and cultural boundaries that were then otherwise difficult to breach. Guardsmen black and white marched together on civic holidays. They attended summer training, and as we will see when the ING is called up for duty in World War 1, they shared many of the same experiences in camp—drilling, parading, messing, skirmishing and lounging. On all these occasions the differences between the colored and white units were extinguished. They wore the same uniforms. They were subject to the same discipline. They had the same aspirations as soldiers. More drew them together than divided them. For James Scott and the others in the 8th, belonging to the ING gave them a chance to taste equality with their fellow white guardsmen. It also gave them the opportunity to share these experiences with men of different social classes. Professor Hannah notes the wide range of jobs listed for men in the ING in the years from 1870–1904. In the 1st Infantry of Chicago, for instance, the largest percentage is from the category self-described as "clerks." However, work categories are spread throughout the regimental companies. So while James Scott enlisted in the National Guard as a fireman in 1913 and registered for the draft as a janitor in 1918; his fellow guardsmen would have included bookkeepers, carpenters, electricians, as well as attorneys and doctors.

As welcoming as the Illinois National Guard might have been to all its members, it did not always employ them equally at times of crisis. A good example was the Springfield riots of 1908, one of the precipitating factors to the formation of the NAACP. In this case, the trouble began when a crowd gathered outside a jail demanding to be given two black prisoners, one charged with murder and the other accused (but later cleared) of rape.[8] Unlike James Scott's experience in Columbia fifteen years later, the Springfield sheriff protected the jailed men by having the nearby fire station ring its alarm while he put the prisoners into a waiting car, which took them to safety. The crowd, angered at this deception, turned on the driver of the car, burning his vehicle and demolishing his restaurant. Now a thousand strong, the rioters began attacking a large residential section of the city, bypassing those houses where a white sheet hung out in front to indicate its residents were of that color. In the hours that followed, mobs burned black homes and beat their residents. They hanged a black barber from a tree. The rampage stopped only when National Guard units—but only the white ones—arrived and shot into the crowd.

7. James Scott's Possible Great Adventure

The next night the rioters regrouped and tried again to attack black homes along with the arsenal where many blacks had taken refuge. Again only white Guardsmen stepped in. But the rioters did not desist. Instead, they turned toward downtown and coming upon an eighty-four-year-old black man a block from the state capitol, they slashed his throat and hanged him. When the riot was over, 40 homes and 24 businesses had been destroyed, and seven people were confirmed dead, with many other deaths said not to be reported. The Springfield riot resulted in 107 indictments, but as with the later trial in Columbia, witnesses were hard to find. In the end one mob leader killed herself, and one man was sentenced to thirty days for stealing.

Five years later in a confidential report, a federal inspector noted that the 8th regiment of the National Guard, the unit James Scott joined in 1910, would *never* be called out for domestic service, because to do so would almost certainly "precipitate a race war." The inspector did say that if the 8th were called up for service abroad, they would make fine soldiers. This turned out to be an accurate prophecy.

By the time Woodrow Wilson considered taking part in what was later called "The Great War," the fighting had been going on more than three years. Eighteen million men had died including four hundred thousand French during the battle of Verdun and a half million British soldiers in the Battle of the Somme. The Allied forces were being depleted at a rapid rate. Wilson's initial reluctance to engage the United States in war in some ways previewed his hesitancy first to draft, then to use the African American soldiers who volunteered to fight.

When the President and Congress finally agreed to declare war in April 1917, the United States had about ten million Negro citizens. On the first day of registration for the draft in June, more than 700,000 black men lined up to enlist. In response, the Selective Service established a quota system; there would be one black recruit taken for every seven white recruits. In addition, the segregation that already existed in the regular Army would continue. By the end of the war 400,000 African Americans had served in the Army and Navy—the Marines and Air Force refused to take black volunteers—but only 42,000 of them had been given the opportunity to fight.[9] The rest worked overseas as cooks, orderlies and truck drivers. Of the black men who enrolled, only a small percentage were offered combat training, and there was only one officer's training school for blacks—this created as a result of extensive pressure first by Joel Spingarn of the NAACP and later by college students at Howard, Fisk, Tuskegee and other black institutions. The 9th and 10th Cavalry and the 24th and 25th Infantry, the segregated units of the standing Army, were sent to patrol the Mexican border or were stationed in Hawaii or the Philippines. None of these trained, veteran soldiers went to Europe.

But there was one group of African Americans who did not need to be drafted. These were the men, 10,000 strong, who belonged to National Guard units in their states. When the call came for the National Guard to be mobilized, they were ready. The Illinois 8th Infantry Regiment reported for federal service on July 25, 1917. They were still the only regiment in the United States Army to have a complete roster of "colored" commissioned officers, and all of those officers were professionals—lawyers, doctors and business owners. Their leader, Col. Franklin A. Denison was an Assistant City Prosecuting Attorney, who after the war became Assistant Corporation Counsel for Chicago. To belong to the 8th was seen as sign of privilege, and consequently they had no trouble filling out their ranks when they were called up for duty that spring.

As eager as James Scott and the rest of his regiment were to join the war effort, they were also aware of the racism in the armed services and in the country. How could they not be? To begin with, there was the incident in Brownsville, Texas, in 1906 when President Theodore Roosevelt ordered all 167 black men in Company B of the 25th Infantry dismissed without honor after they were alleged to have participated in a racial incident in which a white Brownsville citizen was killed and a policeman wounded. The company protested, but to no avail. The following year a Senate investigation revealed the only evidence connecting the soldiers to the crime—spent shells—could have been planted. (And as it turned out, all the men in Company B were found innocent of the charges, though this didn't happen until 1972.)[10]

Two years after Brownsville came the Springfield riot, but the incident that might have made Scott and his regiment reconsider their commitment to their country occurred just as the 8th began to train for the war. In July 1917, three hundred miles south of them in East St. Louis, Illinois, a riot broke out, and like racial violence elsewhere, there were precipitating factors. In this case, an increasing number of blacks coming into the city to find work had made the whites there nervous. When black residents were only a small minority, the rigid segregation policies in East St. Louis worked. But as companies like Aluminum Ore and Swift Packing began to bring in black workers to take the place of white men who were trying to organize, tensions grew. It didn't help matters that in the 1916 local elections, the Democrats won by a small majority and then only because they had accused the Republicans of

7. James Scott's Possible Great Adventure

secretly plotting to bring more black residents into the city to get the Republican vote. With fear comes exaggeration. Below is a letter sent into the *East St. Louis Mail*:

> It is a noticeable fact that whenever revolvers form part of a display of a store window they at once attract attention from passing Negroes. The glitter of polished chrome metal revolver possesses a fascination for the colored sport that is hard to resist, and he has been known to make a series of small deposits with the dealer to obtain the coveted weapon. Our pawnbrokers can tell you that more pistols are pawned by colored men than by any other class. Their idea is that the gun serves the double purpose of defending them against their dreaded foe "de wite man" and as a meal ticket when they get hungry. Negro gun toters are fanatical on the subject of selfprotection and are constantly confiding to each other what they intend to do to the first "bad man" who disturbs their peace. The way to stop about half of this mortal and terrifying practice is to penalize the sale of guns, especially to "cullud folks."[11]

A rumor began that when Independence Day came, blacks—armed with all these revolvers—were intending to massacre East St. Louis whites. This rumor didn't just arise out of the blue. On May 28, shortly after a large group of union representatives met with the City Council and the Mayor, news came that a Negro had just shot a white man during a robbery. As the story was passed along, it became two white women insulted and another shot. A mob gathered and marched downtown shouting, "Take the guns away from the Negroes," and while no one was killed, several black men were beaten severely. The stage was set for more violence.

On the evening of July 1, 1917, a dark car drove through the black section of the city. The men inside fired shots at the houses. Later after another group of so-called Nightriders did the same thing, black residents got ready. When a third car appeared, they fired back, killing the two white plainclothes policemen inside. The next day white citizens began a rampage through the city that would end up killing almost a hundred blacks, many of them women and children. The rioters chopped fire hoses in half then set houses on fire. They shot, beat and lynched any black person they saw, sometimes throwing him or her into the nearby Mississippi River. Local police did little to stop the rioting, nor did the Illinois National Guard when they were called in. (Witnesses reported many of the Guardsmen joined in the burning and lynching.) In the end the number of deaths was hard to determine, because not all the corpses were recovered. The East St. Louis police chief said he thought about 100 blacks were killed. The N.A.A.C.P estimated somewhere between 100 and 200. Six thousand blacks in the city were left homeless after their neighborhood was burned, while only a few of the white rioters were arrested and tried.

In President Wilson's words, what members of the 8th Illinois National Guard were going to fight for was "a world made safe for democracy." Yet what kind of democracy was evident in East St. Louis? Here is Marcus Garvey's view on the subject in a speech he made a few days after the riot occurred:

> The East St. Louis Riot, or rather massacre, of Monday [July] 2nd, will go down in history as one of the bloodiest outrages against mankind for which any class of people could be held guilty. (Hear! hear.) This is no time for fine words, but a time to lift one's voice against the savagery of a people who claim to be the dispensers of democracy. (cheers) I do not know what special meaning the people who slaughtered the Negroes of East St. Louis have for democracy of which they are the custodians, but I do know that it has no literal meaning for me as used and applied by these same lawless people. (hear! hear!) America, that has been ringing the bells of the world, proclaiming to the nations and the peoples thereof that she has democracy to give to all and sundry, America that has denounced Germany for the deportations of the Belgians into Germany, America that has arraigned Turkey at the bar of public opinion and public justice against the massacres of the Armenians, has herself no satisfaction to give 12,000,000 of her own citizens except the satisfaction of a farcical inquiry that will end where it begun, over the brutal murder of men, women and children for no other reason than that they are black people seeking an industrial chance in a country that they have laboured for three hundred years to make great [cheers][12]

Marcus Garvey, born in Jamaica and organizer of the Universal Negro Improvement Association (UNIA), which represented the largest mass movement in African American history, did not always agree with the American-born black leaders. But in pointing out the hypocrisy of a country that would go to war to "make the world safe for democracy" without offering it to its own citizens, he was allying himself with two black leaders who loudly opposed blacks serving in the war. A. Philip Randolph and Chandler Owen began *The Messenger*, a socialist-labor magazine in August 1917 in New York City. Less than a year later they wrote in the *Messenger*:

> The only legitimate connection between this unrest and Germanism is the extensive government advertisement that we are fighting "to make the world safe for democracy," to carry democracy to Germany; that we are conscripting the Negro into the military and industrial establishments to achieve this end for white democracy four thousand miles away, while the Negro at home, through bearing the burden in every way, is denied economic, political, educational and civil democracy.[13]

But they didn't stop there. "No intelligent Negro is willing to lay down his life for the United States as it now exists," they declared.

For many African Americans, participation in the war became a crucial test of how committed the United States really was to the rights of citizenship

7. James Scott's Possible Great Adventure

for all its people, regardless of race. W.E.B. Du Bois, who in 1911 had thrown off his pacifist cloak to argue for resistance against white racists, now presented his view of black participation in the war in an editorial entitled "Close Ranks":

> This is the crisis of the world. For all the long years to come men will point to the year 1918 as the great Day of Decision, the day when the world decided whether it would submit to military despotism and an endless armed peace—if peace it could be called—or whether they would put down the menace of German militarism and inaugurate the United States of the World.
>
> We of the colored race have no ordinary interest in the outcome. That which the German power represents today spells death to the aspirations of Negroes and all darker races for equality, freedom and democracy. Let us not hesitate. Let us, while this war lasts, forget our special grievances and close our ranks shoulder to shoulder with our own white fellow citizens and the allied nations that are fighting for democracy. We make no ordinary sacrifice, but we make it gladly and willingly with our eyes lifted to the hills.[14]

The reactions to this famous "Close Ranks" editorial by DuBois were not unanimously positive. Some black leaders like Hubert Harrison, founder of the Liberty League and the *Voice*, the radical alternatives to the NAACP and *Crisis*, objected strenuously to the line about "forgetting our special grievances" as if lynching and racism could be put aside so easily. Others wondered whether Du Bois's change of heart from his usual pacifist position was due to the commission he was seeking in the Military Intelligence Branch, the agency to which his friend Joel Spingarn belonged and had encouraged him to join. Du Bois denied the connection, but he did accept a commission to the MIB a month after the editorial was published. However, the offer of a commission was later withdrawn when, among other reasons, Southern members of the Branch objected.

How much of this debate between black leaders would Scott have read about? Not much if his newspaper was *The Defender*. As Theodore Kornweibel, Jr.[15] points out in *Investigate Everything: Federal Efforts to Compel Black Loyalty During World War 1*, going into a war created an opportunity for the government to crackdown on those black publications they considered dangerous. Similar to what happened after 9/11 in our own time, acts were passed which often were heavy-handed attempts to suppress dissension and demand patriotism from everyone. Robert S. Abbott, editor of *The Defender*, turned out to be one of the main targets of those charged with investigating disloyalty during the war.

Congress passed the Espionage Act in June 1917. In May of the next year they added the Sedition Act, which made it a crime to publish anything "disloyal, profane, scurrilous or abusive" about the federal government, the armed forces or even the flag. The punishment for a newspaper or periodical found guilty under the Acts was the revocation of a second-class mailing permit, and if convicted by a trial jury, the offending editor or publisher could be imprisoned for up to twenty years and fined $10,000. But even before the Acts were passed, Robert Abbott and *The Defender* had been put under surveillance.

The September 25, 1916, edition of the paper had carried an attack on President Wilson's approval of segregation and a note of encouragement for blacks who attacked an abusive white policeman in Shreveport, Louisiana. A Bureau of Investigation agent in New Orleans quickly began an investigation of the paper to provide evidence these articles tended to "incite murder." After the war began, white southerners renewed their claims *The Defender* was inciting violence against them. This charge was based on the assumption that any reporting of attacks by whites against blacks such as the brutal lynching that continued to occur during the war was tantamount to asking for a retaliation and as such incited violence. For both white Southerners and, as it turned out, agents in the federal government, this sort of racism—black against white—was clearly disloyal to the war cause. Three days after the war began, Abbott was called into the Chicago office of the Bureau of Investigation. He explained that he did, in fact, condemn racism and promote his race in his paper; but he also gave free advertising for recruitment appeals and published editorials supporting enlistment. The Bureau continued to object to Abbott's condemnation of racism, but they could not prove sedition.

When an article in the August 4 1917 *Defender* urged blacks to defend themselves against whites—this after the East St. Louis riots where blacks were attacked by white mobs with little or no interference by the government—scrutiny by another federal agency, the Justice Department, began. But this wouldn't be all the pressure brought to bear. By 1918 both the Post Office Department and the army's Military Intelligence Branch (MIB) had stepped in, using the authority of the Espionage Act to threaten publications they thought dangerous. When a petition by the "Citizens Committee of Patriotic Negro Citizens" appeared—with no date or evidence of origin—suggesting *The Defender* be investigated because of its attacks on the government, the head of the MIB decided to follow up.[16]

The MIB had no real authority to suppress a publication, so they sent an emissary, Major Walter H. Loving, the army's most loyal black investigator

7. James Scott's Possible Great Adventure

and a man already worried about the unenthusiastic response of many blacks to the war, to talk to Abbott. Loving threatened the publisher, and to some extent it worked. Abbott's written reply the following day denied all charges of disloyalty. Hadn't the paper pledged $12,000 in the Liberty Loan drive now going on? And what about his presentation of a regimental flag to the 365th Infantry and the fact that *The Defender* continued to supply space for war loan campaigns? Yes, the policy of the paper was to criticize lynchings, but Abbott had instructed his staff not to encourage racial strife or disrespect for the laws. Major Loving was pleased with this response and forwarded it to MIB headquarters with his assurances he would keep a close watch on Abbott and his paper.

Two other army men were also keeping a close watch on *The Defender*—Joel Spingarn, chairman of the NAACP board, and Emmett J. Scott, who as special assistant to the secretary of war was the highest placed black in the War Department. They were hearing the complaints from within the military that the black press, including *The Defender*, was spreading dissatisfaction. To address this, Spingarn and Scott organized a conference to let black editors and leaders express their race's grievances. The main complaint was the continued lynchings. Added to this were the federal government's unwillingness to hire black civil servants, the Red Cross's refusal to enroll black nurses and the government controlled railroads' segregated conditions. The resolution that came out of this conference was written by W.E.B. Du Bois, and it demanded an immediate end to lynching, but otherwise sounded a conciliatory tone much like Du Bois's "Close Ranks" editorial would a month later, by stating the group's willingness to suspend much of the race's agenda until the war is over.

For the remainder of the war, it was not so much the military that forced Abbott to change his ways, but Post Office authorities who ultimately had the power to confiscate any issues of his paper in which they found inflammatory articles. They could also charge him with violations of the Espionage Act if they found too many of objectionable editorials and stories. One such charge almost occurred when the June 8 edition of *The Defender* carried a front-page story describing a lynching in which a white mob tied its black victim the railroad tracks so the oncoming train would decapitate him and headlined it "Southern Stunts Surpass Hun." A postmaster in Texas sent this issue to the postal solicitor in Washington, who unbelievably concluded this was evidence of "rank race hatred that shows signs of German conspiracy… and stirs in the negro's revolutionary mind not only seditious thought but the seditious act." The attorney for the postal solicitor drafted a letter to be sent to Abbott that warned

> Anything that tends to destroy this harmony and to cause friction between the two races, and that tends to create in the minds of the members of your race the idea that they have no part in the struggle against the Imperial German Government and that they are being just as badly treated by the whites of America as they would be treated by the whites of Germany tends to interfere with the cause of the United States in the war against Germany and should have no place in a loyal newspaper.[17]

To modern readers, the "rank race hatred" the postal solicitor refers to applies less to the headline mentioning Germany and more to the barbaric nature of the lynching described. But in one respect, the postal solicitor was right: an attack of this kind might very well "cause friction between the two races," and destroy whatever harmony existed.

Like many black men before him, James Scott chose to believe that if he proved his willingness to fight for his country, he would be rewarded. He was not a pacifist as evidenced by his joining the National Guard in 1910 when he was in his twenties, and he appears to have enjoyed the training, marching and other military action the National Guard provided since he reenlisted three years later. But even he must have known that almost half of the black population of America had second, third and maybe even fourth thoughts about fighting for a country that allowed them to be lynched and attacked in their own neighborhoods, a country that did not provide equal opportunity for jobs or much of anything else. This is what *The Defender* and other black newspapers were reporting before the war and what they continued to report as the war progressed.

It was said that on July 25, 1917, when the Illinois National Guard was called into action, the entire city of Chicago could hear the fire bells, sirens and whistles that sang out in multiples of five. Members of the 8th Infantry responded by gathering in the Armory at 35th and Forest Avenue to begin their training and receive the supplies they would need after they were called out to join the other National Guard units. The building that housed them, a large three-story structure that also served as a social center for the community—Marcus Garvey gave a speech there in 1919—had been built in 1914-15 as a replacement for the barn previously being used at that location and was the first armory constructed for African Americans in the United States. Inside James Scott and the other members of the 8th who had been called up received their physicals, awaited guns and uniforms, and drilled each day as crowds watched. The regiment's officers usually ate at home while the

7. James Scott's Possible Great Adventure

enlisted men were fed, and fed well, inside the Armory. A reporter from the *Chicago Defender* visited on August 11th and described the dinner of roast beef, pickled beets, corn bread, peach pie and coffee the men had been served that night. He also reported on the delay that was to keep the 8th at the Armory until October, weeks after others of their National Guard units had already gone south.

> According to rumor coming from good sources the Eighth Regiment, Illinois Infantry, now mustered into federal service, will not train in the southland. The report made many mothers, sisters, brothers and fathers glad, and ten hours before the press dispatches reached the street word had gone the rounds and the report was cheered. None were sorry that their kin would not have to stand the rigors of the southland. The more conservative element were indignant. The south should not be allowed to dictate the policy of the U.S. government, especially when it only had a small voice therein. The Eighth should be sent with other Illinois regiments in the very division they belong.[18]

The reporter went on to say that members of the Appomattox Club, a civic organization founded on the principle of racial reconciliation in 1900 by the Chicago's black political leaders, would be sending a protest to Lawrence Sherman, then U.S. senator from Illinois.

As it turned out, this decision not to send any black National Guard troops to train in the south, originally made by the War Department at the behest of some of the Southern states, was eventually rescinded after protests were lodged. Still, it wasn't until Friday, October 12, weeks after their fellow white Illinois National Guardsmen had left, that 8th Infantry National Guard members marched out of their armory onto 35th Street to board a train heading south. Martial music played as crowds turned out to wave good-bye in a chilly wind while a group of about a hundred black policemen in uniform led the procession to Butler Street, two and a half miles away, where the 8th's train was waiting. James Scott and the men of the 8th were finally headed to Houston, Texas, to join their fellow guardsmen at a place called Camp Logan.

Here may be the place to stop to try to answer an important question—was James Scott actually on that train to Camp Logan? That is, did he really fight with the 8th overseas? This was not a question I entertained when I began researching his life. In fact, one of the first pieces of evidence I found was an article in the May 12, 1923, issue of the *Chicago Defender* whose bold headline declared, "LYNCHED MAN WAS WAR HERO," followed by "OLD EIGHTH MEMBER IS MOB VICTIM." The news report went on to say that James Scott had been for many years a resident of Chicago and was formerly a member of the regular United States Army attached to the Eighth Illinois infantry regiment. For a long time, I assumed this was true, that is, that Scott was a medaled member of the 8th Illinois Infantry regiment that sailed to France and fought in the war. Then I discovered another of those "official documents" that had bedeviled me before. This happened because I was invited to participate in an event to honor Scott in Columbia, Missouri.

The event was a ceremony to dedicate for James Scott's grave a new monument, replacing a small metal plaque which had been there. In the fall of 2010 the Reverend Clyde Ruffin of the Second Missionary Baptist Church in Columbia formed a committee that included members of his congregation along with others, including myself, who had previously shown an interest in Scott's life. To learn whether Scott would qualify for a military honor guard at the dedication of his monument, a smaller group within the committee undertook a search for his military service record. In this smaller group were Church members, including the Reverend Ruffin and Rasheedah King, along with others interested in Scott's life. The latter group included Patrick Huber and Doug Hunt, both of whom had written about the lynching, and David Sapp, and myself. Together we undertook a search for Scott's military service record, beginning with three facts we knew. First, James Scott joined the 8th regiment in 1910, because the article in 1915 *Defender* cites his five years of service. Second, from the volunteer enlistment form he filled out in 1913, we knew he had signed up for three more years, which would make him still a member in 1916. Finally, at the time of his lynching, Scott had been described as an honored veteran of World War I. But beyond that headline and article in the *Defender* we really didn't have any other information to clarify his rank and tour of duty. Then we saw his registration card for the draft.

Wouldn't a card signed by Scott dated September 12, 1918—about the same time the 370th began an attack on German forces at Mont des Signes—mean he was in Chicago rather than France? Not necessarily, it turns out. To follow up the discovery of the draft card, I wrote the chief of the Historical Resources Branch U.S. Army Center of Military History, Frank R. Shirer, to ask whether the signed draft card we had found for James Scott, dated September 12, 1918, and issued in Chicago, would indicate Scott had not been overseas at that time. Mr. Shirer contacted a National Archives and Records Administration (NARA) archivist who specializes in World War I records. Here is his reply: the date of the draft card "implies, but does not prove that Mr. Scott did serve overseas with the 370th Infantry." But there was no further information as to why this was so.

The question remained: was James Scott among those who had marched

7. James Scott's Possible Great Adventure

down 35th Street on October 12 to board the train for Texas? Or was he among those who stood on the street to cheer? Fortunately, there turned out to be other clues to help us solve this mystery. Doug Hunt,[19] who has written an excellent book on the lynching, found the first one. In checking the Selective Service Regulations issued by the Office of the Provost Marshall General, he discovered that the September 12, 1918, date represents a registration class under the Selective Service Act of 1917. That is, it does not represent the actual day Scott registered, but instead one of the three classes into which men fell because of their particular ages. The Selective Service Act of 1917 prescribed three registration dates: June 5, 1917, for all men between the ages of 21–31; June 5, 1918, for those men who had become 21 after June 5 of the previous year; and finally September 12, 1918, for those men who were between the ages of 18 and 45.[20]

In Scott's case, he probably registered for the draft before the 8th Infantry was called up, but his card was placed in the September 12, 1918, class because of his age—he was 34 years old when he registered, and thus was in the third group (with a registration card dated September 12, 1918) even though he had registered before that date. His registration lists him as living at 944 Eastwood Avenue and working as a janitor for J. Frost at 4641 Sheridan Road. Described as short, slender, with brown eyes and black hair, he is reported to have no physical disabilities that would disqualify him for service. At the bottom of the card, he has signed his name.

Another person investigating the question of whether Scott served overseas was an enterprising woman from the Second Missionary Baptist congregation named Rasheedah King. She was able to track down and verify that Scott's discharge papers were in the archives of the State of Illinois. Because the committee hoped to have a Military Honor unit at the dedication, Ms. King asked a major in that unit to request the file with the discharge papers be forwarded to the personal record center in St. Louis. Unfortunately, federal regulations say a file like this can only be released to the next of kin, so her plan didn't work. But this did not stop Ms. King or the committee. They sent a request to their local congressman to have the document released to a Military Honors unit in Jefferson City.

Another piece of evidence that James Scott did indeed serve with the 370th in France is the appearance of his name in the "Roster of the Illinois National Guard...."[21] On page 290 of this online document, in the list of corporals in G Company of the 8th regiment, there appears the name "Scott, James." Here we see he enlisted May 15, 1917, his date of muster was August

3, 1917, and he reported for duty July 25, 1917. While "Scott, James" is a common enough name, July 25, 1917, was precisely the day the 8th headed for the Armory in Chicago.

Have we found enough evidence to confirm his service abroad? The evidence given in the paragraphs above, plus the *Defender* article, which was written only four years after the war was over, support the conclusion that James Thomas Scott, Jr., did accompany his National Guard unit to Camp Logan and subsequently France; and that he was indeed a war hero. The Military Honors unit at Jefferson City thought so too. On April 30, 2011, they sent a military honor guard who, as the dedication ceremony ended, presented a twenty-one-gun salute to the man we had all gathered to celebrate.

Having solved this small mystery, we can return to our story of how Scott and the rest of the men in his regiment prepared to fight for their country. Fortunately, in addition to the official history of this period we have the personal accounts of two members of the 8th. Their memoirs are as different in their reactions to events as the two men were in circumstance and worldview. Whom Scott would have agreed with more I can't definitively answer, but I suspect he would have fallen somewhere in the middle.

The first memoir writer from the 8th was Captain William S. Braddan.[22] He served as a chaplain during the war, and wrote *Under Fire with the 370th (8th I.N.G.) A.E.F.* (initials here stand for "Illinois National Guard" and "American Expeditionary Forces"). In it he says he will endeavor "to show by concrete facts how despite the hardships and handicap of prejudice these men emerged from the World's great battle fields of Europe the most decorated Regiment in the A.E.F."[23] This claim, whether true or hyperbole, is indicative of Braddan's intense pride in his regiment and his equally intense dislike of some of the events that occurred to them after their arrival in France. Braddan had joined the military at age sixteen, and when the 8th went to war, he was 46 years old and the pastor of Berean Baptist Church in Chicago. His memoir includes letters home to his congregation.

The other memoir writer from the 8th was a man named Harry Haywood (*aka* "Haywood Hall Jr."). Later in life he became a communist, and entitled his autobiography "Black Bolshevik,"[24] but it covers also his experiences in WW 1. He was born in Nebraska in 1898, and his family moved to Minneapolis in 1913 and to Chicago in 1915. In the winter of 1917, when he was a young man of 19, he joined the 8th regiment of the Illinois National Guard. He did this, he declared, not as much out of patriotic duty as the desire for adventure and travel. By going off to France, Haywood felt he might

7. James Scott's Possible Great Adventure

escape from "the inequities and oppression that was the lot of Blacks in the U.S."[25]

Camp Logan, the place to which Braddan, Haywood, Scott and the rest of the regiment were headed when they left Chicago, was a name that had appeared in the news already as the site of what came to be called the "Houston Mutiny."[26] In the summer of 1917, while the members of Scott's National Guard unit were stuck in the Armory, army officials brought in the Third Battalion of the 24th U.S. Infantry, a black unit with white officers, to guard two military camps being constructed just outside Houston. White residents of the city, especially the police and streetcar conductors, were already worried about the influx of black troops. They felt this was a further threat to the racial harmony of their city. The Third Battalion, many of whom came from the south, began by obeying the segregation laws, but soon they rebelled against the manner in which these laws were enforced. On August 23, 1917, the situation came to a head. A rumor reached the Battalion that one of their men, Corporal Charles Baltimore, had been killed trying to intercede for a black woman being detained by the Houston police. As it turned out, Corporal Baltimore was only beaten and later released, but in response to this rumor and one that a mob of white citizens was heading toward camp, 150 black troops led by Sergeant Vida Henry grabbed their weapons and marched for two hours through the city. They were met by police and by white locals who had armed themselves. Shots were fired, and four black soldiers and fifteen local residents were killed and a dozen others were wounded. Sergeant Henry, learning that the soldiers he led had shot a white National Guard soldier by mistake, killed himself. The troops ultimately fell into disarray, the violence ended, and martial law was declared. In November, a military court was convened in San Antonio to try sixty-three soldiers from the Third Battalion. Thirteen of those convicted were quietly hanged at dawn on December 11. Two more military courts were convened, and sixteen more men were convicted and sentenced to be hanged. But with pressure from black leaders, President Wilson commuted these later sentences to ten years to life imprisonment. In all 110 enlisted men of First Company were found guilty for participating in the mutiny and riot. No white civilians were ever charged.

The train ride down to Texas took several days, and while Chaplain Braddan termed it uneventful, Haywood's recollections were a little different. Knowledge of the events of the Houston Mutiny had, according to Haywood, made the men angry and apprehensive. At the train's first stop below the

Mason-Dixon line in Jonesboro, Arkansas, many of the soldiers felt they were in enemy territory, as Haywood reports:

> It was a bright, warm and sunny Sunday morning. It seemed like the whole town were on one side of the station platform and Blacks on the other. We pulled into the station with the windows open and our 1903 Springfield rifles on the tables in plain view of the crowd.
>
> We were at our provocative best. We threw kisses at the white girls on the station platform, calling out to them: "Come over here, baby, give me a kiss!" "Look at that pretty redhead over there, ain't she a beaut!" And so forth.[27]

Some men, including Haywood, got off the train to crowd into the nearby stores looking for refreshments. When they were not served fast enough, they just took what they wanted. Regimental officers who had been in the front cars of the train were alerted to what was happening. They told everyone to get back on board and gave orders to the guards not to allow anyone off again. In another small town a few soldiers from the regiment debarked and refused to respect the segregated facilities. At another stop soldiers tore down a sign, and at a third, they demanded service in a store, and when they did not get it, they took what they wanted. Occasionally the men on the train were jeered, and in one place people were said to have thrown rocks at them. Haywood concludes his account of the ride down by saying five dollars was docked from everyone's pay once they had arrived to cover the damages the men had caused, and that "we all felt it was a small price to pay for a lift in our morale."

James Scott, along with most of the 8th regiment, arrived in Houston five days after the "Houston Mutiny." Colonel Dennison, the commander of the 8th, was himself from Texas, and understood what his men would have to do to survive the racism there. He counseled them to steer clear of trouble, and for the most part they did so, though after they took umbrage at the Jim Crow laws in the city, they were banned from riding the streetcars. But overall, Dennison's men managed to stay out of trouble both in Texas and later in Virginia where they went for their embarkment.

This avoidance of trouble was helped by the fact the men of the 8th did not have a lot of free time, at least in the beginning of their stay. James Scott and his fellow soldiers arrived in Houston early on the morning of October 18th and were immediately put to work unloading five boxcars of equipment. Then they marched seven miles to what looked like a dense pine forest amid swampland. Their first weeks in camp were spent felling trees, digging ditches and filling in low land so they would have a place to drill. The 8th Infantry

7. James Scott's Possible Great Adventure

ended up training at Camp Logan for almost five months. Along with drilling and rifle marksmanship, they attended classes in chemical warfare, bayonet practice, the use of hand grenades and cooking. Every few days Scott and the rest of the regiment members did practice marches of eight miles.

In early November, Houston officials invited the entire Division to march in a parade down the city streets. Remembering the earlier problems, the question came up whether the 8th would be included. The Divisional commander, General Todd, answered that the whole Division would be present, or none would be. The result, according to both Braddan and Haywood, was that Houston's black citizens greeted the regiment with shouts of joy and encouragement as they marched in close order formation down the streets of the city. Even the *Houston Post,* a white paper, declared "the best looking outfit in the parade was the Negro Eighth Illinois." Still, even with this appreciation by Houston's black and white citizens, the 8th was getting anxious to serve. Finally on March 6, the regiment left the city by train for Newport News, Virginia, arriving four days later at Camp Stewart, three hundred cluttered acres able to quarter 100,000 men though it had been a swamp only a few months before. Like Houston, the city of Newport News was long known as a seat of racial prejudice, so it was with some relief when less than a month later in the early hours of April 6, the men of the 8th, now renamed the 370th regiment of the 93rd Division of the American Expeditionary Forces, were ordered to march silently through the narrow back streets of the city to pier three, where they would board their ship, the *USS Madawaska*. The departure time was to have been secret, but hundreds of friends and relatives lined the dock to see the soldiers off. By 11 a.m. all the men of the 370th were aboard and settling in. Now it was just a matter of waiting for the 371st Infantry to board, and they would be off to the war. At almost midnight, the *USS Madawaska*, now at full capacity, slipped its cables and pushed along by tugs began its journey out to sea. Four hours into the trip, however, the ship ran aground on a sandbar, a navigational error caused by an erroneous government chart. The crew spent the next two days off-loading fresh water until the ship was light enough to be pulled off the sandbar by fifteen tugs. After being re-supplied with water, the ship began its journey again, destination France and the war.

The *USS Madawaska* was traveling a familiar route. From the beginning of April until the end of October 1918 more than 1,600,000 soldiers crossed the Atlantic on troop ships. At the start of America's participation in the war, the U.S. Merchant Marine had few boats large enough to carry the needed troops to France and back. It was not until the British released more ships in the spring of 1918, that the flow of soldiers increased. The ship Scott and his regiment traveled on, the *USS Madawaska,* was originally an ocean liner named *König Wilhelm II,* which the Germans had voluntarily interned in Hoboken, New Jersey, so the British Army would not attack it. When the U.S. entered the war, it was seized and renamed. During the war, the *USS Madawaska*[28] made ten transatlantic voyages carrying almost 12,000 men to France. After the armistice she brought 17,000 back. When sailing she had an average of 39 officers and 550 men aboard and a carrying capacity of 2,400 troops.

Once on board, each soldier was given a cloth tag to wear. On it was written the number of his hatch, the letter of his deck, the number of his bunk, and perhaps most importantly, the number of his raft or lifeboat. This tag would also be punched at each meal. The mess lines on these troop transports were extremely long, winding through various passageways, and up and down stairs almost to the bottom of the ship. Soldiers sometimes ate in gangs of a thousand, all standing and pushing through the mess hall as they chewed their food. The food itself came steamed and unseasoned, and as one soldier put it, was "as palatable as a wet sponge." The garbage resulting from all this food preparation was enormous and could be dumped overboard in containers only on certain favorable nights so as not to leave a trail for subs to follow.

Below deck steel bunks in tiers of three filled the hold with the ceiling often little more than a foot away from the top bunk. The men were allowed to go up on deck but only at certain times. Twice a day Scott and the others had an "Abandon Ship Drill." With a blast of a bugle, they donned their life belts and carrying one blanket rolled up on their shoulders along with a pair of woolen gloves, they rushed to their assigned positions. If they had to leave the ship, they were to throw the rafts overboard, jump in the water and then kick the rafts away from the ship while holding onto the sides. Abandon ship drills were not just protocol. On February 5, 1918, the American troop ship the *Tuscania* enroute to Britain with more than two thousand men aboard was torpedoed and sunk by a German submarine in the North Channel; 230 people were lost, most of them soldiers. Besides lifeboat drills, the men on the *USS Madawaska* did calisthenics on the deck (when they were not being seasick, a fate of many in the beginning of the voyage and during a mid-voyage storm). Immediately after sunset each day, the decks were cleared,

7. James Scott's Possible Great Adventure

the doors and portholes closed. Shortly after that the lights would go out, and the only illumination the soldiers below deck had were a few blue bulbs that gave off a ghostly feeble light.

Fear of submarine attack had also led to the use of convoys to accompany troop ships, so seven days out, another troop ship and an auxiliary cruiser met the Madawaska. On April 20th they entered what was known as the Danger Zone. Several American destroyers and a French dirigible came out to escort the ships in. All the men onboard were ordered to wear their life belts and stay close to the life rafts. Seven sub chasers, small and fast naval ships built especially to guard convoys, joined the convoy. They darted in and out among the troop ships for added protection.

On April 24, four days after they entered the Danger Zone, land was sighted. Everyone rushed on deck to see the outline of a city perched on an enormous shelf of rock. After eighteen days at sea, the *Madawaska* sailed into the harbor at Brest. From the ship, the surroundings looked picturesque. Quaint, old-fashioned buildings lined the streets, and along the shore small wooden boats and barges sat at anchor. For those men used to big American ports, this one looked almost dumpy and certainly provincial. The 370th disembarked on flat-bottomed boats called lighters and were met onshore by children both begging for cigarettes (*"pour le père dans la trench"*) and selling them. Small boys crowded around to ask for pennies and sing songs like "*Hell! Hell! The Gang's All Here!*"

From Brest, the regiment marched seven kilometers to the Pontanezen Barracks, a two story high stone structure behind whose walls Napoleon had housed his troops more than a hundred years earlier. They were there for two days unloading equipment and getting organized. On April 26, 1918, the 370th were ordered down to the railroad yards where they first saw what would become a familiar sight: small boxcars perched on high wheels with the words "40 hommes et 8 chevaux" painted on the sides. These forty-and-eights, as the Americans called them, were only 20.5 feet long and 8.5 feet wide, and despite their name more than forty soldiers usually rode inside. Once loaded in, James Scott and his regiment traveled for two days and nights, crowded, cold and hungry, across the breadth of France until they arrived near the Swiss border at the small town of Morvillars. Here they detrained and passed in review of a French general and his staff. Then they marched two miles to the slightly larger town of Grandvillars, where they found comfortable lodging in the homes of the townspeople.

More than nine months had passed since James Scott had reported for duty at the Chicago Armory. Finally he was here on French soil ready to fight. Imagine what he and the rest of the men felt when the announcement came in Grandvillars that the men of the 370th regiment of the 93rd division of the American Expeditionary Forces would not be fighting under the American flag. Instead they were being given to the French Army.

8

Whose Side Are We Fighting on Anyway?

When President Wilson finally agreed to enter the war in the spring of 1917, he chose John J. Pershing as the commander of the American forces. Pershing, nicknamed "Black Jack" because of his early service with a segregated Cavalry unit, had originally been a champion of the black soldier; but now, knowing President Wilson's reactionary views on race and owing a political debt to several southern Democratic lawmakers, he was less enthusiastic. The decision was made to put black draftees into one of two divisions. The 92nd included men who enlisted when the call came. The 93rd was made up primarily of black National Guard units. It was the 93rd into which Scott's regiment was placed in November 1917, and initially it was a division in name only, without the field artillery, machine guns or engineers usually assigned to a division. Later, when British and American troops made it clear they would not fight in combat with black soldiers, Pershing listened. Most of the 92nd were placed in support units on the assumption black men made better laborers than soldiers. For the 93rd, Pershing had a different plan. When the division got to Europe, he turned its regiments over to French commanders who had long clamored for replacement troops. Thus the 369th, 370th, 371st and the 372nd became the only American regiments completely under French control. (Some regiments in the 92nd were later loaned to the French.)

As biased and inevitable as this decision was, the result was better in some ways for Scott and the other men of the 93rd Division. The French Army had recruited Africans from their colonies at the start of the war. They were used to black soldiers fighting beside them and were therefore more color-blind than their American counterparts. In fact, by the time the 93rd arrived in 1918, some 150,000 Senegalese and Algerians had been at the front. Sent into no man's land as shock troops, these men had a reputation as ferocious fighters, their casualties 20 percent higher than those of regular French Army. As Harry Haywood later remarked when this decision was made,

A Lynching in Little Dixie

> All of our Black regiments were fortunate to have been brigaded with the French. In this respect, the American High Command did us a big favor, unintentionally, I am sure. For as far as we were able to observe, the French made no discrimination in the treatment of Black officers and men, with whom they fraternized freely. They regarded us as brothers-in-arms.[1]

The integration of the American black regiments into the French Army went relatively smoothly, which seems to have caused the U.S. military officials concern. Afraid that black American soldiers would get used to being treated without discrimination, a colonel in the American Expeditionary Forces (AEF) headquarters issued a memorandum on how to behave to the French who would come in contact with American black troops. In his "*Secret Information*,"[2] he explained that it was the unanimous view of the Americans in the states that the races must be kept apart for fear of miscegenation. To keep on the good side of American opinion, he suggested it would be necessary for the French army officers to avoid any intimacy beyond civil politeness with black officers. No eating with them, no shaking their hands, no conversing with them beyond military matters should be allowed. As for the French people, they must be told not to spoil the black Americans and under no circumstances should there be relations between French women (presumed white) and black soldiers. When this document was read in the French National Assembly in July 1918, its members expressed great disapproval. In the end, the French Chamber of Deputies passed a resolution reaffirming the principles of the rights of man and condemning prejudice on the basis of religion, class and race. In addition, they stated they would expect everyone to respect French law and would punish any instances of unlawful prejudice no matter who the perpetrators were. This last was added in response to stories of white American soldiers and military police mistreating black soldiers.

Even with this pledge of equality by the French, it was extremely difficult for the officers and men of the 93rd to be placed under the command of an officer whose language they did not understand, and whose military organization and supplies were unfamiliar. That they subsequently performed as well as they did—Scott's regiment would be moved between at least three different French commanders during the six months they were there—deserves our admiration.

When the men of the 370th arrived at Grandvillars,[3] they were transferred to the French 73rd Infantry Division and billeted for six weeks among the townspeople. The inhabitants were primarily women, children and men

8. Whose Side Are We Fighting on Anyway?

too old for service, and after some initial wariness, they treated Scott and his fellow soldiers with great hospitality. As one French resident stated after black troops were billeted in her village, "the inhabitants are not only convinced that there is nothing of the savage about these men but on the contrary no soldier could be found who was more correct."[4] Haywood (1978, 65) reports that the black soldiers were on their best behavior, and that the French noticed this and contrasted the gentlemanly behavior of the black Americans to the rudeness of the white ones.

It was during this time the 370th exchanged the American gear with which they trained for French equipment. After receiving a long bayonet and a French helmet, Scott traded in his American Springfield rifle for what many of the men felt was the inferior French Lebel model that needed reloading after three shots. He also received and learned to use the French F1 grenade. This weapon consisted of a hollow iron body with the familiar pineapple pattern on the outside to encourage fragmentation. It had a weatherproof primer that required the user to remove a safety cover then pull a pin to release a lever that began the detonation sequence. At that point, Scott was told he had five seconds to get rid of the grenade before it exploded. While French guns may have seemed less desirable, the two quarts of red wine that came with French rations—at least in the beginning—met with approval by most of the American soldiers. Later, after instances of drunkenness, the men received a double ration of sugar instead of the wine. The French soldier usually carried everything with him—clothing, bedding, food and drink, equipment and ammunition. This meant Scott's backpack often weighed more than 88 lbs. (By comparison the British soldier's field pack weighed around 66 lbs.) But the most important contribution the French made to James Scott and the soldiers of the 370th at Grandvillars was serious training in trench warfare.

At the beginning of the Great War, the armies on both sides prepared for what they thought would be a brief conflict. However, with the introduction of bolt-action rifles and machine guns, troops could dig in and stay well defended for a long time. Attacking frontally resulted in a large number of casualties, so the preferred method was to outflank the enemy. After 1914, this maneuver resulted in defensive lines being extended from the North Sea down to Switzerland. By the time the 370th arrived in April 1918, the Western Front had become a long line of interlocking defensive trenches on either side of a space known as "no-man's land." From photographs taken during the war, we can see that many of the French trenches were about seven feet deep and reinforced with sandbags, wooden frames and wire. They were often dug in a zigzag pattern so the enemy could not easily attack from the side if the trench was breached and shrapnel from a bombardment would be contained. The side of a trench facing the enemy was called the parapet and usually had a fire step on it. The rear side, the parados, protected the soldier's back from fragments when shells hit behind him. To see out of a trench without exposing their heads, Scott and the others were instructed to look through a gap between sandbags or a place fitted with a steel plate and hole. While trenches could have boardwalks at the bottom, rain sometimes filled them with mud and water to a level of two feet or more.

Off duty but still in the trenches, Scott learned he would be sleeping in a dugout, a large hole constructed off to the side of the trench with a depth of anywhere from ten to forty feet. The dugout could accommodate up to fifteen men. Because of the danger of gas, there was no ventilation system down there which meant air was still and foul. Nor were there mattresses; soldiers slept on their blankets, and during the night they could feel the movement and listen to the gnawing of the large rodents who were their companions. Here is Harry Haywood on the French rat:

> Undoubtedly there were more rats than men; there were hordes of them. Regiments and battalions of rats. They were the largest rats I had ever seen. We soon became tired of killing them; it seemed a wasted effort. Some of the rats became quite bold, even impudent. They seemed to say, "I've got as much right here as you have." They would walk along, pick up food scraps and eat them right there in front of you! The dark dug-outs were their real havens. When we slept we would keep our heads covered with blankets as protection against rat bites.[5]

Even worse than the rats were the other truly noxious residents in the trenches: lice. These small, pale bugs would nest in the seams of a soldier's uniform and were almost impossible to escape from. Even when clothes were put into large delousing vats and attacked with steam and hot water, some eggs remained. Men tried all sorts of ways to delouse themselves including using a candle to burn the eggs buried in the seams of their clothes. Back from the front lines, soldiers took hot baths and many shaved their heads to lessen the chance of lice there. It has been estimated that 97 percent of men in the trenches had lice. They caused itching and discomfort, and for some unlucky soldiers an affliction even worse: trench fever whose symptoms mimicked those of influenza. In the end, more than 800,000 Allied troops were said to suffer from trench fever during World War 1.

Once Scott and the rest of the regiment got to the front, they would have

8. Whose Side Are We Fighting on Anyway?

looked out from the trenches to see barbed wire lay in tangled coils from waist high to head high. These coils, meant to slow an enemy assault, were often more than forty or fifty feet across and in some places they could even stretch out 200 yards. They were usually laid at night deep into no-man's land so the enemy could not get close enough to toss a grenade into your trench. Later, as the men of the 370th fought on the front, they would learn to wait until their artillery shot through the barbed wire barricades before attempting to move forward.

French commanders also trained members of the 370th on the use of a gas mask. In 1914 the French had been the first to employ gas, in their case, tear gas that made the eyes water but was not poisonous. A year later the Germans introduced the first poisonous gas of the war, chlorine. Because chlorine could be easily detected by smell and sight, it was not as lethal as what came next. Phosphene was first used in December 1915. It was eighteen times more powerful than chlorine and more difficult to detect with an odor some described as that of musty hay. The final gas used in World War 1 was mustard gas. Not as lethal as phosphene, it lasted longer, lingering over battlefields for days. Gas masks were not totally effective against mustard gas, because it could saturate the clothes of a soldier who might then pass it on to the next man with whom he came in contact. And if the liquid form of the gas splashed on a soldier, horrific burns would result. Mustard gas did not kill so much as incapacitate. A few years after the war, one of James Scott's fellow members of the 370th, Corporal Jack Fehrs wrote about his own experience with gas in the war, damning mustard gas as "the devil's own discovery" and describing the effects of chlorine in graphic terms:

> first it causes vomiting, then the gases in the lungs causes a strain of vomiting to tear the tissues of the lungs, these torn tissues causes the lungs to bleed freely, then one is drowned in his own blood. This death is one of the most horrible I have ever seen.[6]

While gas caused only 3 percent of the war's fatalities, it was one of a soldier's greatest fears. Drills were done again and again until Scott and every man in his regiment could put on a gas mask within six seconds. In 1918 when the 370th arrived at the front lines, this was an important skill because approximately one in four artillery shells contained gas of one sort or another.

In the beginning of the war, the common plan of attack by men in the trenches was the call to go "over the top," after which a wave of infantry soldiers would emerge into no-man's land and a hail of enemy fire. As the war continued, however, both sides began attacking at night under the cover of darkness when small patrols, having previously cut the barbed wire, were sent out from advanced posts into no-man's land. By 1918, these infiltration tactics were the norm. Only communication and supplies limited the distance patrols could go forward, though there was always the danger they would be marooned there as later happened to one company of the 370th.

After six weeks of training, the 370th was lucky enough to occupy a quiet section of the frontlines for more than a week before being ordered to board a train on June 12 to begin moving into another sector. Here they joined a French division whose job it was to hold the tip of a salient, or bulge in the line. On June 21 the First and Second Battalions of the 370th moved up into the trenches. It was now almost two months since the regiment had arrived in France and almost a year since the 8th had gathered in the Armory in Chicago to train for war. Although the sector they occupied was fairly quiet with only occasional bombs and gunfire, the sounds and smells of a real battlefield must have taken some getting used to. Beyond the dull roar like thunder of distant explosions, they could hear the sounds of shellings closer in. One soldier described the noise of a shell coming toward him as a faraway moan that would build to a scream before roaring by like a train. If it landed nearby, the ground would shake. Another man from the 370th said that on his arrival at St. Mihiel the rattle of the machine gun fire sounded like "constant raindrops in a storm."

It was sometime during this period in late June that Colonel Dennison became worried about the training the men in his regiment were receiving. He felt they had not had time to get used to their new equipment, and just as they got situated in one division, they were moved to another. When the commander of the French 36th ordered the Colonel to have his men defend an entire sector on the front lines, Dennison told him they were not ready to assume that much responsibility. Soon after this, Colonel Dennison was replaced by a white commander, Colonel T.A. Roberts. It was the first time in its history the 8th Illinois had had a white officer at its head, and initially some of its members didn't like it. Here the regiment's chaplain, Captain Braddan on the subject:

> Col. T. Roberts, the arch enemy, vilifier and traducer of the Negro soldier, the one who delighted to sign his private mail as coming from "The White Hope of a Black Regiment" took temporary command of the regiment on the 12th day of July 1918 at Rarecourt.[7]

As has been the case before, Harry Haywood has a different memory of Colonel Roberts and the day he took over:

8. Whose Side Are We Fighting on Anyway?

Our new white colonel, T.A. Roberts, seemed to be warm, paternalistic and deeply concerned about the welfare of his men. He would often make the rounds of the field kitchens, tasting the food and admonishing the cooks about ill-prepared food. He even gave instructions on how the various dishes should be cooked. Naturally, this made a great hit with the men. Our confidence in him was high because we felt that he was a professional soldier who knew his business.

I remember the day the new colonel took over. The regiment formed in the village square. Colonel Roberts introduced himself. He seemed quite modest. He said that he was honored to be our new commander and that he knew the record of our regiment dating back to 1892 and its exploits during the Spanish-American War.

"Since West Point," he said, "I have always served with colored troops-the Ninth and Tenth Cavalry." He then turned to Captain Patton, our Black regiment adjutant. "Captain Patton knows me, he was one of my staff sergeants in the old Tenth Cavalry." Patton nodded.

The colonel smiled and pointed to our top sergeant. "Over there is Mark Thompson. I remember him when he was company clerk in Troop C of the Tenth Cavalry." He went on to point out a dozen or so officers and non-coms with whom he had served in the Ninth or Tenth Cavalry. "These men will tell you where I stand with respect to the race issue and everything else. We are going into the lines soon and I am sure that the men of this regiment will pile up a record of which your people and the whole of America will be proud."[8]

(Haywood later changed this first positive assessment of Colonel Roberts when he learned other black officers had reported that Roberts took credit for what they did and went behind their backs in trying to replace them. Whether this was true or not, I don't know. But at least in the beginning, not all the men felt as Braddan did about Colonel Roberts.)

The stated cause for the replacement of Colonel Dennison was illness, but as Arthur Barbeau and Florette Henri have suggested in *The Unknown Soldiers: African-American Troops in World War 1*,[9] this exchange came just a month after the white American liaison officer with the French Army had sent a report back to AEF headquarters stating the 370th was not prepared to go to the front because the black officers did not speak French and therefore were unable to get supplies. The liaison officer went on to say he was pessimistic about the 370th's ever being fit for service at the front, although he admitted the regiment had had three different instructors and three different changes of equipment in a period of three weeks. Colonel Roberts, after he arrived, apparently did not share the liaison officer's low opinion of the 370th. As early as August, he was complimenting his men to headquarters, saying they were as willing and apt as most troops.

The regiment did not go to the front lines, and after a month in quiet sector where there were few enemy engagements, they were sent back to rest.

It was around this time three more black officers were relieved of their duty with the 370th. Captain Braddan, never a fan of Colonel Roberts, felt this was the colonel's doing and complained. But more likely it had again been ordered from above. The AEF command had decided at one point in the war that white officers should head all black regiments (a repeat of the decision made during the Civil War.) The 370th managed to retain many of its black officers—only three white officers were in command when the Armistice came—but it's clear the men did not like seeing *any* black officer sent away.

Once again the 370th was reassigned, this time to General Vincendon's French 59th Infantry Division, and it is here they would show their bravery as a fighting unit. The 59th had suffered badly in recent battles and was now under strength. Vincendon reorganized his troops, making two regiments out of what had been three. For the third regiment, he used the 370th, which was twice the size of each of the reorganized French regiments and for this reason would bear the brunt of the fighting to follow. This change of division especially delighted Haywood, who was pleased they had become part of "the famous Armee Mangin," led by General Charles Mangin, who was called "*le boucher*" or "the butcher" by his men. Mangin was one of the strongest proponents for using Africans from the French colonies in the war, which may have been why Haywood was so pleased.

On September 1 Scott's regiment reconvened with the French 59th and together they began to move toward the front slowly taking positions in a sector sixty kilometers north of Paris. They were to be part of what was later known as The Meuse-Argonne Offensive, the biggest and the deadliest Allied offensive in the war. All along the Hindenburg Line, Allied troops were preparing to attack more than forty German divisions who had spent the last four years fortifying the rough hilly terrain the Allied forces were set to invade. The objective was to capture the railroad hub at Sedan, a French city on the Belgian border. This would destroy the Germans' ability to supply their troops and force them to withdraw. In the end, during the six weeks of the operation, the Allies succeeded but only with the loss of more than 26,000 AEF soldiers and almost four times that many wounded.

The movement of troops in mid-September indicated to anyone who was interested—and certainly the Germans were—that a major battle was in the offing. Each night around dusk infantry units would reappear from their temporary quarters to form columns and march to the next destination. Trucks and tractors pulling large guns, cavalry troops, ambulances and command cars would force troops off the road and send up clouds of dust that

8. Whose Side Are We Fighting on Anyway?

made it almost impossible for the weary soldiers on foot to breathe without coughing. On and on the columns of soldiers marched, knowing only they were headed in the direction of the front, but not where. At dawn the marchers would find lodging in the small villages and towns along the way. Equipment would be driven into farm buildings or camouflaged, and the roads would suddenly be empty until another dusk came.

As Scott and his fellow soldiers moved forward, they were greeted with the sights of complete devastation. One town they entered had been so thoroughly demolished that not one house was left standing. The streets were filled with shell holes, and the church was a pile of stones. Even the old cemetery had been torn apart with bones long in the ground now strewn about. It was in one such place Scott and the other men of the 370th were told they would be given two months pay before they headed into battle. As Captain Braddan (1923, 86) later wrote, "it was one of the most stupid things I ever saw, to load a man down with 3,800 francs and send him to the front line trenches where the chances were a hundred to one that he would come out alive." (Given that at the end of the war, the 370th was said to have suffered 20 percent casualties including an officer killed outright, the odds of survival cited by the chaplain were overly dire. But we get his point.)

Another day Scott's regiment began a long, silent march late in the afternoon. The men stretched out in platoons so any enemy fire that hit would do the least harm. They marched light, carrying only two blankets, gun, ammunition, canteen and gas mask. When they reached their destination, they were so exhausted they went directly into the caves the French billeting officer pointed to and immediately fell asleep. It was only in the morning when Scott and the others awoke that they saw and smelled the destruction around them: recently evacuated trenches filled with abandoned equipment, and the bloated corpses of dead soldiers and horses smelling so foul that after dark that night, some members of the 370th asked permission to bury the bodies around them. Later as the big battle for l'Oisne Canal was fought, there would be other smells: the fetid stink of rotting bodies in shallow graves, the odor of creosol or chloride of lime to keep infection at bay, and the lingering acrid aroma of cordite and poisonous gas.

Orders arrived in mid–September for the 370th to move forward so they would be in a better position to support an attack carried out by the French 59th on Mont des Singes, a German stronghold. Companies from the 370th including Scott's left to take a position in front of the German stronghold, and during the next five days they took part in repeated attempts to capture this well defended enemy position as German guns continually bombarded them. In one battle, a platoon of Company F under the command of Sergeant Matthew Jenkins fought its way into a large section of enemy works called Hindenburg Cave, and then turning the Germans' own guns on them, held this position for thirty-six hours without supplies until help arrived. For this, Sgt. Jenkins received both the American Distinguished Service Cross and the French Croix de Guerre. Aggressive close-in fighting continued through September 19 with no discernable change in the lines. Finally the French 59th Infantry received orders to pull their assault forces back into a defensive position. The companies of the 370th were released. It turned out this continuous bombardment by German artillery was meant to cover the withdrawal of their infantry from the area. After intelligence reports arrived indicating the German retreat, French Division headquarters issued orders to the 370th and especially the Second Battalion to pursue the retreating Germans. As the men emerged from their trenches and outposts to go over the top, they found themselves facing a well-executed fighting withdrawal plan by the Germans. A day later Colonel Roberts and Colonel Duncan received word to attack again, but because these orders came late, they had to lead their men across three hundred yards of shell torn land in a ravine as the Germans fired machine guns from a plateau above.

For a little more than a week, the 370th came under severe shelling and fire from German machine guns and rifles. They went days without food when German aircraft or artillery would destroy their supply train. In many places they were under constant fire, and if they stuck a helmet on a stick and raised it above the trench line, it would immediately be hit by a rifle shot. Some men advanced by taking cover in shell holes, often removing dead French soldiers to do so. Patrols from the 370th were sent ahead, crawling on hands and knees in the dark over mud and water so that at first light they could spot machine gun nests.

The Germans had retreated to an area south of a canal. Now they were dug in ready to fight fiercely for this position. From October 4 to October 12 Scott and the other men from the 370th tried to dislodge them. When they were not making direct frontline attacks on German fortifications, they were engaged in patrols and small raids in German territory beyond the trenches both at night and in the daytime. These actions, which included a raiding party to capture a German trench after some ferocious grenade attacks and hand-to-hand combat, and a sortie undertaken to determine the position of German machine guns by providing targets for them to fire at, later resulted in awards for the regiment.

8. Whose Side Are We Fighting on Anyway?

Joint operations with the French forces began again against the German lines with the 370th participating in combat operations and night patrols into German territory. They did this under continual and severe artillery shelling, and it was during this period that Company A lost 35 men and had about 50 wounded when an enemy shell exploded near a mess tent. November 7 found the whole French 59th Division moving forward. They encountered heavy resistance but were able to capture the railroad tracks on the eastern boundary of the division by nightfall. On November 8, Company M of the 370th was ordered to provide covering gunfire while a French company attacked Logny, a village strongly fortified and occupied by the Germans. The French company reached its attack position, but was forced to move back by combined artillery and machine-gun fire. Since Company M had followed the French soldiers through the same gunfire, their commander decided it would be better for them to go forward than retreat. They did so and captured the town. The following morning the commander of the division ordered a general attack across the division's front line. Luckily this coincided with the Germans staging a rapid withdrawal. The next day, November 10, the 370th went in pursuit of the fleeing Germans. By afternoon they had come under heavy German artillery fire that pinned them down until evening when the hostile firing ceased. Scott and the others settled in for the night.

On November 11 at 11 a.m.—the eleventh hour of the eleventh day of the eleventh month—the sound of guns abruptly stopped, and men on both sides stood up for the first time without fear of being picked off by a sniper or shot to pieces by machine gun bullets. As one soldier said, when you have crouched for months, to drop your pack and stand is to feel the way you never thought you could. Scott and the others watched as signal rockets burst above the front lines. German soldiers come out of the parapets of their emplacements to dance and yell like crazy men as they threw their hats in the air. A few of them immediately started across no-man's land hoping to find American soldiers with whom they could barter for tobacco and food. This stopped when orders were issued barring visits to either side for fear spontaneous conflicts might break out. The Germans released the prisoners of war they held, glad to be rid of the responsibility of feeding and clothing them when they had so few supplies themselves; and these soldiers streamed back over the front lines. Everywhere people celebrated. When the 370th regiment marched triumphantly into Signy Le Petit, a small village near the Belgium border, the band was playing French music. A French soldier carried aloft the American flag while a sergeant from the 370th lifted France's tri-color into the air. Only ten hours before the Germans had held the town.

The 370th rejoined its Third Battalion, and they all moved back from the front lines. The fighting was over, but the labor wasn't. Still under French command, Scott and the others were put to work repairing roads and communication facilities. It wasn't until a month after the Armistice, when they passed from French to American command that the 370th could relax. They boarded a train headed for Soissons in northern France. Here their days reverted to the usual drilling, training and playing sports the other American forces were engaging in as everyone waited for orders to go home. For the 370th, those orders came on December 23. The regiment headed for the military base at Le Mans, 414 kilometers away, arriving on Christmas Day, 1918 and staying until January 8. Then Scott's regiment boarded a train to Brest and a return to the Pontanezen Barracks where they had begun their adventure. Finally, on the first day of February 1919 the 370th loaded onto a troop ship named *La France IV*. After almost ten months in France, James Scott and the other surviving members of the 8th Illinois Infantry were going home.

The SS. *La France* IV arrived in New York on February 9. The ship was met by two steamboats filled with well-wishers, and after the 4,000 troops including Scott and his regiment disembarked, they all marched through the streets of the city where they were greeted with great applause and acclaim. Then they boarded regular passenger cars that took them to Camp Upton on Long Island where they were to stay for six days. During this time they had no particular duties, though it did turn out there were to be restrictions on what they could do when they were off duty.

The Y.W.C.A. had created four Hostess Houses at Camp Upton, places where off duty soldiers could entertain their wives and sweethearts. Three of these were staffed with white women and one with black women. Apparently there had been an overflow at the Hostess House staffed with African Americans, so some of the black soldiers, forgetting they were not still in France, had taken their companions to one of the other Hostess Houses. On February 14th the adjutant general of the Camp issued a memorandum to the officers of the colored regiments encouraging them to direct their men to the Hostess House meant exclusively for colored troops and to that location alone. A somewhat parallel problem about segregation/integration had occurred earlier in France. At a military base near Toul, two large rooms had been assigned to the Red Cross. By orders from above, one was restricted to white soldiers, the other to black soldiers. A few of the black soldiers, having experienced France's

8. Whose Side Are We Fighting on Anyway?

absence of racial prejudice, violated orders by entering the "For Whites Only" space. When they refused to withdraw, military police were summoned and arrests were made. Later according to Carter Harrison,[10] the Red Cross captain who reported this incident in his memoir, *With the American Red Cross in France*, the order to segregate the rooms was withdrawn. But by this time, most of the black soldiers preferred to stay where they were.

During their time in France, the 370th Infantry had lost 96 men killed outright. Only one member of the regiment had been captured during all the months they fought the Germans, and in the final stages of the war, they had advanced as many as 35 kilometers or almost 22 miles in one day, fighting against strong resistance. They were the first American troop to enter the French fortress at Laon after Germans had held it for four years. During the last two months of the war one or other of the 370th's units was always under fire. One unit, when sent to a position in front of Mont des Signes, encountered a landscape of enemy bunkers, dugouts and barbed wire. To go forward every man in the unit had to climb over a railroad embankment that exposed him to shelling by the Germans. It was reported later no one flinched. On the Soissons front, Companies F, G, H, I and M took Hill 304 from the Germans, after which the French army with whom they had been fighting named it "370th Infantry U.S. Hill" after them in their honor. For their actions in battle, the men of the 370th were awarded 21 American Distinguished Service Crosses, 68 French Croix de Guerre and one Distinguished Service Medal.

"General Orders No. 4785" is the document that was read to the officers and soldiers of the 370th regiment at first formation after returning to Allied command. In it General Vincendon of the 59th Division of the French Army, their last French commander, thanks the American regiment for fighting so gallantly alongside them in the battles of Acier, Brouze, Laon, Sal St. Pierre and Logny. He goes on to say,

> The blood of your comrades who fell on the soil of France, mixed with the blood of our soldiers, renders indissoluble the bonds of affection that unite us. We have, besides, the pride of having worked together at a magnificent task, and the pride of bearing on our foreheads the ray of a common grandeur.[11]

Contrast these words with those in the memorandum by issued earlier in the war by Linard explaining to the French how they must behave toward African American soldiers in France:

> We must not commend too highly the black American troops, particularly in the presence of [white] Americans. It is all right to recognize their good qualities and their service, but only in moderate terms in keeping with the truth.[12]

Surviving the war must have been a great relief to James Scott. But any hopes he had that he would return to a place that would give him the same chance for equality should have been dashed by his experiences with the AEF over there. World War 1 officially ended with the signing of the Treaty of Versailles on June 28, 1919. A few weeks later on Bastille Day, July 14th, white veterans still in Paris helped celebrated this by marching in a victory parade down the Champs-Elysees. The U.S. Army prohibited African American soldiers from participating.

9

Sweet Land of Liberty

On Saturday, February 15 James Scott and the rest of the 370th left Long Island to board a train bound for Camp Grant, Illinois, with a stop in Chicago. They were finally going home. According to *The Chicago Defender*, "a strange maelstrom of joy and wonderment" swept the city when the old Eighth arrived at the LaSalle Street Station 48 hours later.[1] Offices and schools closed for the day and the downtown thoroughfare was choked with people. The 370th—for they were still officially that until a week or so later—detrained and marched fifteen blocks south to the Coliseum, a large building on Wabash used for conventions and exhibitions. Inside the citizens of Chicago had arranged a reception and lunch for their returning heroes.

News reports said upward to 60,000 people pushed their way into the Coliseum while the police stood helpless at the entrances. Cries of joy erupted as mother found son, and wife reunited with husband. The speakers' box up front held many of the regiment's officers including Colonel Roberts, Lieutenant Colonel Duncan, Captain Prout, and Colonel Dennison. The heads of both the white and black welcoming committees were also up there along with committee members. When the speeches began, the Reverend A.J. Carey, pastor of the Bethel A.M.E. Church, called for the same fair play and equal chance the black soldier had received in the war now to be extended to the black civilian (perhaps not remembering or wanting to remember that the 8th Illinois had been given to the French Army rather than serving with the American forces). A cry of assent went up. Then Lieutenant Colonel Duncan spoke of the men who would not be given that chance, because they had not returned from France, and in the silence that followed, the Star Spangled Banner began to be played. The crowd, many weeping, stood at attention.

It was at this point Big Bill Thompson, mayor of Chicago made his appearance, coming in to shout from the speaker's platform that for their glorious service abroad, the 370th and their posterity would be accorded the "equality of citizenship," which would open the doors of opportunity and allow them to live among all the varied people of this country. Somewhere in this speech Thompson also recited a part of "My country, tis of thee, sweet land of liberty." Food was served around noon, and by a little after 2:30 the regiment was lined up at Sixteenth and Michigan Avenue to march in front of the viewing stand set up on the steps of the Art Institute. The soldiers wore their trench uniforms of helmet and greatcoat and carried rifle, bayonet, and cartridge belt. As the parade headed down Michigan Avenue, crowds swarmed in from both sides so exuberantly they almost disrupted the formation. Finally the men of the 370th reached Grand Central Station, where they boarded the train again for Camp Grant two hours away. It had been a glorious welcome home.

During the next sixteen days while he and the other men of the 370th were processed and discharged, James Scott must have thought about what lay ahead. Did he believe what the mayor of Chicago had said about those who fought for their country being accorded be "the equality of citizenship"? Had he really returned to the "sweet land of liberty"? Between March 1918 when Scott was traveling to France and July 1919 five months after he returned, twenty-five bombings had occurred on the South Side of Chicago, their targets the homes of black families who had had the audacity to move into previously white neighborhoods, and the homes and offices of the black and white realtors who facilitated those moves. The equality black soldiers found in France came not from the Americans but from the French, and now they were back in a country where there were sixty lynchings in 1918, up from 36 the year before.[2]

On March 12, 1919, the 370th regiment officially ceased to exist. Their service to the country was at an end, and they were free to pursue their own lives again. Within a few months, James Scott and the rest of the "Fighting Eighth" would discover Bill Thompson's promises of equality were just so many words as the man who quoted the lyrics from "America" allowed a race riot in his city to continue much longer than he needed to.

In the summer of 1919, with temperatures soaring into the 90s, Chicago citizens headed to the beaches on Lake Michigan.[3] Blacks tended to congregate on the beach at 25th Street where there were free towels and lockers and even a black lifeguard. Further down behind Michael Reese Hospital at 29th Street whites patronized their own beach. On Sunday, July 17, four black boys who would figure prominently in a racial conflict that led to a weeklong riot did not go to either beach. Instead, they walked to a spot they had discovered in between. There they untied a raft they had built and pushed off. None of

9. Sweet Land of Liberty

the boys was an especially good swimmer, but with the raft near at hand, they felt safe enough. As they were floating around enjoying the water, a fight started on the 29th Street beach when some blacks wandered down and were met with threats and rocks. When they returned with confederates, the two sides began to engage in a real rock fight. The four boys had by this time passed by the breakwater at 26th Street where a white man stood on the shore. He was about seventy-five feet away, and he started hurling rocks at them. Thinking it was a sort of game, they easily avoided the missiles until one of the boys, his attention diverted, was hit in the head. He sank into the water trying to grab onto another boy before he went down. The remaining boys began to swim toward the 25th Street beach. When they got there, they told the lifeguard what happened. He sent out a boat, but it was too late. Eugene Williams, seventeen years old, had drowned.

The lifeguards recovered Eugene's body thirty minutes later. The boys who had been swimming with Eugene went with a black policeman from 25th Street to 29th Street where they pointed out the man they thought had thrown the rock. But the white policeman on duty there refused to arrest him, nor did he let the black policeman do so. The boys then ran back to 25th Street to tell the crowd what was happening. Rumors and distortions began to be spread fueling anger on both sides. One black man was arrested, and as the patrol wagon drew up, the man pulled a revolver and shot into a crowd of nearby police, wounding one. He in turn was shot and killed by a black policeman. The sound of additional firing rang out, and the riot was on.

That night Chicago's athletic clubs went into action. These were groups of young white men eighteen to thirty who were sponsored by ward chairmen. Their more innocuous activities included boxing and other sports competitions and an occasional minstrel show. But their primary job was intimidation. All spring they had been trying to provoke a race riot. Now they had just what they needed. Twenty-seven blacks were injured that first night as the clubs announced their intentions to take over their territories. Monday afternoon, as black workers left their jobs at the stockyards, white men were waiting at the gates with clubs, iron pipes and hammers. The workers tried to run away, and in some cases they succeeded in climbing on streetcars only to have the cars surrounded by a white mob. When they jumped off, members of the mob hunted them down and beat them. At the same time this was happening near the stockyards, at the corner of 35th and State, at least four thousand blacks gathered, preparing to fight. When a sixty-year-old white peddler had the misfortune to turn his wagon down 36th Street, he was dragged down and stabbed to death. That evening, carloads of whites drove through the black neighborhoods where snipers waited to fire on them. At the Wabash YMCA, home to many students and veterans, black guards were posted around the building. The men who lived there were at their windows and on their fire escapes waiting. Those who didn't have guns stockpiled stones and bricks to throw. At 35th and Wabash, fifteen hundred blacks stood on one corner while a hundred policemen were in the intersection. Someone threw a brick and the police began firing into the crowd. By Monday evening, the death toll was seventeen with one hundred and seventy-two injured.

Tuesday morning saw a strike by transit workers, which meant no streetcars or elevated trains ran after four in the morning. Black workers stayed home rather than try to walk to work through white areas. The riot spread north to downtown Chicago as white mobs went looking for blacks around the Loop. In railroad stations, restaurants and hotels, black workers were dragged into the street and beaten or shot. By evening the rumors had grown. *The Whip*,[4] one of Chicago's more radical black papers, announced a hundred were dead and a thousand injured, or approximately five times the actual count. *The Defender*[5] reported black homes had been burned to the ground and their unconscious residents thrown into the embers. But it was not only the black papers that fanned the flames of this conflagration. *The Chicago Daily News*[6] had an article about black men attacking white women, and elsewhere a rumor arose that blacks had looted the National Guard armory in Springfield and a black mob was on its way to the city ready to attack. On the North Side (where James Scott lived) that night a crowd of at least five thousand whites hunted down the blacks in their streets. On the South Side, few residents ventured outside.

As Wednesday morning dawned, thirty-one blacks had been killed, and people in the Black Belt were running out of food. Stores had depleted their stocks, and no one was willing to deliver more. Garbage collected on the corners and in the alleyways, and the workers who had not been able to get to their jobs had little or no money. Police were unable or in some cases unwilling to stem the flow of rioters into black areas, and the attacks continued. At the very edge of the Black Belt, where nine black families had settled, members of an athletic club shot at the houses and marched in through the front doors to destroy furniture and light fires. After thirty-seven fires were set within five hours, some of them within minutes of each other, Big Bill Thompson finally decided that unless he wanted the whole area to go up in flames—

and with it the African American support he counted on—he needed help to stop the violence. Thompson called the governor, who in turn called out the state militia. At 10 p.m. 6,200 state militia moved out of their armories and into the seven-block area between 18th and 55th Streets. Using the butts of their guns and the bayonets, and firing only as a last resort, they began to crack down on the rioters. They were helped in this suppression by the rain that began to fall later that night.

It was not until Saturday, two days later, that black meat packers went back to work, and that was only because a police guard had been arranged. On Friday, pay stations had been established at the Urban League, the Wabash YMCA and at a bank in the Black Belt area so the meat packers could be paid. The strike of transit workers ended, and streetcars and trains resumed running on Saturday. However, black stockyard workers still didn't feel safe, so they remained at home until the following Wednesday. When they did return to work, 10,000 white unionists walked out. The state militia officially withdrew on August 8, or almost a week after the riot had begun. Fifteen white men had been killed and 195 injured. Blacks had lost twenty-three and had 342 injured.

"The Chicago Race Riots" is a series of articles Carl Sandburg wrote for the *Chicago Daily News* three weeks *before* the riot began. In them, Sandburg reports on issues like migration, housing and labor conflicts, using material he gathered when he spent ten days talking to black residents of Chicago. Later, Harcourt, Brace and Howe published the articles as a book.[7] In its introduction the journalist and political commentator Walter Lippman declares that until we can house and employ everyone at decent wages and guarantee them their civil liberties and an education, the race problem will continue. Lippman goes on to suggest the ideal lies in what he calls race parallelism, another name for the separate but equal doctrine that had started after the Civil War and been promoted by leaders like Booker T. Washington during the time James Scott was growing up. Separate things often were, but hardly ever equal.

In the articles Sandburg wrote, he makes special mention of the high number of black men who registered for the draft and subsequently fought overseas. Offering that "supreme sacrifice" should entitle them to freedom and equality, he is told by the black residents he interviewed. This was a common sentiment among blacks in the post-war years. The "New Negro" movement had begun in the 1890s as a demand for legal rights along with a program of racial uplift meant to replace the old stereotypes of blacks with new middleclass values. Now, as the black veterans returned, this demand was made more militant, as these veterans and others became more assertive and race proud. The response by white America was immediate. The Klu Klux Klan grew and racial tension across the country broke out in at least eight to ten major race riots in the period between late 1918 and 1919. There were also almost 100 lynchings during this time. Sandburg tells the story of a social survey conducted in the northern counties of Alabama at the behest of a wealthy woman in Chicago. The surveyor discovers that for many blacks who come north, the main attraction is not employment or better wages, but the idea they are going to a place where there are no lynchings. Later Sandburg cites another man who says that each time there is a lynching in the south, the people from that area soon appear in Chicago. Unfortunately, the summer of 1919's race riot provided evidence to Chicago's blacks that even this far north they were not safe from white violence.

Sometime between being discharged from the 370th in March 1919, and January 1920, when the census shows him living in Columbia with his mother and her third husband, James Scott leaves the city he has lived in for almost twenty years. If he was there at the time, did the riots of 1919 influence him? Or perhaps his decision was more personal. His marriage to Lucille Smith had fallen apart. The 1920 census shows him as a single parent of two small children. He may have gone to Columbia because he needed his mother's help. Whatever his reasons, James Scott decided to return to the place where his maternal grandparents and great grandparents worked and raised their families, the place where they prospered before they died. This turns out to be the place where James Scott too will work and prosper and where he will die—though not at so nearly advanced an age as his grandparents had and certainly not as peacefully.

When the U.S. Congress convened in 1919, three bills concerning lynching appeared on the floor. The first two proposed the establishment of committees to study the subject. The third, introduced by Leonidas C. Dyer, a Republican Representative from Missouri, went to the heart of the matter. The Dyer Anti-Lynching bill would make lynching a federal felony. Any state or city official who had the power to protect a person in his jurisdiction but failed to do so, or had the power to prosecute those responsible and failed to do so would be subject to a fine of five thousand dollars, a maximum of five years in jail or both. In addition, any person who participated in a lynching could be jailed for up to five years. And finally, any county in which a lynching took place would be fined ten thousand dollars payable to the victim's family.

9. Sweet Land of Liberty

If a victim was caught in one county and lynched in another, both counties would be liable to the fine.

Because Representative Dyer, like many others, was worried about the increase in lynching that had taken place, especially in the South, he introduced his bill in May 1919. By January 1922 the House had passed it by a vote of 231 to 119, but eleven months later a filibuster led by Southern Democrats in the Senate stalled its passage to the floor for a vote. After several days of trying, its sponsors withdrew the bill. The December 3 edition of the *New York Times* carried an article in which Senator Lee Slater Overman of North Carolina, gave his reasons for joining the filibuster. First denouncing the anti-lynching bill as a partisan attempt by Republicans to solidify the black vote in the North, Overman went on to say, "The decent hard working negroes of the South enjoy every safeguard of the law. They own property, their children go to public schools, and for such as they this proposed legislation is absolutely uncalled for." It is only the "ignorant negroes of the South," according to Senator Overman, who would profit by interpreting the bill as Federal license "to commit the foulest of outrages." This statement makes no sense at all, unless one believes, as the senator from North Carolina apparently does, that it is only the threat of *lynching* that keeps errant Negroes in place. Senator Overman goes on to point out that five of the six senators who supported this bill in the last Congress were defeated for re-election (these included senators from New Jersey, New York, Michigan, West Virginia, and Maryland, which might lead one to believe there could be other reasons besides opposition to lynching that caused the defeat of at least some of these particular senators.)

The Dyer Anti-Lynching Bill, though withdrawn for consideration, stayed on the calendar until midnight, March 3, 1923, when it officially died along with the 68th session of Congress. This means that when a little over fifty-six days later, James T. Scott, one of those "decent, hardworking negroes" Overman mentions, is lynched before a crowd of more than a thousand people, federal officials could do nothing in response. They could not punish the sheriff who did so little to protect his prisoner in the Columbia jail even though he could not have missed hearing the talk of lynching that had occurred earlier in the week. They could not prosecute the men who broke down the jail door to drag Scott out into the street. They could not even fine Boone County for its part in this horrendous act. Instead justice was left to a jury of twelve men, all of whom had grown up in Columbia and the surrounding county. And they carried out this justice in eleven minutes. But I am getting ahead of my story.

When James Scott left Chicago, he brought with him two of his children: Helen, age six and Carl, age five. On the 1920 census form, the three are recorded as living with Scott's mother, Sarah and her third husband, James Brown, a truck gardener who owns a house at 205 First Street in the black section of town. Brown was 65 at the time and his wife 52. James Scott appeared on not one but two census forms in 1920. On the first he is listed as 28 years of age, married and working as a chauffeur for a private family. Three days later, on a second form apparently filled out at the university since there is no mention of Scott's children, mother or stepfather; James Scott is said to be head of the household (Brown held that honor on the first census), 32 years old and working as a janitor. It is not clear who gave this second census taker his information, but several points are incorrect enough (e.g. James Scott, Sr.'s birthplace is recorded as New Mexico along with his son's) that we can probably safely assume it was not Scott himself. But like the first census, this document records him as married, which he was at the time of the census but would not be a year later. The September 27, 1920, edition of the *Columbia Evening Missourian* notes, "James Scott, a negro has filed suit for divorce from Lucille Scott, asking custody of the two children. The case will come in the October term of Court." On January 22, 1921, the same paper lists ten divorces granted that day including the following: "James Scott was granted a divorce from Lucille Scott and awarded custody of their two children."

During the years James and his mother Sarah were living in Chicago, Columbia's population had almost doubled. In 1900 the city had 5,651 residents. Twenty years later there were 10,392. The city grew in prosperity during those years too. The university had added a school of journalism, a school of commerce and a department of economics; and a year after Scott's return, the Boone County Hospital opened. 1921 was Missouri's centennial year, and all around the state celebrations were held. But those who were paying attention knew the state's growth was showing signs of slowing down, as if the best years might be behind them. Increasingly, rural Missourians were leaving the middle of the state to move to the two large cities, which sat on its edges. Sometimes those moving didn't stop there. From 1910 to 1920, Missouri dropped from being the seventh largest state in the country to the ninth. While the state continued to be more rural than urban in 1921, the urban centers had become proportionally larger. Seventy percent of city dwellers lived in St. Louis and Kansas City. Next in size came St. Joseph, which wasn't really growing, and Springfield, which was. Columbia occupied a place in the third tier down—those cities of more than ten thousand.

9. Sweet Land of Liberty

Though Missouri's numbers as a whole were decreasing, there was one segment of the population that was growing faster than all the others in the years after the War. This was its black population. In 1920 blacks accounted for 5.2 percent of the state's residents, which made it the only non-southern state with a black population of more than 5 percent. While this represented a decrease from 60 years earlier when 10 percent of Missouri's residents were black, at the time James Scott returned to Columbia, proportionately more blacks were coming into Missouri than whites. What they found was a racial situation that had not changed much since Reconstruction. Segregation remained firmly in place. The state constitution mandated it in school, and it existed by custom rather than law in such places as hotels, restaurants, theaters and even hospitals. When in 1917 the U.S. Supreme Court ruled that ordinances enforcing residential segregation or racial zoning were unconstitutional, whites in Missouri chose other means to keep the races separate, including the bombing of black homes in St. Louis and Kansas City. Influential city papers like the *St. Louis Post-Dispatch* quickly denounced these extreme acts of violence, but the papers also continued to run mildly racist—if such a concept even exists—articles and jokes.

Another sign of the feelings Missouri whites had for blacks around the time James Scott decided to return was the tightening of the state anti-miscegenation law in 1921. Miscegenation laws, or bans on sex and marriage between races, were not new. As early as colonial days, laws against sex and marriage between whites and non-whites were created and enforced, in part to dissuade slaves and Native Americans from joining forces as oppressed people. That these prohibitions didn't altogether work is shown by the fact that by the time the American Revolution started, there were between 60,000 and 120,000 colonial residents with "mixed heritage." Taken from the Latin, *miscere* "to mix" and *genus* "race," the name "miscegeny" didn't actually appear until 1863 when journalists created it to discredit the Abolitionist movement. State laws against miscegeny were still strong eight years later when the first attempt to ban interracial marriage on a federal level through a Constitutional amendment was made—by a Democrat from Missouri. Representative Andrew King's proposal to make interracial marriage illegal nationwide came when he realized the ratification of the Fourteenth Amendment—which would give emancipated slaves equal civil rights—might provide a basis for declaring state anti-miscegenation laws unconstitutional. Representative King did not have to worry. It took another 96 years for the federal government to act. Even after the Fourteenth Amendment was ratified, most state laws against miscegenation still existed, though some northern and western states repealed their anti-miscegenation laws beginning in the late 1800s. Nevertheless, a large majority of whites in the United States continued to believe interracial marriage was wrong if not illegal. As late as 1950, an astounding 96 percent of Americans polled were against it.

There is a debate among scholars as to the basis for these anti-miscegenation laws. Some feel sexual fears play the greatest part in this sort of racism while others identify economic exploitation and the wish to deny blacks the same cultural status as whites. Whatever the cause or causes, the strengthening of Missouri's anti-miscegenation law in 1921 was a sure sign the state's white population felt endangered. And that feeling remained. As late as 1964, the marriage of a white person to a black person could result in two years in the state penitentiary. Only in 1967 did interracial couples become free to marry in the state. The case of *Loving v. Virginia* went to the United States Supreme Court, which ruled *all* bans on interracial marriage were unconstitutional. So finally, the last sixteen state laws against miscegenation were invalidated. Representative Andrew King of Missouri had his fears confirmed—72 years after he had died.

The house Scott lived in when he first returned to Columbia was owned by his stepfather, James Brown, at 205 North First, about two blocks north of Broadway above the Columbia Cemetery. From here Scott had about a half-mile walk to campus and the Medical School where he worked. Gertrude Carter, whom he would marry a year later, lived four blocks away with her parents in a house on Walnut. A Columbia native, Gertrude was born in 1899 or 1900 (census reports as we have come to expect differed on the year.) After attending Frederick Douglass School, Gertrude went on to get her teaching degree from Lincoln Institute Jefferson City. By 1920 she was back teaching first and second grade at her old grade school, Douglass Elementary.

Gertrude and James probably met at the church they both attended, Second Baptist Church at 407 East Broadway. Second Baptist was the same church whose initial site had been on land provided by Scott's great grandfather. In February 1921, a month after he received his divorce from Lucille, James and Gertrude were married at the church. J.L. Caston, the same man who would later arrange for a lawyer for Scott when he was charged, conducted the service. The couple moved into 501 North Third Street, a home in a middle-class neighborhood where some of their neighbors included teachers from Gertrude's school two blocks away.

At Douglass Elementary, Gertrude was paid about seventy-five dollars

9. Sweet Land of Liberty

a month, almost as much as the white teachers in Columbia's public schools. James earned sixty-five dollars a month, which is exactly what his fellow white janitors received from the university. Thus, they were relatively affluent members of their community. While they rented rather than owned their house, James did own a car, something not had by many other Columbia residents, black or white. Described in later newspaper articles as a practically new Hupmobile, it was reported Scott had originally paid six hundred dollars for it. Though no longer a familiar name like the Ford Model T, the Hupmobile was produced from 1909 to 1940 by a company started by Robert Hupp, a former employee of Oldsmobile and Ford. Given the price he paid and the year, Scott would most likely have owned a Model R with a touring body style from 1918 or 1919. In other words, this was a car very similar to the ones he would have seen in France carrying American officers or acting as ambulances. Advertised in 1918 as "The Comfort Car," the Touring model seated three in the back and two in the front, and had running boards on both sides and a twin bumper in front. Like his brother Akers, who was working as a chauffeur for a private family in Evanston in 1920, James too is listed in that year's census as a chauffeur. Owning and driving an automobile like the Hupmobile in Columbia would certainly have been seen as a sign of affluence and perhaps even effrontery, given that its owner was black. We can only imagine how much it cost him emotionally to sign over its title three years later to the lawyer who was hired to defend him.

Life appears to have gone well for Scott after his return to Columbia. Unlike some others in the black community, he had a full-time job with a dependable income. He had been awarded custody of his two youngest children, Helen and Carl; and he was married to the daughter of a well-known family in Columbia. We know from census reports Gertrude's parents James and Annie Carter lived with their four children at 403 North Fifth Street in 1920. This was the same address they had occupied ten years earlier. They had been married for 25 years, and James worked as janitor first at the Elks club, then at an apartment house. His wife Annie, Gertrude's mother, was a laundress in 1910, but by 1920 could afford to stay home to care for her family.

Before he was lynched, James Scott's name had appeared in Columbia papers only four times. The first two involved his divorce. The third came on August 4, 1922, when *The Columbia Evening Missourian* carried the following story:

A Lynching in Little Dixie

NEGROES CELEBRATE TODAY
Emancipation Day Brings 1,000 Visitors Who Make Merry.

The first event of the program for Emancipation Day, which is being celebrated in Columbia today by negroes from Mexico, Centralia, Boonville, Sedalia, Jefferson City and several other nearby towns, was the parade through the business sections of town at noon. Sam O'Neal, James Scott and Clarence Crosswhite lead the parade, at the head of which was the American flag, and were followed by the Moberly band. About twenty-four automobiles and trucks draped in colored bunting were in the procession. The Fulton minstrels and the Columbia Jazz Hounds also furnished music. At least 1,000 out-of-town negroes are here today to take part in the celebrations.

After the parade the crowds gathered at the Fair Grounds where the afternoon was full of entertainment. A ball game between Columbia Blues and Centralia Cubs, dancing, a merry-go-round, picnic, dinner and speaking by several prominent out-of-town negroes made up some of the events of the afternoon. Besides the minstrel show and dance tonight there will also be extensive displays of fireworks.

Emancipation Day is celebrated each year throughout the entire state, but perhaps at no other town is more enthusiasm shown than at Columbia, this being one of the older southern towns. Many of the negroes who witnessed today's celebrations can remember the days of slavery when such a day as Emancipation Day was only dreamed of.

Thirteen days later, a fourth article appears, in the August 19, 1922, edition of *The Columbia Evening Missourian*, mentioning James Scott and Emancipation Day:

CALKINS LOSES LAW SUIT.
Unless He Appeals Case Will Have to Pay $100.

A verdict in favor of the plaintiffs was returned by a jury of six yesterday in the case of Sam O'N'eal William Burton, Ralph Bass and James Scott, negroes, against J.M. Calkins, proprietor of the Rock Bridge Amusement Farm. This verdict compels the defendant, in case he does not appeal, to pay the plaintiffs $100 for the privilege of operating his merry-go-round on the fair ground during their celebration Emancipation Day.

According to a contract between the two parties Calkins was to pay the four men in charge of the Emancipation Celebration, $100 for allowing him to operate his merry-go-round concession during the celebration. Calkin, however, stopped payment on a check for the $100, which he had given them after he was compelled to stop his machine because of lack of water for his engine. He asserted that the men had agreed to furnish him with water and filed a counter charge, against them for $100 which was the amount he claims he lost while the machine was forced to remain idle. The plaintiffs served a writ of attachment on the machine when payment on the check was stopped, and it has been held by the constable since that time.

This report of four black black men suing a white man for breach of contract and receiving an affirmative verdict might provide us with some reassurance about the fairness of the judicial system in Columbia, that is, until we learn

9. Sweet Land of Liberty

how quickly another Columbia jury less than a year later settled a far more important case involving a black man. What these appearances in the newspaper do prove is how James Scott had returned to Columbia to become one of its more active black citizens. Whether this kind of visibility influenced what happened next in his life I can't say. But given the general tone of relations between the races in Columbia at this time, it can't have helped.

10

The Last Week

> There is, therefore, only one thing left to do; save our money and leave a town which will neither protect our lives and property, nor give us a fair trial in the courts, but takes us out and murders us in cold blood when accused by white persons.[1]

These are the words any black resident of Columbia might have proclaimed after James Scott was dragged from jail and lynched. However, they were written by Ida B. Wells in 1892 after she learned three of her friends, men who ran a successful black grocery in competition with a white store across the street, had been arrested for defending themselves, then taken from jail and lynched. Similar sentiments were heard among blacks in Columbia a little more than thirty years later, though few actually left town. Instead, they kept quiet, burying this event almost as effectively as my own family did. What appears here are the facts of James Scott's last week of life taken from newspaper articles and later accounts written by Patrick Huber and Doug Hunt.[2] Well's phrase, "when accused by white persons" has special resonance. It is what caused me to begin my search for James Scott's life. In Wells' words, it became for me the "only one thing left to do."

According to reports that appeared the next day in the papers, on Friday, April 22, 1923, at about around 3 p.m.—though the time was never that exact—a heinous event took place on the west side of Columbia. Regina Almstedt, a teenage schoolgirl and the daughter of a university professor, was walking home from an after-school music lesson when she encountered a Negro on the Stewart Street Bridge near her house. The man told her there was a small child on the railroad tracks below them, and he was afraid a train might strike the child. Looking over the railing, Regina saw nothing. No, the man said, the child is further along around the bend. So with the impulsiveness of a fourteen-year-old, Regina scrambled down the bank and began walking in the direction the man indicated. Soon she noticed he was following

10. The Last Week

her. She hesitated then began to run up the hill beside the tracks. The man ran after her and forced her down. He put a belt around her neck and a rag in her mouth. At this point he either did or did not have sex with her. (Initial newspaper reports said Regina fought him off with her umbrella and gave him a fifty cent piece she had in her pocket to leave her alone.) While all this was going on a railroad crew passed below. Perhaps this commotion scared the man off, because, again as reported by the local papers, her assailant got up and ran away but not before making her promise not to call for help until he had escaped. Some accounts said her assailant asked her forgiveness and had even given her a reason for the attack; he was getting even because a white man had stolen his wife. Left bruised and in shock, Regina climbed up the hill, then walked the remaining blocks to her house on Garth Avenue, fainting several times along the way. When she finally got home, a doctor was called, as were the police. And here the story, at least as far as it concerns James Scott's guilt or innocence, gets more interesting.

That same afternoon Police Chief Ernest Rowland and his patrolmen went down to the site of the attack with two bloodhounds borrowed from a neighboring police force. There they found a pair of overalls Regina said her attacker had carried under his arm. One of the bloodhounds was able to follow this scent through the woods and into a white section of town until the path veered east toward Sharp End, the black business district of Columbia. Once there, the bloodhound followed the scent into a restaurant owned by George Scott (no relative of James) at Fourth Street and Walnut. When the dog became confused, the police brought him outside again, and less assuredly he followed the smell a few hundred feet east along Walnut before stopping. The police interviewed people in or around the restaurant, and because of the bloodhound's actions, concluded Regina's attacker had probably ordered a meal inside. (Later as more evidence accrued this theory would be superseded by another, more reasonable one.)

In the immediate aftermath of the Friday attack, Regina had given the police a description of her assailant as a Negro of anywhere from twenty-five to thirty years of age with a Charlie Chaplin moustache and clothes that gave off a strong chemical smell. The next day, Saturday, as people gathered to whisper about this terrible crime and the *Columbia Daily Tribune* inflamed the situation by reporting Regina's clothes had been torn to shreds and her body bruised and lacerated, Chief Rowland sent his entire force into the black sections of town to rout out and arrest any man wearing a Charlie Chaplin moustache. This dragnet caught James Scott in its web, and by that afternoon, he was in jail. From there he was taken to the Almstedt home, where from thirty feet away on the porch, Regina declared him to be her attacker, crying out, "Oh! Those are his eyes!" and "Don't let him come any nearer!" Or so it was reported in the newspapers. My aunt made this identification a little more than twenty-four hours after she had been attacked.

Sunday afternoon, Regina along with her parents went downtown to the office of Columbia prosecutor, Ruby Hulen. While hiding in an anteroom, she listened to Hulen interviewing four black prisoners. Again, she identified Scott by voice as the man who had attacked her. When the four men were brought into the anteroom, she picked out Scott in the line-up. Later, when the chief of police produced vials of chemicals for her to smell, Regina reacted strongly to the one holding formaldehyde, a chemical it was assumed Scott would have come into contact with at his job at the medical school since it was used to preserve specimens there. With these pieces of evidence in place, the police and the county prosecutor believed they had all they needed, though surprisingly Hulen did not immediately give Scott's name to the press. Nor did he file any charges against Scott at this time. The prisoner continued to maintain his innocence, saying he was at the medical building during the period of the attack, a statement two white witnesses partially collaborated having seen Scott at 3 p.m. and again at 5 p.m. But no one could be found to say he or she had seen him for the two hours in between.

For the next five days James Scott sits in a dark cell in the county jail. Does he believe he will get a fair trial at some point? He hasn't even been charged. All this changes on Friday morning when a witness—who is never identified—comes forward to say he or she has seen Scott at 4th and Walnut the afternoon of the attack. Scott was allegedly walking south toward campus with a bundle under his arm. For providing this information, the informant hopes to receive the reward that is being offered—$200 from the city, $925 from various civic groups and $300 Prosecutor Hulen has applied for and received from the state. Once more my aunt is brought in to identify Scott, this time at the courthouse in front of additional witnesses. It is 3 o'clock in the afternoon, almost the same time this nightmare began a week before. After she affirms her identification, Scott is again returned to his cell, while Regina and her parents adjourn to the office of the prosecutor to talk with him about the charge and the subsequent trial. Doug Hunt, who has written a mesmerizing account of this period in a small book called SUMMARY JUSTICE, believes that it is at this moment the prosecutor hears for the first time from Regina's father, Hermann Almstedt, that Regina has indeed been raped.

10. The Last Week

Professor Almstedt goes on to tell Hulen his daughter will be ready to testify fully when the case comes to court. It is not vengeance he seeks, my grandfather adds, but a fair trial for the accused.

Perhaps now is time to talk about eyewitness accounts of a crime. According to the Innocence Project, the non-profit legal clinic associated with the law school at Yeshiva University, eyewitness misidentification has played a role in more than three-quarters of convictions later overturned by DNA testing. Of course, there was no DNA testing in 1923. But eyewitness testimony has always been known to be unreliable, just as it has always been known to strongly affect a jury. Hugo Münsterberg,[3] a professor at Harvard, discussed the problem as early as 1908 in his book ON THE WITNESS STAND, and years later Supreme Court Justice William Brennan concurred with Münsterberg, noting the inherently suspicious nature of this evidence. Eyewitness identification can be especially unreliable when what is called "suggestive eyewitness identification procedures' are followed. These include using a "show up procedure" when only one suspect is present, and failing to tell the eyewitness the culprit may not be in the line-up. The Columbia police used both procedures in the case of James Scott. But again, this was 1923, and they were common practice. I cannot help but wonder, though, if this basic unreliability of eyewitness testimony was the reason Ruby Hulen did not immediately charge James Scott when my aunt, then an adolescent white girl who had just been attacked by a black man, identified him. James Scott was well spoken, gainfully employed and even owned a car. He was married to a schoolteacher and enjoyed the status of a middle class black man in Columbia. He said he wasn't there, and witnesses, white witnesses, had been found to back up his statement he was at work, at least at 3 p.m. and 5 p.m. On the other hand, my aunt truly believed she had identified the right man. Most eyewitnesses, once they make an identification, do not back down. But how many black men had she seen closely in her young life? Studies in recent years have shown that errors in facial recognition occur much more frequently between races. That is, most people "see" or process the racial information but not the facial information of an individual of another race. Victims can tell you whether their attacker was white or black, but they do not always see individual differences within a race. Regina described her attacker as a Negro, and she said he had a moustache like Charlie Chaplin. Only later, according to the newspapers, did she remark on his eyes, and that is when she was presented with James Scott at a distance of thirty feet. I have tried this myself, and making an assessment of the uniqueness of a person's eyes from thirty feet away is almost impossible. So whether on Saturday afternoon, only twenty-four hours after the attack, she suddenly remembered her attacker's eyes or whether this was something the newspapers created, once she had identified James Scott, there was probably no going back, or at least not until it was too late.

When Ruby Hulen informed James Scott he was to be charged with assault on Friday afternoon, Scott, presumably with the help of his minister, the Reverend J. Lyle Caston of the Second Baptist Church, hired Emmett Anderson, a well known local white lawyer who was president of the county bar association to represent him. To secure Anderson's services, Scott signed over the title to his car. On Saturday morning, April 28th James Scott was officially charged. Accompanied by his lawyer, he was removed from his cell and taken before Judge H.A. Collier of the circuit court. Asked if his first name was James, Scott replied in the affirmative, and the indictment was corrected from Charles to James. Judge Collier then set the trial date for May 21. A few minutes before this, Scott and the others in court learned he would be charged not with assault but rape.

After the arraignment the Reverend Caston left the courtroom to call George Vaughn, a black lawyer from St. Louis. How Caston chose Vaughn, I don't know for sure, though the Reverend Caston had lived in St. Louis at one time. Whatever the reason, he made what turned out to be a good choice. Not only was the St. Louis lawyer on the train to Columbia by four, but after the lynching, it was Vaughn who stayed to write an account of what had gone on for the NAACP. Born in 1885 to former slaves, George L. Vaughn received a law degree from Walden University in Tennessee and after serving overseas during World War 1, he set up a law practice in St. Louis. Vaughn was active in Democratic politics, and in 1919 he founded Citizen Liberty League, a group that sought to put more African Americans in elected office. Because The St. Louis Bar Association did not admit black lawyers, Vaughn became president of the Mound City Bar Association, which had been especially created for African American lawyers. But his greatest achievement came later when in 1948 he argued successfully before the Supreme Court against racially restrictive real estate covenants. This was the landmark case of *Shelley v. Kraemer*, and in his oral argument, he famously called these restrictive covenants "the Achilles heel" of U.S. democracy.

When the Friday newspapers reported Regina's identification of Scott as her attacker, Columbians began calling for justice for the accused to be swift. Earlier in the week, the *Kansas City Post* reported a lynching should

10. The Last Week

be expected if angry citizens captured the "fiend." Now with the victim's identification of her attacker confirmed and the information provided by the secret witness well known, James Scott had been all but declared guilty. The Saturday evening edition of the Columbia *Daily Tribune*, carried on its front page the same message the *Kansas City Post* had earlier suggested:

> There has been much talk of mob activity and many men of sound judgment who do not believe in mob law are of the opinion that if it is positively proven that the negro is the man who committed the crime the taxpayers should be saved any costs that might accrue from a trial and that summary justice should be dealt to him.[4]

Inside, on the editorial page, the *Daily Tribune's* editor, Edward Watson made explicit what had been implied on the front page of his paper. He told white men in Columbia that as champions of womanhood they must provide the rapists now in jail ("brutes and supercriminals") with "swift justice." Watson wrote of rapists in the plural, because along with Scott, there were two other black men, Ollie Watson and Jadie Scott (no relative to James) in jail. They had been charged with raping two black schoolgirls a week or two earlier. Because their victims were black, they were never truly in danger, but we will hear Ollie Watson's name again.

The townspeople of Columbia were not unfamiliar with measuring out swift justice. In 1853 a slave by the name of Hiram fell prey to this manner of morality. As William F. Switzler[5] tells the story in his 1882 book, *The History of Boone County, Missouri*, compiled "from the most authentic official and private sources," there was a daring attempt at rape made near dark on the night of August 12, 1853. A young woman, her married sister and the sister's child were returning from a funeral on horseback. They had stopped so the young woman could take down some poles across their path, and as she was putting them back, a Negro man entirely naked emerged from a nearby thicket. The struggle that ensued was reported to have gone on for ten minutes, and it was so loud the horse which the married sister and her daughter were seated on reared, throwing them both to the ground. The sister was disabled, but the little girl scrambled up and ran to a nearby house where she alerted the owner about what was happening. He rushed back with her, but on hearing the approaching footsteps, the Negro assailant disappeared into the thicket.

Men gathered and a number of Negroes were arrested including Hiram, who was owned by a man living ten miles south of Columbia. Circumstances pointed to Hiram, but he was discharged after being brought informally in front of two local justices. When people continued to have strong feelings about his guilt, a warrant was issued, and he was arrested again and put in jail. Four days later on a Saturday he was brought to trial. A large group of people gathered outside the Court House, most of them convinced of Hiram's guilt and impatient with the details of a trial. What they wanted, reported Switzler was "summary vengeance." The trial began and progressed without interruption until about three in the afternoon. At that point some of the crowd, unable to control their frustration, rushed into the courtroom to put a rope around the defendant's neck. The rope was cut by one of Hiram's defense lawyers, a well known Columbian by the name of J.S. Rollins. Almost at once the crowd put another rope in its place. As with Scott nearly seventy years later, the mob dragged Hiram down the Court House steps then down Broadway to a bridge over Flat Branch at the western end of the town. But they did not stop there. Instead they continued to a woods where they attempted to hang him. However the rope broke. At that point the mob began to talk of burning him. Hiram was saved from this fate by the intervention of his counsel, Major Rollins, who along with several other respected men of the community arrived to talk to the crowd. These men were able to calm the group down while beseeching them to allow a fair trail to continue. The prisoner was led back by those who had initially taken him to the jail to await recommencement of his trial on Monday. On Sunday Hiram confessed to the crime and implicated several other Negroes who, he said, had plans to commit a similar act.

When court convened on Monday, an even larger number of people argued against waiting for conviction now that Hiram's guilt was known. The father of the victim came forward and like my grandfather spoke to the crowd. He did not, he said, object to summary vengeance, only the manner in which it was done, suggesting that he preferred hanging to burning. Others spoke to the crowd, telling them that if they were determined to hang the defendant, they should do so in a decent and cool manner. One of Columbia's most esteemed citizens, Eli E. Bass, Esq., was chosen chairman of this impromptu meeting. Ever the democrat, he asked those in favor of burning to say "aye." Then he put forward the proposition of hanging, and to this a large majority assented. Not everyone present voted; a large portion of the crowd disapproved of either action, but as with the Scott lynching, they did not intervene. With hanging the chosen method, a committee was appointed to assemble the supplies: a rope, a cart in which to convey to prisoner to the place of execution, and a coffin. In addition the committee was given the task of forcing open the jail doors to secure the prisoner. A Mr. King was appointed to head

10. The Last Week

the committee, and he in turn chose nine men to help him carry out these tasks. Around noon, the ten men proceeded to the jail and while the sheriff protested, forced open the door to the cell and took Hiram out. A large group of people followed them to a grove of trees northwest of town where the Negro was hanged and buried. *The History of Boone County, Missouri* not only notes the precise spot, a woods now part of a pasture belonging to Dr. and Mrs. Arnold, but lists the men who formed the committee to carry out this task.

Hiram was not the only black man to be "decently" lynched in Columbia. In 1889, a boy of seventeen was thrown from the third floor of the Court House with a rope around his neck. His name was George Bush, and he had been accused of molesting the five-year-old mulatto daughter of the woman he worked for. His arrest came late on a Thursday afternoon, and by the early hours of Saturday morning he was dead, his body swinging from a half-inch rope, a thick rubber gag over his mouth, and, according to a newspaper report, a sign on his chest which said, "Don't Cut Down 'Till Seven a.m. This Is What We Intend To Do With All Those Who Commit This Crime. (signed) White Caps." The men who carried this out had knocked at Sheriff Evans' door around one a.m. Saturday morning. When the sheriff asked who it was, a voice identified himself as "Constable Edwards" and said he had a prisoner. Sheriff Evans opened the door to find a man, his hat pulled low over his face, standing there. By the time he realized it wasn't Edwards, the man had pushed his way inside and grabbed the sheriff's keys. Three or four other men followed. They were all heavily armed and masked. Without a word, they began to unlock the doors leading to the cells. When they reached a cell that held two black men, the man with the keys asked which one was George Bush. The youth stepped forward and was seized and gagged. They led him back out past the sheriff and his family. Sheriff Evans later reported that Bush had given him a look of appeal but could not talk because of the gag. By now twenty to twenty-five men had gathered outside in the dark. They led Bush to the Court House front door and stopped. At a signal by their leader, the men assumed a military formation. Three of them stepped forward to take Bush inside. A few minutes later his body came hurling out a window on the third floor. With that, they turned and marched double file down the street. The headline to the next day's *Columbia Herald* called them "The Committee of Safety." It was clear to everyone whose safety was meant. These men thought themselves the direct descendants of those who had formed the "slave patrols" of an earlier time, and like the slave patrols, no legal recourse was made against them. Their own "summary vengeance" went unpunished.

James Scott may not have known of the Reverend Caston's call to George Vaughn, but he would have been temporarily comforted to know of Vaughn's arrival by dinnertime that night. After eating a meal with the Reverend Caston and his family, Vaughn and Caston went to the Stewart Street bridge to inspect the scene of the crime. From there they walked over to Emmett Anderson's office, near the courthouse, to discuss the case. Around 11 p.m. a deputy sheriff knocked on Anderson's office door, and taking the white lawyer out into the hall, told him a mob was forming by the old courthouse. Be careful, he warned Anderson. Anderson returned, and with the help of Caston and Vaughn, they turned out all the lights then looked out to see a group of as many as three dozen men walking toward the jail. The Reverend Caston left immediately to check on the safety of his family, taking Vaughn with him. When they came out onto the street, they found themselves surrounded by a crowd of white men and boys and even some women. From the direction of the jail, they could hear shouts and cries. Caston led Vaughn down a smaller street as they tried to avoid the mob now surging toward the courthouse and the jail.

For Sheriff Fred Brown, there was no avoiding the crowd. As he crossed the courthouse square, he met a group of at least four hundred white men. Some had been drinking, but most were sober—and agitated. They demanded the key to Scott's cell. Sheriff Brown said no and told them to disperse. A few did, but most only retreated a short distance. The sheriff continued on to the jail. A few minutes later, ringleaders of the mob decided to try to get in through the jailer's quarters, which sat at the back section of the building. Did James Scott hear the brick that crashed through the kitchen window not that far from his cell? Did he understand what was happening as the men tried to batter down the outside door? From inside, the jailer, a man by the name of Wilson Hall, reportedly shouted out to them, "This is my home. You can't go through here, and the first man who attempts it, I'll kill him." This would be the first and only time the mob encountered the actual threat of gunfire, and they responded by withdrawing, acknowledging, as one man said, that Hall had every right to defend his own home—also, perhaps, acknowledging none of them was willing to be killed to carry out this plan.

Sitting on his bunk in his cell, wrapped in a blanket, James Scott, along with cellmates Ollie Watson and Jadie Smith, must have known they were in

10. The Last Week

danger. And since they were black men living in Columbia, Missouri, in the year 1923, they had some idea of what that danger was. The mob renewed their attack on the jail, this time going to an unguarded door on the north side. Swinging a heavy axe, one man broke the padlock, and those in front pushed into a dark corridor. (Some time earlier, the jailer or the sheriff had turned off the power.) The men pounded on the bars of a nearby cage holding two white prisoners, demanding to know where Scott was. It may not have been possible, but I hope Scott heard these men lie for him, telling the crowd that he had been taken to the Fulton jail for safekeeping. Not believing the prisoners' claim, the mob pushed further down the corridor, bodies filling all the available space until they came to two doors that separated the Negro section of cells from the white. The first door was iron. Either it had been left unlocked by accident or someone in the crowd had a key. The second door was a latticed steel grillwork filling the doorframe. This door was locked. Those in the mob who had sledge hammers and chisels began to go to work trying to break open the hinges. It was said the sound of hammers hitting steel carried for several blocks, so it is not difficult to imagine how loud those same blows must have rung in Scott's ears. Still, the noise seemed not to worry Columbia's chief of police. As he crossed the courthouse square, someone asked Chief Rowland why he wasn't inside trying to stop this. Rowland told the man not to worry; the mob would never get in the jail.

As the hammering continued, George Vaughn and the Reverend Caston walked back up Walnut toward the courthouse. The white crowd was by then so large it filled the lawn of the square and flowed out onto several side streets. Coming closer Vaughn and Caston could hear the joking and the laughter. Vaughn later described it as a picnic atmosphere, and he was appalled. He took down the license plate numbers of several cars that had pulled up, then he and Caston returned to the parsonage so Vaughn could call the governor. In the corridor of the jail, the pounding continued, and one hinge snapped. But the mob inside was getting impatient. The acetylene torch and gas tank that had been offered earlier from outside the jail were now brought in. When the torch was lit, faces appeared out of the dark like masks. Soon the second hinge and the main latch were dismantled. The men nearest the door pulled it down, shouting in triumph as this next to last hurdle was surmounted. Scott and the prisoners in the cell with him could hear the clang of metal as the door was shoved aside. Despite their initial exuberance, the mob started down the dark corridor cautiously. Near the end of the corridor was a short passage leading to the jailer's kitchen. It was separated from the cell area by two doors, one solid and one grated. If one or both were open, the jailer and the sheriff could easily fire on the men in the front of the mob.

Earlier Sheriff Brown, listening to hammering, had called Ruby Hulen to tell him he needed help. Now when the phone rang inside the jailer's quarters, it was not Hulen calling back, but the governor, Arthur Hyde, telling Brown he had ordered out the National Guard. They were gathering across the street from the jail at the armory, so help should soon be there. In the meantime, the governor instructed Brown to do everything he could to keep Scott safe. Governor Hyde had already had a lynching happen while he was in office. Two years before a teenager named Roy Hammond had been hanged from a tree and shot over and over again in Bowling Green, Missouri, a small town about 85 miles northeast of Columbia. He didn't want any more trouble.

When the men in the dark corridor saw the kitchen door was closed, they felt safe enough to turn on their flashlights and begin their search for Scott in the two cells that held Negro prisoners. Other men were pushing in from behind, one of them carrying the torch which was again lit. Light flowed into the recesses of the cells as they began to cut through the lock on the cell they thought contained Scott. Just then the kitchen door opened, and Judge Collier, who had earlier charged Scott and set a trial date, stepped up to the grill. Behind him stood Sheriff Brown. Brown called out to one of the men, "George Barkwell, won't you listen to Judge Collier?" Barkwell raised his hand to stop the work, and the crowd turned to listen. James Scott was listening too. The following dialogue comes from Doug Hunt's well-researched account in *Summary Justice*:

"Men, you don't know what you're doing. This is a bad case, a very bad case, but we should let the man have a trial by jury. I've set the trial date myself. It's less than three weeks away, and I've no doubt it will be a speedy trial."

"Get the damned nigger!" someone shouted from the back of the crowd.

"We're going to hang this damned nigger anyhow!" shouted someone near the front.

"Let a jury of your own people decide this man's guilt or innocence," Judge Collier pleaded.

"To hell with juries! We know juries. We'll be our own jury."

Collier tried another tack. "I speak in the name of the father of the girl, who has been wronged more than any of you. He wants this man to have a trial."[6]

10. The Last Week

By this time the mob had become noisy and impatient, so when Ruby Hulen shouted through the grate for the men at least to wait long enough to hear what Hermann Almstedt had to say, someone in the back promised to lynch him too. But the men at the head of the mob, the ones closest to the sheriff, the judge and the prosecuting attorney, hesitated, realizing officials now knew who they were—mutual recognition seemed to exist between mob leaders and officials. In those few seconds, James Scott must have thought he had been saved. But as with many mobs, those in the back who were more likely to feel anonymous began to taunt the men by the cell door. A young man pushed his way forward to grab the torch and resume cutting. Suddenly the corridor went dark. Another member of the mob, worried that burning acetylene in such a crowded space would blow them all up, had cut the hose and was trying to carry the tank away. He was stopped by a man with a revolver, and snapping on their flashlights again, the men nearest the cell refitted the hose and relit the torch. The lock was cut, and men pushed their way into the cell demanding to know which of the prisoners was Scott. Seated on his bunk, a blanket around his shoulders, Scott said calmly he was the man they wanted. Before he could move, they grabbed him and shoved him out into the corridor. Men on either side kicked and pushed at him as a rope was placed around his neck and he was practically dragged out onto the courthouse lawn. James Scott was not a big man. According to police reports, he was 5'4' tall and weighed 135 lbs. Surrounded by a crowd of more than a thousand white men, women and boys, all eager for his demise, did he flash back to France and the attack on Mont Des Signes or the woods of Bois de Mortier? There the enemy had been equally fierce, but hidden, and he had been part of an armed group on the other side. Now it appeared no one was on his side.

Back in the kitchen of the jailer's quarters the officials who had stood behind the grated door were talking. What they said exactly remains unrecorded, but George Vaughn, who wrote a report of this night for the NAACP, believed Sheriff Brown proposed to go outside to recapture his prisoner using firearms if necessary. Ruby Hulen, the prosecutor, objected. He argued there were only six of them—the sheriff, his deputy, two policemen, Judge Collier and himself—and the crowd had grown huge. Most, of course, were just curiosity seekers, but if the six of them were forced to fire, innocent bystanders might get hurt. (How anyone in this crowd could be called innocent is something we are left to ponder.) Because the prosecutor outranked the sheriff, he won the argument. Hulen and Brown went out onto the porch of the jailer's quarters without guns. The sheriff asked the crowd for help in getting Scott back into custody. He said a car was coming to take the prisoners to another jail. The prosecutor pleaded with the mob to let justice take its course. He was, he said, almost certain to get a conviction. No one responded.

Scott, listening to this, could hardly have taken much consolation in Hulen's words. He knew he was innocent, but how to explain this to the enormous sea of angry white faces, most of them calling out for his murder? It is said that at this point Scott asked to see his father one last time. I am a little suspicious of this detail, since Scott's biological father had died many years earlier, and his mother was now married to a local man, James Brown. It could have happened, but I don't think Scott had given up yet. I don't think he thought of anything being "one last time." But he soon would. A man in the crowd yelled, "Take him to the Stewart Bridge. Hang him." Now Scott understood exactly what this mob wanted to do with him. Another man, seeing some movement at the armory, warned they should get him away quickly. Men began to push, then drag Scott by the rope around his neck. "Don't pull me. I will go," he is said to have told his captors. Then turning to a reporter for the university paper, he again professed his innocence. "I am not guilty. I swear it."

Pushed and pulled along by his captors, Scott fell to the ground several times on the way down 7th to Cherry, then south on 6th to Stewart Road, but he somehow managed to get back on his feet. Cars honked in front of him. People crowded in from all sides. Scott probably did not see a black face among them. By the time they reached the Stewart Street Bridge several blocks away, he was bleeding from the ears and nose. Here with arc lights set up, he saw even more white people filling the bridge and the ravine below. They spilled up onto the hill on the other side. Led by the rope around his neck, Scott was pulled to center of the span. Was it at this point he realized he was going to die, murdered by this pack of white people whom he had lived among for only three years? Apart from his experience in the war, James had led a quiet life. In Chicago he lived and worked on the north side of the city away from the riots and slums. Leaving Chicago for Columbia, he had gotten a steady job at the university and married a schoolteacher. He went to church each Sunday and even owned a car. Yet here he was, surrounded by an enemy he always knew he had, but one who up to now had not directly attacked him. He was alone in the middle of this murderous mob, without any protection except the knowledge of his own innocence, and clearly that was not going to be enough.

10. The Last Week

At this point someone decided the rope around Scott's neck was too short and thin to do a proper job, so a man was sent off to get a longer, thicker one. It was while the lynching party was waiting for a new rope that my grandfather appeared on the bridge, pushing his way through the crowd. Ruby Hulen had probably called him, or perhaps he just heard the commotion from his house a few blocks away on Garth Avenue. Whatever the reason, Hermann Almstedt came back to the same spot where his daughter had met her attacker not eight days before. He came to try to stop what he saw as a miscarriage of justice. He did not know Scott was innocent. In fact, he had every reason to believe him guilty. But my grandfather was a man who had seen how prejudice worked when World War 1 began, and his German classes had been cancelled at the university. He believed in justice and the rule of law. I will quote from what the newspapers reported as my grandfather's words that night. I do not know if they were quite this noble, but I do know he was courageous, walking onto that bridge, surrounded by more than a thousand people eager to see Scott hanged, to deliver a speech he knew would be unpopular:

> I have been wounded to the very heart of this affair, wounded far more than any of you. Don't besmirch your hands with this deed. I plead with you to let the law take its course with this man. I ask it of you in the name of law and order and the American flag."[7]

In response to this plea, the crowd hissed and booed. A man near my grandfather told him to shut up or "we'll lynch you too." When my grandfather turned to go, James Scott's hopes of being rescued would seem to have gone with him.

But one more time Scott argued for his innocence. Leaning against the railing, bruised and bleeding, he told them he could never have harmed a child. He had a fifteen-year-old daughter of his own. He had never touched a white woman in his life. The person who did this was his cellmate, Ollie Watson. Ollie had confessed to him that afternoon. As Scott spoke, he looked imploringly at one face after another. Most just stared back, but one or two responded. Maybe we should investigate his claims, one man said. He sounds like he is telling the truth. For a few seconds, Scott may have felt hope, but this feeling was dashed as he heard others calling out to get it over with. From below came a voice yelling to throw him down. "We'll take care of him," he heard. Turning to a young man near him, he said, "I know I haven't a chance. They won't listen to me. Won't you say something?" This was Charles Nutter, a student in the journalism school at the university and a stringer for *The*

Kansas City Star. Nutter probably did speak then, but even more bravely, he later testified at the trial of the only man to be charged in the lynching. Charles Nutter couldn't save James Scott that night, but like my grandfather, he had the courage to try.

A large white man pushed his way up to Scott, a twenty-foot rope in his hands. He took the shorter rope from around Scott's neck and used it to tie Scott's hands behind his back. Then he tied one end of the new rope onto the bridge railing and with the other end he made a noose, which he lifted to Scott's head. When Scott felt the rope encircle his neck, he went to his knees to pray. "Oh Lord, have mercy on an innocent man," he implored. The large man put his hands under Scott's arms and with fingers squeezed in on his chest lifted him to the railing. With the cheers from the crowd and cries of "Over the railing with him" all around him, Scott looked straight into the large man's face and said, "I will jump. You don't have to push me." But as with everything that had happened to him since he had been arrested in his own home more than a week before, no one listened. The large man stuck his hands out and shoved Scott over the railing. As he toppled down, he called out one last time, "I am innocent." Scott's feet struck the top of a small tree, his body jerked upwards, and with a nauseating pop his neck snapped. After a few seconds of silence, the crowd began to laugh. This may have been the most evil sound of all that night, and I am glad James Scott did not hear it.

Within thirty minutes the crowd had disbanded. Cars drove away. College students walked a few blocks back to campus. Some of Columbia's most powerful citizens returned to their homes. At three a.m. the coroner arrived to cut down the corpse. James Scott's body was taken to the Parker Funeral Home, probably by order of the Reverend Caston, and a later examination showed he had died instantly of a broken neck. Scott's neck was swollen and burned, but apart from a small cut on his left temple, his face was unmarked.

The beating my aunt had given her attacker with an umbrella just eight days before apparently left no signs.

11

The Aftermath

In a way, James Scott's biography should end now. His life is over, having been taken from him early on a Sunday morning in April 1923 by men the prosecutor will later erroneously call "roughnecks." What was not over and still needs to be described is the "life" of the place where all this happened. I originally set out to solve two mysteries—what James Scott's life was like before he became a victim of a lynching, and how a place like Columbia, Missouri, could provide a crowd of more than a thousand people to watch a lynching. This chapter speaks to the latter mystery.

When on Friday afternoon before the arraignment my grandfather told Prosecutor Hulen he did not seek vengeance, he may have been among a majority in Columbia, but it was a silent majority. After the lynching was over and newspapers across the country began to condemn all Columbians, not just the men actively involved; people began to speak up. White residents turned to one another to ask how this could have happened. In the black community, residents knew how lynchings happened, but many were surprised one had happened here. Excuses from those in charge quickly followed. Missouri Governor Hyde, who had been alerted by George Vaughn to what was going on, defended himself and the local National Guard, saying they did all they could since only 35 minutes had elapsed between the time he was called and when Scott was removed from his cell. (Vaughn remembered a different timetable with more than an hour between these two events.) Colonel Williams, the commander at Battery B of the National Guard, declared his men could have responded more efficiently and even stopped the lynching if they had been called earlier. The fault, he said, was not his, but the sheriff's. He should have asked for help sooner. (Those who identified many of the men in the mob as members of Battery B might dispute Colonel William's claim.) And not to let town officials off the hook, Charles Ellwood, a professor of sociology at the university—the same man who oversaw William Elwang's 1903 thesis on blacks in Columbia—said he had tried to warn Mayor McDonald a mob was forming after he heard, on the Saturday morning before the lynching, angry comments about the Almstedt girl's attack. The mayor told him not to worry.

What happened in Columbia in the days and weeks following the lynching was not surprising according to Sherrilyn Ifill, a civil rights lawyer for seventeen years who wrote *On the Courthouse Lawn: Confronting the Legacy of Lynching in the Twenty-First Century.*[1] In her study of lynchings along the eastern shore of Maryland during the first half of the twentieth century, she notes some basic commonalities. One is the willingness of participants in a lynching to act without disguise as happened in Columbia. This, she says, indicates the participants feel they will never face punishment within their community. Another common feature is the complicity of average white citizens in a lynching, again as happened in Columbia. For blacks this confirms whites are not to be trusted. Nor can blacks trust the legal system to give them justice. According to Ifill, there is no record of *any* white person ever being convicted of murder in the lynching of a black person. In fact, however, at least one such case did occur in Missouri twenty years before James Scott was lynched. On June 4, 1903, a Joplin, Missouri, white man, Samuel Mitchell, was sentenced to ten years' imprisonment for his part in the April 15 lynching death of Thomas Gilyard, a black man who also lived in Joplin. However, this conviction for second-degree murder was later overturned, so in an important sense, Ifill is correct. But her most powerful observation about the common features of lynchings is this one: they are inevitably followed by silence in the white and the black communities. A day or two after the lynching, Sheriff Brown told a reporter, "I just wish that the papers would let the matter rest." Most Columbians agreed. Even my grandfather, who had spoken up as the lynching was happening, made this statement to the press: "We want to try to forget this trouble as soon as possible and lift the cloud that has been hovering over my home for more than a week."

Those who did not want to forget and who pressed most strongly for action against mob members came from outside Columbia. Many of them belonged to the NAACP, the group originally founded in response to aggression against blacks. John L. Love, president of the Kansas City chapter, sent a telegram to Governor Hyde urging " a rigid investigation and prosecution of the Columbia lynchers." He also telegraphed the St. Louis chapter for cooperation in a statewide demand for prosecution, and he contacted Walter White, assistant secretary of the national NAACP telling him he hoped for the national NAACP's assistance in this demand. White telegraphed back to

11. The Aftermath

assure Love he had it. Meanwhile George Vaughn stayed on in Columbia to write up a report for NAACP headquarters in New York City. His first communication to them was a telegram on April 30 to White announcing he had been an eyewitness to the mob's actions. In his reply, the NAACP assistant secretary asked Vaughn to send his report by Thursday so White could release it to the media. Vaughn sent him eight typewritten legal size pages on which he described what he has seen and heard on Saturday night and early Sunday morning.[2]

The final section of Vaughn's report is entitled "SCOTT INNOCENT," and here the lawyer lays out some of what he would have been used in Scott's defense had he been given a chance. One issue he notes is the changing chronology of the original attack. Regina initially reported the attack occurred at 2:30 but later changed the time to 3:30. Vaughn cites one witness, a white man, who accompanied Scott in a truck that arrived back on campus at 3:10 after they had gone to burn carcasses used in the dissecting room of the medical building where Scott worked. Scott then cleaned and polished floors and woodwork in the medical building until 3:45. This time too was collaborated by a white witness. So while no witnesses had yet been found to verify Scott's contention he had continued cleaning and polishing until 5, there was a white witness who placed him in the medical building fifteen minutes after my aunt had been attacked and another white witness who had seen him there at five. Vaughn then makes another interesting, but flawed, observation:

> The strange thing about the girl's identification is that Scott had worked at the university for some time and nearly every body out there knew him. The girl's father is a professor in the school and his family live on campus with him. The daughter must have seen Scott about there many times, even if she did not know his name.

In point of fact, my aunt and her family did not live on campus. They lived on Garth Avenue several blocks away. Nor was there any reason to believe my aunt would know James Scott by sight. My grandfather taught in a building some distance from the Medical Building where Scott worked. It is not likely Scott would have strayed far from his place of employment. Perhaps what Vaughn was attempting was a proposal for an alternative explanation for why Regina Almstedt had identified James Scott as her attacker not once, but three times. As I mentioned earlier, mistaken identity is not an unusual occurrence. Why my aunt mistakenly picked out Scott can never be conclusively answered. That she had made a mistake, however, was becoming increasingly clear, even without Vaughn's incorrect supposition.

Pressure by the NAACP, along with the negative comments that were appearing in both state and national newspapers about Columbia and its university, forced authorities to act. On Monday morning after the lynching State Attorney General Jesse W. Barnett and Prosecuting Attorney Ruby Hulen met in Jefferson City to announce a grand jury would be called two days later to look into the lynching. Hulen sounded optimistic in his promises of at least a dozen indictments, but we have to wonder if he truly believed this. Yes, he and other local authorities could identify many of the men involved, but where would they get a grand jury that was, as he described, "composed of citizens with respect for the law"? At the same press conference, Attorney General Barrett, who had assigned his assistant attorney general, Henry Davis, to help with the prosecution sounded equally positive about the outcome. "I know the people of Boone County, and I know that they are not the kind to let this assault upon law and order go unpunished." The fact that the people of Boone County, with very few exceptions, had allowed an assault on law and order to go on from approximately ten p.m. Saturday night to one-thirty Sunday morning seems to have escaped the Attorney General's notice.

When on Thursday, May 3, the grand jury voted to indict George Barkwell, a former city councilman and local contractor for second degree murder, and four other men were charged with obstructing an officer in Scott's lynching, the indictment showed opinion about the rightness of the lynching was more divided than it might have seemed on the night it occurred. On the other hand, quite a few of Columbia's most illustrious citizens showed their true colors. The president of the Boone County Trust Company, William A. Bright, not only helped post Barkwell's bond, but he told the sheriff to send any more men in the mob who might be charged to him. "I'll make bond for them until you fellows around the courthouse holler 'Enough!'"[3] he is reported to have said. In all, seventeen prominent Columbia businessmen provided the twenty thousand dollar bond for Barkwell, doing so within thirty minutes of his arrest. These men included another bank president, a city administrator, three lumberyard operators, two contractors and the county collector. Neither the men charged nor those who supported them by posting their bonds were the "roughnecks" Ruby Hulen had originally suggested were leaders of the mob, perhaps in a vain attempt to save Columbia's reputation. Nor were any of those directly involved, it should be noted, from the university community. Boone County and Columbia's middle class showed their true colors (or color), too. When H.H. "Hamp" Rowland, a forty-six-year-old farmer and relative of Columbia's chief of police, was arrested, ten carloads of his fellow farmers from Harrisburg, eighteen miles

11. The Aftermath

away, followed him to Columbia to help post his five thousand dollar bond. Twenty-two of these men signed their names ten minutes after the bond had been written. They were added to the signatures of a local real estate agent, a New York insurance representative and a former sheriff. Another of the men charged, Marvin Harris, a harness maker whose shop was on South Eighth Street in the city, had his bond posted by several nearby shop owners and five retired farmers. In posting these bonds, those in the farming and business communities who believed in "summary justice" came together to support the men who had carried it out. For Nina March, who along with her husband had signed Hamp Rowland's bond, the matter could not be clearer. All women, she said, should be interested in supporting the men who had stepped up to defend women's honor. On May 8 attorneys for the five defendants united to file not guilty pleas for their clients. Judge Ernest Gantt of Audrain County ordered the cases tried separately during the next term of the Boone County Circuit Court.

Because the lawyers for George Barkwell, the first defendant to be tried, felt the usual judge presiding over the Circuit Court, David Harris, was biased against their client, it was again Judge Gantt who called court to order shortly after 9 a.m. on July 9, approximately two months after the indictments and 71 days after James Scott had been lynched. The courtroom, already warm on this summer morning, filled as spectators pushed their way in to watch jury selection. Judge Gantt called up the first twelve men summoned for jury duty, and the lawyers for both sides began their questions. Seven of the twelve said they believed in mob law or they felt Barkwell should never have been charged. Two of those announced they would probably not convict *any* white man for a crime committed against a Negro. One of the possible jurors did say he was against mob law, but then he added, "if I had been the daddy of the child, there wouldn't have had to have been any mob law." Somehow Judge Gantt found four of these first twelve qualified to sit on the jury. They included the man who admitted he would have taken the law into his own hands.

More possible jurors were summoned and questioning continued. The courtroom onlookers applauded those who said mob law was appropriate on some occasions, and murmurs of approval arose when someone suggested this trial shouldn't even be happening. By the afternoon of the first day, the pool of potential jurors needed replenishing. Fifteen new faces appeared after lunch, and that evening Wilson Hall, the jailer, and Officer Pless King, his deputy, went out to find more. "Citizens with respect for the law" were turning out to be harder to find than Hulen had thought. Twenty-one possible jurors presented themselves the next morning at nine at the courthouse. Some were dismissed outright because they were related to the principals in the trial including the prosecutor himself. As selection got down to the last group, the atmosphere in the courtroom became audibly partisan. Everyone questioned said he was for mob law in certain circumstances, and each answer was cheered by the crowd. In the end, of the eighty-three men (and it was only men) summoned, more than a quarter were dismissed because they said they believed in mob law in some situations. Five were let go when they declared they saw no reason to prosecute a white man for "hanging a nigger." This difficulty in finding a relatively unbiased jury reflected the sentiment of most of Columbia and Boone County white residents at the time. Prosecuting the alleged lynchers served no real purpose and only kept the event in the public eye longer. As Ifill pointed out, silence is the normal reaction by a community to a lynching that has occurred there.

To an extent, those who wished the whole thing would quickly go away got their wish. Wednesday morning, July 11, over five hundred people, including a small cadre of blacks, crowded into the courtroom to hear the opening statements by lawyers for both sides. The prosecution's case as stated by Ruby Hulen was simple: "I believe testimony will trace the defendant from the courthouse columns until he tied a rope around the neck of the negro and pushed him backwards from Stewart Bridge." Hulen went on to describe the hours it took to break into the jail, the refusal by mob leaders to stop when instructed to do so by officers of the law, and the composure of the victim throughout. Barkwell had four lawyers defending him. In his opening statement, one of them, Senator—he kept this title long after serving—Frank Harris began by telling the jury what a righteous and law-biding citizen his client was. Then he moved on to his essential argument. Focusing on the crime the victim of the lynching had allegedly committed, he described in lascivious detail the attack and the subsequent identification of Scott by the victim. The implication was easy enough for all to draw: Scott deserved to be lynched, and a great many people in Columbia thought so. However, declared Senator Harris, Scott was not lynched by the defendant. In fact, George Barkwell had tried to stop the crowd that night at the jail, and as for being the man who put the rope around Scott's neck, this was a completely unfair accusation. Testimony would show that his client was standing on the other side of Stewart Bridge when Scott was pushed off.

After a recess for lunch, testimony began. Prosecutor Hulen called Sher-

11. The Aftermath

iff Brown, who testified he had seen George Barkwell outside Scott's cell but could not say for certain who had burned the locks off the door. Judge Collier, Deputy Hall and Officers King and Miller agreed they had seen Barkwell in the jail corridor and said it had been he who raised his hand to quiet the crowd so Judge Collier and Prosecutor Hulen could try to persuade them to stop their attack on the cell. In cross examination, the defense lawyers did not dispute the identification of the witnesses, but instead focused on the inaction of Sheriff Brown in protecting the victim when he knew a lynching might occur. When defense lawyer and Democratic Congressman Samuel Major again referred to Scott's guilt by asking Sheriff Brown if the Negro taken from the cell was the same one identified by Regina Almstedt, Hulen jumped up to protest. This time with the jury out of the courtroom, Judge Gantt agreed with Hulen that whatever Scott may or may not have done, the jury was charged with determining Barkwell's actions not Scott's. He sustained Hulen's objection that the defense's repeated references to the rape were only being done to inflame the jury.

Testimony moved on to what happened on the Stewart Street Bridge. Hulen's first witness was Francis Misselwitz, a recently graduated journalism student who was now working for the *St. Louis Post-Dispatch*. Misselwitz had come up from St. Louis on the 6:15 train when he heard there might be a lynching in Columbia. He didn't see anything initially, but around 11 that night someone told him a crowd was gathering. He arrived at the jail just in time to see the last hinge on the hallway door burnt off. When the mob started toward the bridge, Misselwitz rode there in a car and followed my grandfather onto the bridge. He found himself standing right by James Scott, and in a subsequent article for his paper wrote "A big man elbowed his way to the negro, and, in silence, placed a one-inch noose over his head." This same man tied the loose end of the rope to the bridge, then after pushing Scott over the side with both hands, disappeared into the crowd. Asked by the prosecutor if the big man he had seen on the bridge was in the courtroom, Misselwitz hesitated. The man who had done this was the same size and build as Barkwell, Misselwitz admitted, but he hadn't actually seen his face. Doug Hunt, in his account of the lynching and trial, suggests Misselwitz may have been influenced by a job offer that came shortly after Misselwitz's lynching article appeared. Without an application or interview, Dean Walter Williams offered Francis Misselwitz a faculty position in the School of Journalism from which he had so recently graduated. Whether any other stipulations accompanied this offer we will never know. Certainly Misselwitz understood the mood of Columbia after the lynching. Forgetting a face was only a small part of forgetting the whole incident.

A witness to the lynching who did not forget a face turned out to be Charles Nutter, at the time a twenty-year-old journalism student who had been close to Scott from the moment he was taken out of the jail to his arrival on the bridge. Like Misselwitz, whom he was standing right in front of, Nutter heard Scott profess his innocence to the crowd and proclaim the guilt of Ollie Watson, who had confessed to Scott earlier and shaved three times a day in their cell so that a "Charlie Chaplin" mustache would never appear. Unlike Misselwitz, Nutter was able to identify George Barkwell as the man who put the noose around Scott's neck, lifted him onto the railing and shoved him over. Prosecutor Hulen asked Nutter where exactly he was standing when this happened, and Nutter repeated that he was right next to Scott. In fact, Barkwell had pushed him back into Misselwitz in order to reach Scott. How was the defense going to refute this testimony? The cross-examination was rough. Asked if he could describe the clothing the defendant wore, Nutter said he could not. Then how could he be sure the man he saw was Barkwell? Nutter replied that with the arc light and the moonlight, he was certain of his identification. Besides, a man in the crowd had called him "Barkwell," and Nutter, ever the reporter, had verified both the first and last name with another man standing near him in the crowd. If this were so, asked Congressman Major, then why hadn't Nutter reported it in his article in the *Missourian*? Nutter replied that he did not want to risk having Barkwell sue for libel. When the defense lawyer reminded him truth was an absolute defense against libel, Nutter agreed, but said it just wasn't done in stories like this. So then, pressed Major, why didn't he report the name to the police instead of waiting for the grand jury? To this Nutter answered that he had reported the name the same night to Officer Pleas King. Hulen's last witness was another journalism student by the name of Foster Hailey. Hailey had been in the jail perching on top of Scott's cell—which has bars on all sides and the top—when he had seen Barkwell "monkeying with" the tank after the acetylene torch went out. Here the defense in cross-examination merely focused on the imprecision of Hailey's words. Had he seen Barkwell do something specific with the tank besides what he called "monkeying"? Hailey admitted he had not.

The defense's strategy was clear with the first witness they called. Emmett Smith, chief cashier in the Exchange National Bank, testified his friend George Barkwell was standing right next to him on the north side of the

11. The Aftermath

bridge when Scott was hanged. Another of Barkwell's friends, Pierce Neidermeyer, son of a socially prominent family in Columbia, said that not only was Barkwell standing by him when Scott was lynched but earlier he had seen George on the courthouse lawn holding his hand up to the mob in an attempt to stop the march to the bridge. When the prosecution's turn came for cross-examination, Ruby Hulen asked Neidermeyer if he had talked to Barkwell after the lynching, and if so, what was said. Neidermeyer said they had met in the street, and Barkwell had asked if Neidermeyer remembered seeing him at the lynching. Another witness, Roy McDonald, a clerk with the MTK railroad, confirmed Smith's story that he had been talking to Barkwell on the north side of the bridge away from the actual lynching spot. By the time court recessed Wednesday night, the choice of whom to believe was clear to the jury.

On the second day of the trial, the defense, not content with eyewitnesses who placed Barkwell off the bridge, called Hollis Edwards, the Columbia *Daily Tribune's* city editor, to be a witness. Asked by Senator Harris if he had written the lead story on April 27 about the victim's identification of James Scott as her attacker, Edwards had barely replied in the affirmative when Prosecutor Hulen objected. Judge Gantt sustained the objection, but this did not stop the lawyer for the defense. Holding up the editorial section from April 28 and already knowing the answer, Harris asked Edwards who had written the editorial. Hulen again objected, and again Judge Gantt sustained it. In what was to be the final straw, Harris pointed to the article on the front page of the April 29 *Daily Tribune* which included the suggestion there was an agreement among "men of sound judgment" that Boone County taxpayers might be saved the cost of a trial for James Scott. Who, asked Harris, had written this article? The judge sent the jury out and after conferring with both sets of lawyers, allowed the defense one more question on the matter, though it and the answer would be stricken from the record before the jury returned to the courtroom. Harris asked Edwards who had supplied him with the information for the article, and Edwards replied he had gotten his information from Sheriff Brown, Chief Rowland and Prosecutor Hulen. When the jury returned, Harris asked permission of the judge to read the charge that had been filed against James Scott by the prosecutor on the morning before the lynching. Ruby Hulen's decision to charge Scott with "the crime of rape" was heard and taken in by everyone in the courtroom.

By 11 that Thursday morning, Barkwell's lawyers were ready to give their closing arguments. Again, they pressed home the notion that because James

Scott had been charged with rape, he was already seen to be guilty, otherwise why would the prosecutor have brought him up on this charge? (Somehow George Starrett, the defense lawyer who pursued this line of reasoning, did not see its fatal flaw—that is, the same prosecutor had now brought up George Barkwell on the charge of second degree murder. Was *he* therefore guilty?) As for the witnesses who had seen Barkwell at the jail, yes, he had been there, but just like the sheriff and prosecutor, he had been trying to stop the crowd from taking Scott. The one witness who thought he saw George Barkwell put a rope around the victim's neck was not from here. Members of the jury did not even know him. If they were to believe Charles Nutter's testimony, they would be calling three of the town's more prominent citizens liars, and who was willing to do that?

When Ruby Hulen got his turn to speak, he began with the comment one of the defense lawyers had made that Hulen and his co-counsel were prosecuting Barkwell merely to make a point. Barkwell, Hulen said, had been indicted by the grand jury on the basis of credible evidence. It was his duty therefore to prosecute the case. And, he added, lawyers for the defense appeared to have a strange notion of duty, since one of their number was employed as a well-paid congressman in Washington, yet was sitting here today earning additional money defending George Barkwell. At this, the lawyer in question, Samuel Major, jumped to his feet to demand Hulen withdraw this accusation; maybe Hulen didn't know, but the jurors certainly did that Congress was not presently in session. The prosecutor quietly withdrew his comment, then went on to summarize the facts of the case, focusing especially on the vicious attacks the defense had made against the character of Charles Nutter. At 2:10 the jury retired to deliberate and eleven minutes later they returned to give their verdict. Cheers erupted in the courtroom as George Barkwell was declared not guilty of second-degree murder. Less than an hour later, Hulen dismissed charges of obstruction against "Hamp" Rowland. And when in a few more days, Columbia residents presented a petition to Hulen to dismiss the charges against the other three, he, in consort with the defense, arranged to continue the cases indefinitely. The reasons given by the residents included "the trial will keep alive bad feeling."[4]

On that early April Sunday morning when Sarah Brown learned her son had been killed, she was so distraught that according to George Vaughn's report to the NAACP, she collapsed and had to be carried to bed where she pleaded with the Lord to let her die. Later that day, James' brother Akers arrived from St. Louis to console his mother, and the next day, Scott's three

11. The Aftermath

children were brought down from Chicago, where they had been staying. Anna was then fifteen, Helen had turned ten earlier that month, and the youngest, Carl, was eight and a half. What a terrifying place Columbia, and perhaps the whole white world, must have seemed to these children.

James Scott's body had been taken to the Parker Funeral Home on the corner of Tenth and Walnut, and the next day hundreds of men and women from Columbia's black community filed by the casket to pay their respects and to talk among themselves. While those intent on lynching Scott dismissed his story about his cellmate confessing to the rape, many in the black community had no trouble believing it. Only a week before the lynching, the man Scott had named—Ollie Watson—and another man had been charged with viciously attacking and raping two young black girls to whom they had given a ride.

On Wednesday, May 2, the Reverend Caston led a funeral service for the deceased at Sarah Brown's home on First Street, and at 10:30 that morning Scott's body was buried in the nearby Columbia Cemetery. One day later this notice appeared in the *Columbia Missourian*,

CARD OF THANKS

We take this means of thanking our many friends and the community at large, for their kindness and sympathy shown us in our bereavement in the death of our dear husband, son and brother. Especially do we thank the Rev. J. L. Caston for his untiring efforts in every way to help. We also thank our friends for the beautiful floral offerings. We thank the undertaker for his efficient service and patience. Signed, Mrs. G. L. Scott, wife; Mrs. Sarah Brown, mother; Akers Scott, brother.[5]

Other newspaper articles in that summer mentioned James Scott, but did not appear in any of the Columbia papers. "Wrong Man is Lynched Girl Tells Parents" was the title of a brief article in the July 14 *Chicago Defender*, just two days after George Barkwell's acquittal. The story reported that Regina Almstedt had gone with her mother to Mexico, Missouri, in July to identify another man as her attacker. This was Ollie Watson, the same man Scott had said confessed to him when they were in jail together. Watson, along with his co-defendant, Jadie Scott (no relation), had been moved to the Mexico jail soon after James Scott was taken by the mob, and his trial for the attack on Ernestine Huggard, the black Columbia schoolgirl, was to begin the next day. Earlier in the week, Prosecutor Hulen had asked the Mexico jailer not to allow Watson to shave. He made this request so Regina might be able to see the "Charlie Chaplin moustache" Watson wore in the months before his arrest. But somehow the whiskers over Watson's lip never grew. Whether he pulled them out or scraped them off in some manner, we will never know. But even without his moustache, my aunt identified Watson as her attacker.

The Chicago Defender was not the first newspaper article to mention the possibility of Scott's innocence. The *St. Louis Argus*, a black newspaper, reported Regina's identification of Ollie Watson on July 5, the day that Prosecutor Ruby Hulen took her to the jail where she made that identification. Just one day later, the *St. Louis Post-Dispatch* (which employed Francis Misselwitz, a witness in the George Barkwell trial) published an article with the headline "State May Try to Prove Innocence of Lynched Negro." What makes these two articles interesting is that they appeared *before the Barkwell trial began*, yet Prosecutor Hulen, the same man who had accompanied Regina and her mother to Mexico, Missouri, *did not mention the possibility James Scott was innocent*. Nor did any newspaper in Columbia run these articles. James Scott had been laid to rest, and except for articles immediately following his lynching and the perfunctory trial of Barkwell, little would appear in Columbia papers about his death and its aftermath, until Barton Grover Howe published his five part series in the 2002 *Columbia Missourian*—the same series that introduced me to James Scott and my aunt's role in his life and death.

12

Still Partially Cloudy

> Dear John: Yours was received and so glad to get it. John, I want to leave here right away, but have not got the money. We all fear something is going to happen because things are awful critical just at the present time. We can't tell just yet, but we've got a good many who have left, some gone to the country, some left town. You ought to know that every white man who gets arrested for this lynching is let out right away on bonds. The authorities feel they've got to do something on account of the state university.[1]

While the unnamed correspondent in this letter published in the *Chicago Defender* after James Scott's lynching is anxious to leave Columbia, many other black residents of Columbia stayed including some of James Scott's closest relatives. But like the letter writer, they did so with the knowledge they were living in a place that would not protect them and even worse, one that did not punish those from whom they might need protection.

It was said that Gertrude Scott, James's third wife, never recovered from the trauma of her husband's lynching, and perhaps that's true. We do know she moved back in with her family after Scott's death, because the 1930 census shows her living in the home of her parents, James and Annie Carter at 401 Walnut. Also there are Gertrude's three brothers and a sister. Gertrude is still living in the Carter family home in 1940, but now she is married to a man named Elvis Stephens from Grand Rapids, Michigan. According to a notice in the September 6, 1930, *Chicago Defender*, the couple was married September 5 in Jefferson City, Missouri. They had gone there with four of their friends. The other change in Gertrude's life by 1940 is that she no longer teaches school. Instead at age 39, she works as a maid at Stephens College. Her appearance in the 1940 census is the last official notice I find for her, though she is indirectly referred to in a Mexico, Missouri *Weekly Intelligencer* news article on December 3, 1936, which reports an automobile accident between a car driven by E.C. Stevens and a local farmer. Gertrude wasn't present at the scene, but she is recorded as the owner of the Ford V-8 sedan her husband was driving. (The Stevens-Stephens discrepancy in her husband's last name brings to mind all the other mistakes that have been made in recording names. Remember Akers-Acres in the 1900 census?) I was unable to find a death certificate for Gertrude, but it seems likely she lived the rest of her life in Columbia, the place where she was born and where her first husband was lynched.

James Scott's mother also stayed on in Columbia after her son's death. The 1930 census shows Sarah Brown living with her third husband James at 205 N. First Street, the same address her son returned to when he left Chicago with his two youngest children. Sarah was in this house on Saturday, February 3, 1940, when a terrible accident happened. Here is the *Columbia Daily Tribune* news report:

Burns Are Fatal to Mary Brown, Negress

Mary Brown, 75-year-old Negress, died yesterday afternoon at 5:45 o'clock at the Boone County Hospital as a result of burns she received when her house caught fire last Saturday afternoon. She lived at 205 North First Street.

Fire Chief Tom Walden said the fire started from an overheated stove in the room in which the Negress lived. Her daughter said she was accustomed to sitting near the stove, usually wearing a shawl which was thought to have caught fire and burned her back, hips and neck severely.

Firemen gave the aged Negress emergency treatment before she was rushed to the hospital in an ambulance. Several Negro men passing the house rushed in and carried her out as the flames spread and badly scorched the interior walls of the room. Her husband and several children survive.[2]

This report, while presumably accurate as to the cause of her injuries, misnames Sarah, calling her Mary, which was, in fact, the name of James Brown's previous wife who died in 1913. Then there is the matter of the daughter. In the 1900 census, Sarah is recorded as having three children, yet only Akers and Scott appear in later censuses. Was there a daughter born before or after them? I am tempted to believe a news report that gets the name of the main party wrong might also have misidentified one of the women the reporter talked to. A more reasonable explanation for the mention of a daughter is this: we know that in 1945 Ella Brown Lane, daughter of Sarah's third husband, James Brown, was living with her father at 205 N. First. This is probably the "daughter" (actually step-daughter) the reporter talked to. The *Columbia Missourian* (Feb. 4, 1940) has a similar news article about the fire, though they refer, more accurately, to Sarah as "Mrs. James Brown."

According to her death certificate, Sarah Brown had lived for 74 years,

12. Still Partially Cloudy

four months and three days. In that time she had survived the early death of her first husband and the lynching of a son. She left behind a third husband and stepchildren from that marriage. She also left behind another son and three grandchildren. The woman who was born Sallie Akers had traveled as far west as Las Vegas, New Mexico, and as far east as Chicago. But in the end she came back to Columbia. Did she ever lament this decision, one that undoubtedly influenced James to return too in order to be near her? Sarah Akers Scott Clemens Brown had been born at the end of one war, lived through another and died at the beginning of a third. She had watched her son go off to fight for his country, came back safely, then be killed in her hometown. In the almost seventy-five years she was alive, Sarah had seen the world change dramatically. The telephone, light bulb, automobile and airplane had come into being, as had penicillin and other drugs that promised better health and a longer life. Congress passed amendments to the Constitution that gave her and other African Americans equal rights in a white world. But nothing could give her back her son. That she stayed in the same place where he was killed is perhaps a testament to her belief in change, or maybe it is a testament to her belief that she and her family would be no safer elsewhere.

James Scott's brother Akers didn't share his mother's feelings about Columbia. He did return for his brother's funeral in 1923, and he came back to bury his mother in 1940, but in neither case did he stay long. It was Akers who provided the information for his mother's death certificate, though in his grief he could not remember where his grandparents were born, facts he had known earlier when questioned by census takers. After his mother was buried Akers returned to Kansas City, where he lived for another eight years. His death certificate records him as passing on May 25, 1948, at 12:25 in the morning. Akers Charles Scott is incorrectly said to be almost 60 years old (he is probably four years older than this) and the cause of death is diabetic acidosis, a life-threatening condition caused by lack of insulin in the body. Whether he knew he had diabetes and didn't monitor it well or discovered it only at a late stage, I am not sure. In those years many people died of undetected diabetes. According to his death certificate, Akers spent just one day in Wheatley-Provident Hospital, a facility set up In Kansas City in 1914 to serve black patients. At the time of his death Akers had been living in Kansas City for eleven years and was working as a hotel clerk at the Booker T. Hotel at 1821 Vine Street in Kansas City. The person who provided the information for his death certificate was his wife, a woman named Lillie Ford Scott then living at 2027 Troost in Kansas City. Besides not knowing his correct birth year, Lillie was unable to provide the names of her husband's parents or where they came from. We know from the 1940 census that Akers had met Lillie at least eight years before when he was a boarder in her household at 2317 Forest Avenue in Kansas City and worked as a laborer on the WPA project aimed at controlling flooding in the area. Like his brother's neighborhood in Columbia, all of the places listed on Aker's death certificate have now either been torn down (the hotel and his house) or abandoned (the hospital).

Akers had led a peripatetic life. More than likely he had been born in Columbia then as a baby made the trip west with his parents to New Mexico. In 1900 when Sarah and James were living together in Chicago, Akers was living and working on a farm fifty miles south in Indiana. Ten years later he too is in Chicago, this time with his mother and brother and his brother's family in the household of Sarah's second husband on the north side of Chicago. Akers is still unmarried and works as a canvasser for a wholesale grocery. Between 1910 and the time he registers for the draft—dated like his brother's on September 12, 1918—he moves to the South Side of Chicago on Prairie Avenue. Now he is employed as a chauffeur and mechanic for the East Chicago Transfer and Express Company just over the border in Indiana. On his draft registration he lists his nearest relative as his mother whose address is Columbia. From this we can conclude two facts: Sarah left Chicago sometime between 1910 and 1918, and Akers has remained unmarried. In 1920, the census records Akers still working as a chauffeur, but this time for a private family, the Altons, in Evanston, Illinois. The head of the household is Carol Alton, the director of a "gent's furnishing store," and Akers lives in along with Carol's family and two more servants, both female. What is particularly interesting is that on the 1920 census Akers is recorded as a widower. So, sometime between the date Akers signed his draft card and January 10, 1920, he has married then lost his wife. Who she was and when she died I was never able to find out, and the next time Akers' name appears is when his brother is lynched in 1923. Newspapers report he has come up from St. Louis, where he may have been living at the time, though I couldn't find any records. Nor could I find him in the 1930 census. But because of information in the 1940 census, we know that around 1937 he moved to Kansas City, where he will spend his final years. The 1940 census describes Akers as a widower, so it would seem he didn't marry again after his first short marriage until he met Lillie Ford in Kansas City. None of the censuses show his having children, and his obituary refers by name only to his step-children and one cousin, Mayme Hardrick, daughter of Dora Akers, one of his mother Sarah's sisters.

12. Still Partially Cloudy

While Akers appears not to have had any children, we know his brother did, and the question of what became of them is difficult to answer. Anna would have been around 15 years old at the time of her father's death. Helen was almost exactly 10 and Carl, a young boy of eight and a half. James had been awarded custody of Helen and Carl after he divorced Lucille in January 1921. Yet newspapers reported the children returning from Chicago for their father's funeral. So they were either visiting relatives there at the time of their father's death or perhaps they had returned to live with their mother after his marriage to Getrude. If the latter, they would have gone back to Chicago after the funeral. Anna had a different mother from the younger two, so presumably she was living with Scott's first wife, Grace in Chicago both before and after the lynching. She may never have seen her half-siblings again.

By the time of the next census in 1930, Helen would have been at least 17 and may no longer have been living at home. I could not find her listed anywhere. Carl, however, does appear in the 1930 census. He is living in East Chicago, Illinois, with someone named Lucile Patterson, a widow said to be 32. The household consists of Lucile as head along with three boarders, one of whom is listed as Carl Scott, age 15. All are black, and the other two renters are older men who work in construction and at the steel mill. Could Lucile be Carl's mother? Though recorded on the census as one of the boarders, Carl reports his father was born in "Mexico" and his mother in Missouri—just where Lucile Patterson was born. Another piece of evidence for the supposition that Lucile Patterson is Lucile Scott is this: in answer to the census question of when she was first married, Lucile Patterson replies 16—the same age Lucille Smith was when she married James Scott. Neither of these facts would be enough to prove Carl is living with his mother in 1930—after all, lots of women are named Lucile (or Lucille) and some of these Luciles get married at 16—but then I find the piece of evidence that is. In the Cook County, Illinois Index of Marriages a Lucille Scott is recorded marrying Don A. Patterson on March 16, 1922. So now we know Lucile Patterson was originally Lucille Scott, and Don Patterson has apparently died sometime between his marriage in 1922 and 1930, when Lucile is listed as a widow.

On May 20, 1937, Carl applies for his Social Security card approximately seven months after the first cards are issued. He is now living at 3712 Pennsylvania Avenue, East Chicago, Indiana, about a half mile from where he had been staying with his mother seven years earlier. According to his application, he is 22 and was born on October 11, 1914, in Chicago. He lists his parents as James Scott and Lucelle Smith and writes down that he is working at Club

Oasis, a restaurant located at 103 Plummer Street in Calumet City, Illinois. This is approximately seven miles from his home. Three years later the 1940 census records him back living in the same household as his mother, and the good news is that his sister Helen has joined them there. They are all staying with Lucille's cousin, a man named Walter H. Davis in a house at 3237 139th Place in Robbins, Illinois, about fifteen miles west of East Chicago and southwest of Chicago. According to the census, they moved there sometime after 1935. (In Carl's case, we know this is sometime after 1937 because of his social security application.) The 1940 census shows the following work history for the residents of 3237 139th Place: Walter worked in a steel foundry as a crane operator, and while he made $660.00 for 52 weeks of work in 1939, he is now seeking employment. Walter's cousin Lucille made only $21 working as a housekeeper for a private family during the three weeks in the previous year, and Carl, whose occupation is listed as musician with a private orchestra, earned nothing in 1939. Helen is said to be a "new worker," and like her brother has no income listed. If the earnings for Carl, his mother and his sister seem slight, we have to remember 1939 was near the end of the Great Depression. All three members of the Scott family answered yes to the question "seeking work," which may be why Lucille and her children had to move in with her cousin.

As for their educational backgrounds, the census records Walter, age 46, as finishing four years of elementary school, while Lucille is said to have finished four years of college. Carl and his sister have both had four years of high school. Lucille's age is 38 in this census, but if she were really 16 when she married James Scott in 1910, she would be at least 45. In fact, it appears all the Scott family members have shaved years off their ages. Carl is recorded as 21 here, yet his social security form lists his birth year as 1914, so he would be 26 in 1940. Helen's birth certificate, which we have seen, records her birth date as April 1, 1913. But on the 1940 census she is listed as 22, another loss of five years. Both Helen and Carl are listed as single, while this time their mother is said to be divorced. So in the ten years between the two censuses, Lucile may have married and divorced again. Or—and given our experience with official records—one of these census designations was incorrect. In any case, as I continue to trace Carl's life, I note that registration for the draft for the Second World War begins in 1940. Carl would have been 26 years old, so I assume he would have registered. Unfortunately, because of privacy laws, the registration cards for men his age are not available to anyone but family members. So the next time I see Carl's name, it is on the Social Security Death

12. Still Partially Cloudy

Index. Carl Earl Scott died on April 27, 1993, in Gary, Indiana. According to my calculations he would have been 78 years old and lived one day short of 70 years without a father.

After Helen Scott's appearance on the 1940 census with her brother and mother, I could find no further records for her. Unlike her brother, whose last name never changed, there is a good chance Helen married and took the name of her husband. But I have been unable to discover evidence of such a marriage. Scott's first daughter, Anna by his wife Grace, has been equally untraceable if not more so. After she came down from Chicago for her father's funeral, she seems to have disappeared. I have not been a very good detective as far as James Scott's descendants are concerned. This was particularly disheartening when the committee to put a monument on Scott's grave began their own search. They envisioned a service that would honor Scott and redeem his name—though most people in Columbia, at least most African Americans, already knew the wrong man had been lynched. For his survivors, this event would have had special meaning.

For the rest of us who gathered on a warm Saturday morning in April 2011 at the Second Missionary Baptist Church and cemetery, the day had its own signficance. It gave Columbians a chance to come together in a gesture of strength and healing. The group that made all this happen, the James T. Scott Memorial Committee, had been formed the previous November at the instigation of the Reverend Clyde Ruffin of the Second Missionary Baptist Church, the church James Scott and his family had attended. The Reverend Ruffin, who also teaches at the university, was assisted by University of Missouri Professor Emeritus Douglas Hunt, whose essay[3] on the lynching received honorable mention for Best American Essays for 2004, and whose later book, *Summary Justice: The Lynching of James Scott and the Trial of George Barkwell in Columbia, Missouri, 1923*, was published in 2010. The committee also included twenty-two hardworking church members and Columbia residents. Their goal was twofold: to make the lynching of James T. Scott publicly recognized and to raise money for a larger, more prominent headstone in the cemetery where Scott had been laid to rest. To accomplish this they held fund raising events and gathered oral histories of second-hand accounts of the lynching and the impact it had on racial divisions in Columbia. (The material generated by this effort—five CDs, three DVDs, and one computer disc—is now part of James T. Scott Memorial Collection at the State Historical Society of Missouri.)

Professor Patrick Huber, who had earlier written about the lynching in

A Lynching in Little Dixie

the Missouri Historical Society's *Gateway Heritage* magazine (vol. 12, no. 1, Summer 1991) contributed a two-page biography of Scott in the dedication program. He was aided by material given to him by several researchers and historians including Doug Hunt, Rasheedah King, Clyde Ruffin, David Sapp and myself. In the program and at the memorial service, three men, in addition to James Scott, were honored: first, my grandfather, Hermann Almstedt, who tried to stop the lynching; second, Charles Perry Nutter, who stood by Scott on the bridge and at Scott's request, spoke to the crowd to try to stop them, and later not only wrote newspaper stories about the lynching but also was the only witness at Barkwell's trial to provide the full truth, and strong evidence for Barkwell's guilt in leading the lynching; and third, the Reverend Jonathan Lyle Caston, Scott's pastor who arranged for George Vaughn, the special NAACP representative and a lawyer, to come to Columbia; afterwards, Vaughn very publicly sought justice for James Scott.

If I needed it, the event confirmed for me the importance of what I had been trying to do ever since I read my aunt's name in that April 2003 *Columbia Missourian*. What existed for so long in the dark—in my family and in Columbia's black and white communities—had with this gathering moved out into the light. Despite cloudy skies, it was a day filled with illumination and redemption.

Now the question is how well have I succeeded in my own task to bring material into the light? I set out to solve two mysteries: who was James Scott and how could more than a thousand people stand by as he was lynched? What I have written here is based on the evidence I found during the years I did research. It took me longer than I anticipated, and in the end, I don't know how truly successful I have been. For instance, I never even found a photograph of the man whose life I was investigating. I did manage to accumulate enough facts to create a basic chronology of James Scott's life staring with his birth in or around 1884 in Las Vegas, New Mexico, and ending abruptly on April 29, 1923, in Columbia, Missouri. And I was able to fill in some details. According to his death certificate, James T. Scott lived for 35 years, six months and 23 days (though it is more likely he lived three years longer than this.) During this time, he married three times, had five children, two of whom died in early childhood, worked as a laborer, fireman, chauffeur and janitor, joined the National Guard, fought with distinction in World War 1, purchased his own car, and sought and received custody of his daughter and son. Then he was lynched.

Those are the facts of his life, and in a sense, they solve part of the mys-

12. Still Partially Cloudy

tery of who James Scott was. But when I set out I wanted to tell his story in the same way I remembered those stories being told in my childhood biographies. They had a development and a theme. Is the theme I have chosen—the history of racism that surrounded Scott as he and other blacks grew into adulthood at the end of the nineteenth century and the beginning of the twentieth—an appropriate one, or merely the one I have imposed in order to make Scott's life have a point? From the little I can conclude by looking at the evidence, James Scott did not demand his rights in the way W.E.B Du Bois hoped that black men would. But neither was he the kind of black man who believed in accommodation as Booker T. Washington suggested. In Chicago, Scott did not live among the majority of his fellow blacks on the South Side of the city but apart from them on the north side of the city where he was in the minority. From the information on the census reports, we can see that he and his family lived in predominantly white neighborhoods but always in houses or apartment buildings where all the other residents were black. James Scott was clearly proud to be an African American. He joined the 8th Illinois National Guard, whose roster had only black officers. He fought with a black unit in the war. None of Scott's immediate family married outside their race. James Scott was not perfect. No one is. But the simple facts of his life allow us to see a man who worked hard, loved his children and sought connection throughout his life. We can view him mainly as a victim, but that would be a mistake. The James Scott I have tried to describe here is a man to be admired. That is what we did on April 30, 2011, and I hope that is what the reader of this short biography will do now.

When James Scott moved to Columbia after the war, he was choosing a place unlike any other in his earlier experience. Born in a town in the New Mexico territory with a population of just over 2,000 in the 1870s, by the time he was sixteen, he was living in a northern city whose population in 1900 was just under 1,700,000 people. Twenty years later when he left to go to Columbia, this figure had grown by a million. And while Chicago had a substantial area of segregation, as we've seen, James did not live in it. He lived and worked on the north side of the city, away from the strict racial divisions of the south side. Columbia too had a segregated section where almost all of the black residents lived. This was hardly surprising given its location in an area of the state formerly known as Little Dixie. In attempting to solve the mystery of how more than a thousand people here could watch a man be lynched, I have traced the history of Columbia as it grew from a settlement of wooden cabins to the site of the state university and two additional colleges.

A Lynching in Little Dixie

What that history makes clear is that Columbia was founded by people whose social roots and culture came from the south. They were men and women who before the Civil War and for sometime afterwards believed slaves were property. What those beliefs evolved into was a general feeling that blacks, while now free, remained inferior and other. Predicated on this notion was much of what happened in Columbia in the years after the turn of the century. Even after black men risked their lives in World War 1, the idea that they were equal to whites was never even entertained. And the more blacks demanded that they receive the rights due to them, that they be treated as equals, the more many white Americans, in Columbia and everywhere, became fearful, and that fear turned into anger. Would James Scott have been lynched if he had been a white man accused of raping a fourteen-year-old girl in Columbia? Of course not. The two black boys accused of raping a black teenager two weeks before were not even considered for "summary judgment." Blacks were not equal to whites, which is what made the idea of a black man interfering with a white girl so heinous.

There is no mystery why the men who broke into the jail and dragged James Scott out to be lynched acted the way they did. In 1923, 29 black men died this way. The mystery was so few tried to stop it. Columbia was filled with intelligent people—professors, students, businessmen and their spouses. To accuse these people of cowardice is too easy. Not many of us are willing to face a huge crowd acting in a way we object to. But the question remains—how many of those thousand or more people really objected to what was happening? Not enough to come together and step forward, it turned out.

My grandfather wanted to disperse the clouds covering his house after his daughter's attack, and he felt the way to do that was with silence. I don't agree. James Scott was a real man with a real family and a real life. We cannot bury his life in silence. Nor can we bury the fact that thousands of people watched as he was lynched. If we don't talk about the evil that was done to him, we will be condoning that evil ourselves.

My aunt made a mistake. She made it three times, and when she finally corrected the mistake, it was too late. But she did not kill James Scott. People living in a particular place at a particular time did this. My hope was that by learning more about the history of that time and place, I could solve the mystery of how so many people could watch a man be lynched without trying to stop it. In the end, I don't think I found an answer. But I did lift some of the clouds, and with words, not silence.

Chapter Notes

Introduction

1. The articles my cousin was referring to first appeared in a five part series beginning online and in print May 5, 2003. Howe, Barton Grover. 2003. "Legacy of a Lynching," *Missourian* (Columbia, MO). May 3–8. https://www.columbiamissourian.com/news/local/legacy-of-a-lynching/pdf_d011a4fa-8963-11e5-824c-ef3e5ef91961.html.

2. Accounts of the attack on my aunt appeared in several Missouri newspapers including the Columbia *Missourian*, *Daily Tribune* and *Herald-Statesman*; the St. Louis *Post-Dispatch*, *Globe-Democrat* and *Argus*; the Kansas City *Star*; and the Mexico *Ledger*. Specific citations appear in a very well researched article about the lynching by Huber, Patrick J. 1991. "The Lynching of James T. Scott: The Underside of a College Town." *Gateway Heritage* 12:1 (Summer).

3. This quote is taken from Wright, Marie T., 1993. "Augusta Stevenson and the Bobbs-Merrill Childhood of Famous Americans Biographies." *Indiana Libraries*. Volume 12, Number 1. https://journals.iupui.edu/index.php/IndianaLibraries/article/viewFile/16712/pdf_176.

4. Rampersad, Arnold. 1983. "Biography, Autobiography and Afro-American Culture." *The Yale Review*, 1–16.

5. For another view on the idea of a white biographer for a black subject, see Rampersad, 1983.

Chapter 1

1. James, P.D. *Talking About Detective Fiction*. New York: Knopf, 2009. 174.

2. This information is from Billington, Monroe Lee. 1994. *New Mexico's Buffalo Soldiers, 1866 1900*. Boulder, CO: University Press of Colorado.

3. Switzler, William F. *History of Boone County Missouri Written and Compiled from the Most Authentic Official and Private Sources*. St. Louis: Western Historical Company, 1882. 492. https://ia600502.us.archive.org/32/items/historyofbooneco01stlo/historyofbooneco01stlo.pdf.

4. Richardson, Barbara J. *Black Directory of New Mexico: Black Pioneers of New Mexico, a Documentary and Pictorial History*. Rio Rancho, New Mexico: Panorama Press, 1976.

5. Perigo, Lynne. *Gateway to Glorieta: A History of Las Vegas, New Mexico*. Boulder, CO: Pruett Publishing Company, 1982.

6. Perigo, 1982, 68.

7. Cabeza de Baca, Fabiola. *We Fed Them Cactus*. Albuquerque: University of New Mexico Press, 1994. 84.

8. Perigo, 1982, 168.

9. Santa Fe Route. Chicago: Poule Brothers Printers, 1885. http://railroads.unl.edu/documents/view_document.php?Scope%5B0%5D=national&sort=rend&order=asc&per_page=20&page=29&id=rail.ATS_06_1885.001.

10. Lewis, Nancy Owen. "Seeking a Cure, Transforming New Mexico: The Lungers and Their Legacy." *New Mexico History*. Org, 12 July 2012. http://newmexicohistory.org/people/lungers-and-their-legacy.

Chapter 2

1. Unless specifically referred to in the text, the primary sources I relied on for information about Little Dixie before the Civil War were the following. Hurt, R. Douglas. *Agriculture and Slavery in Missouri's Little Dixie*. Columbia: University of Missouri, 1992; also, Stone, Jeffrey C. *Slavery, Southern Culture, and Education in Little Dixie, Missouri, 1820–1860*. Abingdon-on-Thames: Routledge, 2006.

2. Meyer, Duane G. *The Heritage of Missouri, Third Edition*. Springfield: Emden Press, 1982. 316.

3. Subsequent data on slave numbers comes from McGettigan, James W. Jr., 1978. "Boone County Slaves: Sales, Estate Divisions and Families, 1820–1865." *Missouri Historical Review*. Volume 72, Numbers 2 (January) and 3 (April).

Notes—Chapters 3, 4 and 5

4. McGettigan, January, 1978, 183–184.
5. Stone, 2006, 22.
6. Stone, 2006, 34.
7. McGettigan, January, 1978, 187.
8. McGettigan, January, 1978, 192.
9. McGettigan, April, 1978, 275–276.
10. McGettigan, April, 1978, 293.
11. McGettigan, April, 1978, 294–295.
12. Stone, 2006, 40.
13. Bruce, Henry Clay. *The New Man: Twenty-Nine Years a Slave, Twenty-Nine Years a Free Man.* Lincoln: University of Nebraska, 1996. 12.
14. "Lewis & Clark County, Montana Biographies," 2006. *MTGenWeb Project.* November. http://www.rootsweb.ancestry.com/~mtlewisa/BioB.htm.
15. "United States Census, 1860, Gilbert Robinson, 1860." *FamilySearch.* July 2011 https://familysearch.org/ark:/61903/1:1:MHCB-3PC.
16. Crighton, John C. *A History of Columbia and Boone County.* Columbia: Computer Color-Graphics, Inc., 1987. 186–187.
17. *Missouri Intelligencer,* January 24, 1835.
18. Switzler, 1882, 163.
19. Atherton, Lewis E. 1944. "Life, Labor and Society in Boone County, Missouri, 1834–1854, as Revealed in the Correspondence of an Immigrant Slave-Owning Family From North Carolina, Part 2." *Missouri Historical Review,* XXXVIII, 424.
20. Subsequent quotes come from Switzler, 1882, 377–382.

Chapter 3

1. *Missouri Statesman,* March 15, 1861.
2. Switzler, 1882, 402–403.
3. Switzler, 1882, 407.
4. Switzler, 1882, 408.
5. Switzler, 1882, 409.
6. Crighton, 1987, 150.
7. Crighton, 1987, 157.
8. *Columbia Evening Missourian,* August 24, 1921.
9. Switzler, 1882, 423.
10. Crighton, 1987, 176.
11. Blassingame, John W. 1964. "The Recruitment of Negro Troops in Missouri during the Civil War," *Missouri Historical Review,* 58 no. 3, 338.

Chapter 4

1. Crighton, 1987, 189–192.
2. Crighton, 1987, 191–192.
3. Greene, Lorenzo J., Gary R. Kremer, Antonio F. Holland. *Missouri's Black Heritage,* Revised Edition. Columbia: University of Missouri Press, 1993. 91.
4. *The New Constitution of the State of Missouri: As Revised, Amended, and Adopted in Convention, Begun and Held in the City of St. Louis, on the Sixth Day of January, Eighteen Hundred and Sixty-Five; and Ratified; by the People, at an Election Held on the 6th Day of June,* 1865, 5. https://archive.org/details/newconstitutiono00miss.
5. Williams, Henry S., 1920. "The Development of the Negro Public School System in Missouri." *The Journal of Negro History,* vol. 5: 149.
6. *Columbia Statesman,* June 28, 1867, page 3, column 4.
7. Rollins, James Sidney (1812–1888), *Letters, 1870–1885* (C3014), State Historical Society of Missouri, roll 1.
8. *Missouri Statesman,* May 1, 1885, page 2, column 3.
9. *Missouri Statesman,* January 9, 1885, page 3, column 3.
10. *Report of the Public Schools of the State of Missouri,* 1890 (Volume 40). Tribune Printing Company, 33.
11. *Columbia Statesman,* May 24, 1867, page 2, column 3.
12. Crighton, 1987, 191.
13. Grenz, Suzanna Maria. *The Black Community in Boone County, Missouri 1850–1900.* Diss. University of Missouri, 1979. 179.
14. *Missouri Statesman,* December 27, 1872, page 3, column 2.
15. *Missouri Statesman,* April 23, 1886, Page 2, Column 7.
16. *Boone County Missouri Marriage, Book 1,* page 119.
17. Research for a booklet on James Scott's life produced in 2011 in connection with the dedication of his memorial was done by several people including David Sapp, who supplied these clues to a possible identification of Scott's father.
18. Switzler, 1882, 803.

Chapter 5

1. Wright, Richard and Edwin Rosskam. *12 Million Black Voices.* New York: Viking, 1941. (reprint: 2002, New York: Basic Books) 99–100.
2. Many books about black Chicagoans focus on the south side of the city, but James and his family lived on the north side. Nevertheless, the following are of particular interest: Drake, St. Clair and Horace R. Cayton. *Black Metropolis.* Reprint: Chicago, University of Chicago Press, 1993; also, Spear, Allan H. *Black Chicago: The*

Making of a Ghetto 1890–1920. Chicago: University of Chicago Press, 1967.

3. *The Professional World*, November 8, 1901, page 1, column 5. http://chroniclingamerica.loc.gov.

4. Spear, 1967, 29.

5. Chicago Commission on Race Relations. *The Negro in Chicago; a Study of Race Relations and a Race Riot in 1919*. Chicago: University of Chicago Press, 1922. (reprint: New York, Arno Press, 1968), 102.

6. Wells, Ida B. 1893; 1999. *The Reason Why the Colored American Is Not in the World's Columbian Exposition*. Reprint by Chicago: University of Illinois Press.

7. McCammack, Brian. 2010. "My God, they must have riots on those things all the time": African American Geographies and Bodies on Northern Urban Public Transportation, 1915–1940." *Journal of Social History*, 43 (4), 979. https://scholar.harvard.edu/brianmccammack/publications/%E2%80%98my-god-they-must-have-riots-those-things-all-time%E2%80%99-african-american-geo.

8. Grossman, James R. *Land of Hope: Chicago, Black Southerners, and the Great Migration*. Chicago: University of Chicago Press, 1991. 183.

9. Grossman, 1991, 185.

10. Spear, 1967, 35.

11. Sernett, Milton. *Bound for the Promised Land: African American Religion and the Great Migration*. Durham: Duke University Press, 1997. 144.

12. Wood, Junius B. 1916. *The Negro in Chicago: How He and His Race Kindred Came to Dwell in Great Numbers in a Northern City; How He Lives and Works; His Successes and Failures; His Political Outlook*. Chicago: Chicago Daily News, Dec. 11–16, 19. https://archive.org/stream/negroinchicagoho00wood/negroinchicagoho00wood_djvu.txt.

13. Wood, 1916, 19.

14. Wood, 1916, 19.

15. Chicago Commission on Race Relations, 1968, 524.

16. Spear, 1967, 53–54.

17. A very good history of the paper is found in Michaeli, Ethan. 2016. *The Defender: How the Legendary Black Newspaper Changed America*. New York: Houghton Mifflin Harcourt.

18. Suggs, Henry Lewis. *The Black Press in the Middle West, 1865–1985*. Westport, CT: Greenwood Press, 1996.

19. Scott, Emmett J. 1919. "Letters of Negro Migrants of 1916–1918," *Journal of Negro History* 4, 290–340.

20. Scott, 1919, 290–340.

Chapter 6

1. 103 issues of *The Professional World* from 1901 through 1903 can be viewed on the Library of Congress Chronicling America website: http://chroniclingamerica.loc.gov/lccn/sn89066321/issues/1901/.

2. Ellwood, Charles A. *Sociology and Modern Social Problems*. New York: American Book Company, 1910. https://archive.org/details/sociologymoderns00ellwuoft.

3. Ellwood, Charles A. 1925. "The Menace of Racial and Religious Intolerance." *NCSW Proceedings*, 18–26. ("NCSW" resulted from a name change in 1917 to the "National Conference of Social Work," which was changed again in 1956 to the "National Conference on Social Welfare.")

4. *Columbia Daily Tribune*, May 12, 1923 cited in Huber, Patrick. 1991."The Lynching of James T. Scott: The Underside of a College Town." *Gateway Heritage magazine*, 12.

5. Elwang, William Wilson. *The Negroes of Columbia: A Concrete Study of the Race Problem*. Columbia: Department of Sociology, University of Missouri, 1904. iv. https://archive.org/details/sociologymoderns00ellwuoft.

6. Elwang, 1904, 3.

7. Elwang, 1904, 5.

8. Elwang, 1904, 10.

9. Elwang, 1904, 18.

10. Elwang, 1904, 20.

11. Elwang, 1904, 20–28.

12. Elwang, 1904, 29–32.

13. Elwang, 1904, 33–37.

14. Elwang, 1904, 38.

15. Elwang, 1904, 38–44.

16. Elwang, 1904, 45.

17. Elwang, 1904, 51.

18. Elwang, 1904, 51–52.

19. Elwang, 1904, 53.

20. Elwang, 1904, 56–59.

21. Elwang, 1904, 60–62.

22. Elwang, 1904, 63.

23. Elwang, 1904, 65.

24. Elwang, 1904, 66.

25. Elwang, 1904, 66–67.

26. Elwang, 1904, 67.

27. Elwang, 1904, 68.

28. Elwang, 1904, 69.

29. McCord, Charles Harvey. 1906. *Negro Criminality*. Master's Thesis, University of Missouri, 30.

30. McCord, Charles Harvey. *The American Negro as Dependent, Defective and Delinquent*. Nashville, TN: Benson Printing, 1914. 225.

31. "The Negro in Columbia." 1911. *University Missourian* (Columbia), March 29, 2.

32. "The Negro in Columbia," 1911, 2.

33. "The Negro in Columbia," 1911, 2.
34. "The Negro in Columbia: Black Population Is at a Standstill, the Death Rate Being Two and a Half Times That of White People." 1913. *University Missourian*, January 10, 2.
35. "The Negro in Columbia: Black Population Is at a Standstill, the Death Rate Being Two and a Half Times That of White People." 1913, 2.
36. "The Negro in Columbia: Black Population Is at a Standstill, the Death Rate Being Two and a Half Times That of White People." 1913, 2.
37. Jindrich, Jason. 2002. "Our Black Children: The Evolution of Black Space in Columbia, Missouri." MA thesis, University of Missouri, Microfilm, University of Missouri Libraries.
38. *Evening Missourian*, Dec. 28, 1915.
39. Larson, August F. *A Housing Survey of Columbia, Missouri*. Columbia: University of Missouri, 1919.

Chapter 7

1. Barbeau and Floret, 1974, ch. 4; Ellis, Mark, 2001, *Race, War, and Surveillance: African Americans and the United States Government during World War 1*, ch. 5. Bloomington: Indiana Univ. Press.
2. *The Argus* was published in St. Louis, 1835–41, with a focus on AfricanAmerican issues. Cf. http://chroniclingamerica.loc.gov/lccn/sn84020176/.
3. Scott's enlistment form was sent from this archive: *The National Personnel Records Center, Military Personnel*, about which you can learn at https://www.archives.gov/st-louis/military-personnel.
4. Cf. http://www.blackhistoryheroes.com/2010/02/black-soldiers-in-american-wars-eighth.html. Also cf. www.8thinfantry.org/history.html.
5. Cf. http://archives.chicagotribune.com/1898/05/27/page/2/article/john-c-buckner-is-striving-to-get-a-command.
6. This is from the March 25, 1899 edition of the *Appeal*, a Black newspaper founded in June, 1885 in St. Paul, Minnesota. http://www.aaregistry.org/historic_events/view/appeal-newspaper-was-popular-20th-century-black-america.
7. Hannah, Eleanor. 2007. "Soldiers Under the Skin: Diversity of Race, Ethnicity, and Class in the Illinois National Guard, 1879–1916." (online at) *American Nineteenth Century History*, vol. 8, Issue 3, Taylor and Francis. 293–323.
8. Merritt, Carole. 2008. *Something So Horrible: The Springfield Race Riot of 1908* (a catalog) at https://www.illinois.gov/alplm/museum/learning/documents/race_riot_catalog_2008.pdf. Cf. also Senechal de la Roche, Roberta. *In Lincoln's Shadow: The 1908 Race Riot in Springfield, Illinois*. Carbondale: Southern Illinois University Press, 2008.
9. Cf. Keene, Jennifer D. 2002. "A Comparative Study of White and Black American Soldiers during the First World War," *Annales de Demographie Historique*, 71–76, 86 (fn.7).
10. Evidence for exonerating the soldiers was first described in Weaver, John D. *The Brownsville Raid*. College Station: Texas A&M University, 1992.
11. The East St. Louis Mail is described as published in East St. Louis in Saint Clair County, Illinois, from 1914 to 19??. http://chroniclingamerica.loc.gov/lccn/sn87082765/.
12. Garvey's speech was published in the *New York Globe*, July 11, 1917, and appears in Early, Gerald (ed.) *Ain't But a Place: An Anthology of African American Writings about St. Louis*, 300. St. Louis: Missouri Historical Society Press, 1998.
13. *The Messenger*, July, 1918. *The Messenger* was an important political and literary magazine by and for African American people in the early 20th century.
14. From the July 1918 issue of *Crisis* (vol. 16, no. 3, 111–114). Cf. https://www.marxists.org/history/usa/workers/civil-rights/crisis/0700-crisis-v16n03-w093.pdf.
15. Kornweibel, Theodore, Jr. 2002. *Investigate Everything: Federal Efforts to Compel Black Loyalty During World War 1*. Bloomington: Indiana University Press.
16. This petition, and reactions to it, are discussed in Kornweibel, 2002, 123 ff.
17. Lamar to Abbott, 13 June 1918, B-47522, RG 28, PO, NARA (National Archives and Records Administration).
18. "An Elaborate Dinner," *Chicago Defender*, August 11, 1917, 6.
19. Hunt, Doug. 2011. *Summary Justice: The Lynching of James Scott and the Trial of George Barkwell, in Columbia, Missouri, 1923*. Amazon, Kindle edition.
20. Cf. Leach, Jack Franklin. *Conscription in the United States: Historical Background*. Rutland, VT: C.E. Tuttle Pub. Co, 1952.
21. Cf. online: *Roster of the Illinois National Guard and Illinois Naval Militia as Organized When Called by the President for World War Service*.
22. Braddan, William S., c. 1923. *Under Fire With the 370th (8th I.N.G.) A.E.F.*; under this title, the book is archived online. In his preface Braddan says the 8th was "composed largely of

men from Berean Baptist Church and Congregation" [his Chicago church].
23. Braddan, 1923, ch. 11.
24. Haywood, Harry. *Black Bolshevik: Autobiography of an Afro-American Communist.* Chicago: Liberator Press, 1978. (All references are to Ch. 2.)
25. Haywood, 1978.
26. Haywood, 1978, reports an account from *Crisis* concerning the Houston Mutiny.
27. Haywood, 1978.
28. Information about the Madawaska and transporting troops to France is based on the following: Braddan, 1923, ch. 6.; Roberts, Frank E. *The American Foreign Legion: Black Soldiers of the 93d in World War.* Annapolis, MD: Naval Institute Press, 2004. 63–65; Hallas, James H., ed. *Doughboy War: The American Expeditionary Forces in World War I.* Boulder, CO: Lynne Rienner Publishers, 2000. (reprint: Mechanicsburg, PA: Stackpole Military History Series).

Chapter 8

1. Haywood, 1978, 65.
2. This "Secret Information Bulletin Concerning Black American Troops" was published in Du Bois, W.E.B. 1919, in his editorial in *The Crisis*, May, 16–17; it also appears in Haywood, 1978, 54–55, and Barbeau and Henri, 1974, 114–115.
3. Unless specifically referred to in the text, the sources underlying the present account of the life of an American black infantry man in France during WWI are the following: Barbeau and Henri, 1974; Braddan, 1923; Hallas, 2000; Haywood, 1978; Mason, Monroe, and F. Arthur. *The American Negro Soldier with the Red Hand of France.* Boston: Cornhill Company, 1920; Roberts, Frank E. *The American Foreign Legion: Black Soldiers of the 93d in World War I.* Annapolis, MD: Naval Institute Press, 2004. 122–128; Scott, Emmett Jay. *Scott's Official History of the American Negro in the World War.* Chicago: Homewood Press, 1919. (http://shsmo.org/manuscripts/columbia/c3014); Sweeney, W. Allison, *History of the American Negro in the Great War.* Chicago: Cuneo-Henneberry, 1919. 153–176 (reprint by Johnson Reprint Corporation,1980); Williams, Chad L. *Torchbearers of Democracy: African American Soldiers in the WWI Era.* Chapel Hill: University of North Carolina Press, 2010; Williams, Charles H. *Negro Soldiers in World War I: The Human Side.* New York: AMS Press, 1923. (1970 reprint).
4. Cf. Keene, Jennifer D. "French and American Racial Stereotypes During the First World War." *National Stereotypes in Perspective:* *Americans in France, Frenchmen in America.* William Chew, editor. Amsterdam: Rodopi Press, 2001. 266. https://www.chapman.edu/our-faculty/files/publications/keene-jennifer/French%20and%20American%20Racial%20stereotypes.pdf.
5. Haywood, 1978, 58.
6. Corporal Fehrs' descriptions are included in the following collection of narratives from African American soldiers who served in WWI: Withers, Zachary, ed. *Heroes of 1918: Stories from the Lips of Black Fighters.* Chicago: O. Walker, 1919. Photos and excerpts from the book were found in 2017 at http://illinoisrbml.tumblr.com/post/113353615756/as-part-of-our-ongoing-commemoration-of-world-war.
7. Braddan, 1923, 71.
8. Haywood, 1978, 56.
9. Cf. Barbeau and Henri, 1974, 122–124, 127.
10. Harrison, Carter Henry. *With the American Red Cross in France, 1918–1919.* Chicago: R.F. Seymour, 1947.
11. This order from General Vincendon is quoted in Haywood (1978, 67).
12. Quoted in Du Bois, 1919, 16–17.

Chapter 9

1. "Throngs Greet 8th," *Chicago Defender*, p.3, Feb. 22, 1919; cf. also an editorial on the same topic, p. 2.
2. http://www.chesnuttarchive.org/classroom/lynching_table_year.html.
3. Sources for this section are the newspaper articles cited, and the following: Tuttle, William M. *Chicago in the Red Summer of 1919.* New York: Atheneum, 1970; also, McWhirter, Cameron. *Red Summer: The Summer of 1919 and the Awakening of Black America.* New York: Henry Holt, 2011.
4. *The Whip* (Chicago newspaper), August/September, 1919.
5. "Ghastly Deeds of Race Rioters Told," *Chicago Defender*, September 2, 1919.
6. "300 Armed Negroes Gather; New Rioting Starts; Militia Next," *Chicago Daily News*, July 28, 1919.
7. Sandburg, Carl. *The Chicago Race Riots.* New York: Harcourt, Brace, and Howe, 1919.

Chapter 10

1. Wells-Barnett, Ida B. *Southern Horrors: Lynch Law in All Its Phases.* New York: New York Age, 1892. EBook #14975.

2. Cf. Hunt, Douglas 2010, and Huber, Patrick 1991. The newspapers are the *Columbia Evening Missourian* and *The Columbia Daily Tribune*. Both begin coverage in their April 22, 1923 issues, and increase coverage on April 30 because of the lynching and the subsequent grand jury investigation of it.

3. Münsterberg, Hugo. *On the Witness Stand: Essays on psychology and Crime*, Garden City, NY: Doubleday, Page, 1908, 1917. Https://Archive.Org/Details/Onwitnessstande00goog.

4. Columbia, *Daily Tribune*, Apr. 28, 1923.

5. Switzler, *The History of Boone County, Missouri*. St. Louis: Western Historical Company Press of Nixon-Jones Printing Co., 1882. https://ia600502.us.archive.org/32/items/historyofbooneco01stlo/historyofbooneco01stlo.pdf.

6. Hunt, 2010, 26–27.

7. Hunt, 2010, 34.

Chapter 11

1. Ifill, Sherrilyn. *On the Courthouse Lawn: Confronting the Legacy of Lynching in the Twenty-First Century*. Boston: Boston Press, 2007.

2. Vaughn, George L., a report (letter) to Walter F. White of the NAACP, May 2, 1923. The original is in the Library of Congress; a reprint is in the *St. Louis Argus*, May 4, 1923.

3. Reported in Hunt, 2010, 53.

4. Quotation from Huber, 1991.

5. *Columbia Missourian*, May 3, 1923.

Chapter 12

1. "Lynchers Scare Columbia, Mo., Folk From Town," *Chicago Defender*, May 19, 1923, 3.

2. *Columbia Tribune*, Feb. 4, 1940.

3. Hunt, Douglas G., 2004.

Bibliography

This section is divided into three parts: "Books and Articles," "Archives of Governmental and Business Documents," and "Newspapers." Websites are usually not given in the bibliography, but are found instead in the *footnotes*. (A few exceptions are websites that provide the best description for a source.)

Books and Articles

Atherton, Lewis E. 1944. "Life, Labor and Society in Boone County, Missouri, 1834–1854, as Revealed in the Correspondence of an Immigrant Slave-Owning Family From North Carolina, Part 2." *Missouri Historical Review*, vol. 38: 408–429.

Barbeau, Arthur E., and Henri Florette. 1974, 1996. *The Unknown Soldiers: African-American Troops in World War I*. 2nd ed. New York: Da Capo.

Billington, Monroe Lee. 1994. *New Mexico's Buffalo Soldiers, 1866–1900*. Boulder: University Press of Colorado.

Blassingame, John W. 1964. "The Recruitment of Negro Troops in Missouri during the Civil War." *Missouri Historical Review*, 58 no.3, 326–337.

Braddan, William S. 2007. *Under Fire with the 370th Infantry (8th I.N.G.) A.E.F. "Lest You Forget": Memoirs of the World War*. San Diego: University of California, Internet Archive.

Bruce, Henry Clay. 1996. *The New Man: Twenty-Nine Years a Slave, Twenty-Nine Years a Free Man*. Lincoln: University of Nebraska.

Cabeza de Baca, Fabiola. 1994. *We Fed Them Cactus*. Albuquerque: University of New Mexico Press.

Chadbourn, James Harmon. 1933. *Lynching and the Law*. Chapel Hill: University of North Carolina Press.

Crighton, John C. 1987. *A History of Columbia and Boone County*. Columbia: Computer Color-Graphics, Inc.

Drake, St. Clair, and Horace R. Cayton. 1993. *Black Metropolis*. Reprint. Chicago: University of Chicago Press.

Du Bois, W.E.B. 1918. "Close Ranks." *The Crisis*, v. 16, July, p. 111. Online: https://www.marxists.org/history/usa/workers/civil-rights/crisis/0700-crisis-v16n03-w093.pdf.

_____. 1919. "An Essay Toward a History of the Black Man in the Great War." *The Crisis*. Vol. 18, no. 2, 63–87.

Early, Gerald (ed.). 1998. *Ain't But a Place: An Anthology of African American Writings About St. Louis*. St. Louis: Missouri Historical Society Press.

Ellis, Mark. 2001. *Race, War, and Surveillance: African Americans and the United States Government during World War I*. Bloomington: Indiana University Press.

Ellwood, Charles A., 1910. *Sociology and Modern Social Problems*. New York: American Book Company.

_____. 1925. "The Menace of Racial and Religious Intolerance." *NCSW Proceedings*, 1925. 18–26.

Elwang, William Wilson, 1904. *The Negroes of Columbia: A Concrete Study of the Race Problem*. Columbia: University of Missouri.

Greene, Lorenzo J., Gary R. Kremer, and Antonio F. Holland. 1993. *Missouri's Black Heritage*. Columbia: University of Missouri Press.

Grenz, Suzanna Maria. 1979. *The Black Community in Boone County, Missouri 1850–*

Bibliography

1900. Columbia: Diss. University of Missouri.

Grossman, James R. 1991. *Land of Hope: Chicago, Black Southerners, and the Great Migration*. Chicago: University of Chicago Press.

Hallas, James H. (editor). 2000. *Doughboy War: The American Expeditionary Force in World War I*. Boulder, CO: Lynne Rienner Publishers.

Hannah, Eleanor. 2007. "Soldiers Under the Skin: Diversity of Race, Ethnicity, and Class in the Illinois National Guard, 1879–1916." *American Nineteenth Century History*. Vol. 8, Issue 3. Oxford: Taylor and Francis, 293–323.

Harrison, Carter H. 1947. *With the American Red Cross in France, 1918–1919*. Chicago: Ralph Fletcher Seymour.

Haynes, Robert V. 1976. *A Night of Violence: The Houston Riot of 1917*. Baton Rouge: Louisiana State University Press.

Haywood, Harry. 1978. *Black Bolshevik: Autobiography of an Afro-American Communist*. Chicago: Liberator Press.

Howe, Barton Grover. May, 2003. "Legacy of a Lynching." *Missourian* (Columbia, MO). https://www.columbiamissourian.com/news/local/legacy-of-a-lynching/pdf_d011a4fa-8963-11e5-824c-ef3e5ef91961.html.

Huber, Patrick J. 1991. "The Lynching of James T. Scott: The Underside of a College Town." *Gateway Heritage* 12:1 (Summer).

Hunt, Douglas G. 2004. "A Course in Applied Lynching." *The Missouri Review*, Volume 27, Number 2 (Summer), 122–170.

_____. 2010. *Summary Justice: The Lynching of James Scott and the Trial of George Barkwell in Columbia, Missouri, 1923*.

Hurt, R. Douglas. 1992. *Agriculture and Slavery in Missouri's Little Dixie*. Columbia: University of Missouri.

Jindrich, Jason. 2002. "Our Black Children: The Evolution of Black Space in Columbia, Missouri." M.A. Thesis, Columbia, Missouri. Microfilm, University of Missouri Libraries.

Keene, Jennifer D. 2001. "French and American Racial Stereotypes During the First World War." *National Stereotypes in Perspective: Frenchmen in America: Americans in France*. Ed. William Chew. Amsterdam: Rodopi Press, 261–281.

_____. 2002. "A Comparative Study of White and Black American Soldiers During the First World War." *Annales de Demographie Historique*, 71–90.

James, P.D. 2009. *Talking About Detective Fiction*. New York: Knopf.

Kornweibel, Theodore, Jr. 2002. *Investigate Everything: Federal Efforts to Ensure Black Loyalty During World War I*. Bloomington: Indiana University Press.

Larson, August F. 1919. *A Housing Survey of Columbia, Missouri*. Columbia: University of Missouri.

Leach, Jack Franklin. 1952. *Conscription in the United States: Historical Background*. Rutland, VT: C.E. Tuttle Pub. Co.

Mason, Monroe, and F. Arthur. 1920. *The American Negro Soldier with the Red Hand of France*. Boston: Cornhill Company.

McCord, Charles Harvey. 1906. *Negro Criminality*. Master's Thesis, Columbia: University of Missouri.

_____. 1914. *The American Negro as Dependent, Defective and Delinquent*. Nashville, TN: Benson Printing Company.

McGettigan, James W., Jr. 1978. "Boone County Slaves: Sales, Estate Divisions and Families, 1820–1865." *Missouri Historical Review*. Volume 72, Numbers 2 (January) and 3 (April).

McWhirter, Cameron. 2011. *Red Summer: The Summer of 1919 and the Awakening of Black America*. New York: Henry Holt.

Merritt, Carole. 2008. *Something So Horrible: The Springfield Race Riot of 1908*. https://www.illinois.gov/alplm/museum/learning/documents/race_riot_catalog_2008.pdf.

Meyer, Duane G. 1982. *The Heritage of Missouri, Third Edition*. Springfield: Emden Press.

Michaeli, Ethan. 2016. *The Defender: How the Legendary Black Newspaper Changed America*. New York: Houghton Mifflin Harcourt.

Münsterberg, Hugo. 1908, 1917. *On the Witness Stand: Essays on Psychology and Crime*. New York: Doubleday, Page.

Perigo, Lynne. 1982. *Gateway to Glorieta: A History of Las Vegas, New Mexico*. Boulder, CO: Pruett Publishing Company.

Rampersad, Arnold. 1983. "Biography, Autobiography and Afro-American Culture." *The Yale Review*, vol. 73, 1–16.

Richardson, Barbara J. 1976. *Black Directory of New Mexico: Black Pioneers of New Mexico, a Documentary and Pictorial History.* Rio Rancho, New Mexico: Panorama Press.

Roberts, Frank E., 2004. *The American Foreign Legion: Black Soldiers of the 93d in World War I.* Annapolis, MD: Naval Institute Press.

Rollins, James Sidney. *Letters, 1870–1885.* State Historical Society of Missouri, roll 1. http://shsmo.org/manuscripts/columbia/c3014.

Sandburg, Carl. 1919. *The Chicago Race Riots.* New York: Harcourt, Brace, and Howe.

Scott, Emmett J. 1919, 1969. *Scott's Official History of the American Negro in the World War.* Chicago: Homewood Press; New York: Arno Press.

———. 1919. "Letters of Negro Migrants of 1916–1918," *Journal of Negro History.* 4, 290–340.

Senechal de la Roche, Roberta. 2008. *In Lincoln's Shadow: The 1908 Race Riot in Springfield, Illinois.* Carbondale: Southern Illinois University Press.

Spear, Allan H., 1967. *Black Chicago: The Making of a Negro Ghetto, 1890–1920.* Chicago: University of Chicago Press.

Stone, Jeffrey C. 2006. *Slavery, Southern Culture, and Education in Little Dixie, Missouri, 1820–1860.* Abingdon-on-Thames: Routledge.

Suggs, Henry Lewis. 1996. *The Black Press in the Middle West, 1865–1985.* Westport, CT: Greenwood Press.

Sullivan, Patricia. 2009. *Lift Every Voice: The NAACP and the Making of the Civil Rights Movement.* New York: New Press.

Sweeney, William Allison. 1919. *History of the American Negro in the Great World War; His Splendid Record in the Battle Zones of Europe, Including a Resume of His Past Services to His Country in the Wars of the Revolution, of 1812, the War of the Rebellion, the Indian Wars on the Frontier, the Spanish-American War, and the Late Imbroglio with Mexico.* Chicago: Cuneo-Henneberry.

Switzler, William F. 1882, 2009. *History of Boone County Missouri Written and Compiled from the Most Authentic Official and Private Sources.* St. Louis: Western Historical Company.

Tuttle, William M. 1970. *Chicago in the Red Summer of 1919.* New York: Atheneum.

Weaver, John D. 1970, 1992. *The Brownsville Raid.* New York: Norton.

Wells-Barnett, Ida B., 1892. *Southern Horrors: Lynch Law in All Its Phases.* Release date as EBook #14975, February 8, 2005.

———. 1893, 1999. *The Reason Why the Colored American Is Not in the World's Columbian Exposition.* Reprint of 1893 pamphlet. Champaign: University of Illinois Press.

Williams, Albert E. 1999. *Black Warriors: A Chronicle of African Americans in the Military.* West Conshohocken, PA: Infinity Publishing, 45. Reprinted.

Williams, Charles H. 1923, 1970. *Negro Soldiers in World War I: The Human Side.* New York: AMS Press.

Williams, Henry S. 1920. "The Development of the Negro Public School System in Missouri," *The Journal of Negro History.* vol. 5.

Withers, Zachary (ed.). *Heroes of 1918: Stories from the Lips of Black Fighters, Dedicated to the Brave Whose Lives Have Made Our Flag Immortal.* (Chicago?: 1919?)

Wood, Junius B. 1916. *The Negro in Chicago: How He and His Race Kindred Came to Dwell in Great Numbers in a Northern City; How He Lives and Works; His Successes and Failures; His Political Outlook.* Chicago: Chicago Daily News, Dec. 11–16.

Wright, Marie T. 1993. "Augusta Stevenson and the Bobbs-Merrill Childhood of Famous Americans Biographies," *Indiana Libraries*, Volume 12, Number 1, 11–21.

Wright, Richard and Edwin Rosskam. 1941, 2002. *12 Million Black Voices.* New York: Viking.

Archives of Govermental and Business Documents

Boone County Missouri Marriage, Book 1, 119.

Chicago Commission on Race Relations. 1922, 1968. *The Negro in Chicago; a Study of Race Relations and a Race Riot in 1919.* Chicago: University of Chicago press; reprint: New York: Arno Press.

Bibliography

"Lewis & Clark County, Montana Biographies." *MTGenWeb Project*. November 2006. http://www.rootsweb.ancestry.com/~mtlewisa/BioB.htm.

The National Personnel Records Center, Military Personnel. https://www.archives.gov/st-louis/military-personnel.

The New Constitution of the State of Missouri: As Revised, Amended, and Adopted in Convention, Begun and Held in the City of St. Louis, on the Sixth Day of January, Eighteen Hundred and Sixty-Five; and Ratified; by the People, at an Election Held on the 6th Day of June, 1865, 5. https://archive.org/details/newconstitutiono00miss.

Report of the Public Schools of the State of Missouri, 1890 (Volume 40). Tribune Printing Company.

Santa Fe Route. 1885. Chicago: Poule Brothers Printers. http://railroads.unl.edu/documents/view_document.php?Scope%5B0%5D=national&sort=rend&order=asc&per_page=20&page=29&id=rail.ATS_06_1885.001.

"United States Census, 1860, Gilbert Robinson, 1860." *FamilySearch*. July 2011 https://familysearch.org/ark:/61903/1:1:MHCB-3PC.

Newspapers

Appeal, St. Paul, Minnesota, 1885–1923.
Argus, St. Louis, 1835–41.
Chicago Defender, 1905-present.
Chicago Tribune, 1898-present.
Columbia Missouri Statesman. Published from 1860–1874 in Columbia by William Switzler, but from 1874 to 1913 it was sometimes called *Missouri Statesman* or *Columbia Statesman*.
(Columbia) Missourian, 1908-present (variously called *University Missourian, Daily Missourian, Evening Missourian*, or *Columbia Evening Missourian*).
Columbia Daily Tribune, 1904-present.
Columbia Herald-Statesman, 1913–1917, 1924–1938.
East St. Louis Mail, 1914–19??.
Kansas City Star, 1885-present.
Mexico Ledger, Mexico, MO, 1855–1956.
Missouri Intelligencer, May 4, 1830–Dec 12, 1835.
New York Globe, 1904–1923.
The Professional World, Columbia, MO, 1901–192?
St. Louis Globe-Democrat, 1852–1986
St. Louis Post-Dispatch, 1878–present.

Index

Abbott, Robert S. 67, 71, 103–106, 184
Akers (aka Robinson), Gilbert (maternal great-grandfather of James T. Scott) 26, 39–40, 44–45, 47, 49, 51, 92, 182*ch*2*n*15
Almstedt, Hermann B. 4, 73, 146–7, 155, 157, 178
Almstedt, Regina (aunt of Patricia Roberts) 4–6, 8, 21, 60, 93, 144–148, 158, 161, 165, 169–170, 178, 180–181
American Expeditionary Forces (AEF) *see* 8th Infantry of the Illinois National Guard
The American Negro as a Defendant, Defective, and Delinquent 83
The Argus 96, 170, 181, 184, 186, 190
Armistice 114, 124, 127–128

Baptist Female College *see* Stephens College
Barkwell, George 154, 162–170, 177–178, 184, 188; trial 152–156, 162–168
Bell, Montgomery, 17
Black employment 55–57, 60–61, 65, 67–69, 135, 176
Black newspapers 67–68; *see also The Chicago Defender*; *The Professional World*
Black soldiers 98–100
Boone County, 32–35, 47–48, 51–52, 76, 80, 87, 137–138, 149–151, 162–164, 167, 172, 182*ch*2*n*3, 183*ch*2*n*16, 183*ch*2*n*19, 183*ch*3*n*13, 183*ch*4*n*16, 186*ch*10*n*5
Bradden, Cap. William S. 110–113, 122–125, 184, 185*ch*7*n*22, 185*ch*7*n*23, 185*ch*7*n*25; 185*ch*8*n*3
Brest, 115, 128
Brown, Fred (Sheriff) 152, 154–155, 160, 165, 167
Brown, Sarah *see* Scott, Sarah
Buckner, Maj. J.C. 97, 184*ch*7*n*5

Cabeza de Baca, Fabiola 17, 181*ch*1*n*7
Camp Logan 107, 110–111, 113
Carter, Gertrude *see* Scott, Gertrude
Caston, the Rev. Jonathan Lyle 140, 148, 152–153, 158, 169, 178
The Chicago Defender 61, 96, 104–108, 110, 131, 169–171, 183*ch*5*n*17, 184*n*18, 185*ch*9*n*1, 185*ch*9*n*5, 186*ch*12*n*1

The Chicago Race Riots 135–136, 185*ch*9*n*7
The Childhood of Famous Americans 6–7, 179, 181*intro.n*3
Christian Female College *see* Columbia College
Churches for African Americans in Chicago 62–64, 77–78, 110, 131, 184, 185*ch*7*n*22
The Civil War in Columbia, Missouri 29–44
"Close Ranks" 103, 105; *see also* Du Bois, W.E.B
colleges 72
Columbia: black churches and education of black people 40–49, 52, 63–64, 71, 77–79, 81–82, 84–85, 88, 92, 102, 135, 176, 181*ch*3*n*1; black employment and businessmen 28, 47–48, 75–77, 93; black housing, sanitary conditions, health, and amusements in Columbia 40, 49–52, 63, 79, 85–94, 135, 184*n*39; early history and 19th century lynchings 27–31, 149–152; segregated neighborhoods 91–94; *see also* Akers, Gilbert; Lang, John, Sr.
Columbia College 28
Columbia Missourian 3–5, 169–170, 172, 178, 181–184, 186
Crighton, John C. *see A History of Columbia and Boone County*

Defender *see Chicago Defender*
Dennison (Denison), Col. Franklin A. 68, 100, 112, 122–123, 131
Du Bois, W.E.B. 8, 9, 95, 179, 185*ch*8*n*2, 185*ch*8*n*12; *see also* "Close Ranks"
Duncan, Col. 126, 131
Dyer anti-lynching bill 136–137

8th Infantry of the Illinois National Guard (earlier called 9th Infantry; aka 370th regiment of the 93rd Division of the American Expeditionary Forces) 96–98, 100, 102, 106–110, 112–113, 115–119, 121–129, 131–132, 136, 184*ch*7*n*22; Black commissioned officers 97, 99–100, 106, 111–112, 114, 118, 123–124, 128–129, 131, 141, 164–165, 179; French command 116–117

191

Index

Ellwood, Charles 73–75, 81–83, 88–89, 159, 183*ch*6*n*2, 183*ch*6*n*3
Elwang, William Wilson 9, 75–82, 85, 89, 94, 159, 183*ch*6*n*5–28
Espionage Act 103–105
eyewitness accounts 147–148

Fisk, Gen. Clinton 41–42, 72, 85
Frederick Douglass School 46, 84, 88, 140
French attitudes toward Black soldiers 117–119, 129

Garvey, Marcus 102, 106, 184*ch*7*n*12
Gas warfare 121
General Orders No. 4785 of General Vincendon 38, 124, 129
Grandvillars 115–116, 118–119
Great Depression 15, 176
Great Migration 54, 58, 61, 67, 183*ch*5*n*8
Guitar, Odon 33–34

Haywood, Harry, 110–113, 117, 119–120, 122–124, 185*ch*7*n*24, 185*ch*7*n*25, 185*ch*7*n*26, 185*ch*7*n*27; 185*ch*8*n*1, 185*ch*8*n*3, 185*ch*8*n*5, 185*ch*8*n*8, 185*ch*8*n*11
Henry, Sgt. Vida 111
History of Boone County Missouri 28–32, 149, 151, 181*ch*1*n*3, 186*ch*10*n*5
A History of Columbia and Boone County 40–41, 48, 50, 182*ch*2*n*16; 182*ch*3*n*6, 182*ch*3*n*7, 182*ch*3*n*10; 182*ch*4*n*1, 182*ch*4*n*2, 182*ch*4*n*12
Howe, Barton Grover 170, 181
Huber, Patrick 2, 108, 144, 177, 181*intro.n*2, 183*ch*6*n*4, 186*ch*10*n*2, 186*ch*11*n*4
Hulen, Ruby (prosecutor) 146–148, 154–155, 157, 159, 162, 164–170
Hunt, Douglas 2, 108–109, 144, 146, 165, 177–178, 184*ch*7*n*19, 186*ch*10*n*2, 186*ch*10*n*6, 186*ch*10*n*7; 186*ch*11*n*3; 186*ch*12*n*3

Ifill, Sherrilyn *see* lynching
Illinois National Guard 96, 106; *see also* 8th Infantry of the Illinois National Guard
Investigate Everything 103, 184*ch*7*n*15

Jailer of Columbia (Wilson Hall) 152–156, 163
James, P.D. 11
Jim Crow laws 55, 62, 112

Kansas-Nebraska Act 29–31
King, Pleas (Officer) 163, 165–166
King, Rasheeda 108–109, 178
Kornweibel, Theodore, Jr. *see Investigate Everything*

Lang, John, Jr. 47–48,
Lang, John, Sr. 27, 40–41, 45, 47, 51, 71, 92
Las Vegas, New Mexico 21–31

Linard, Colonel 118, 129, 184*ch*8*n*2
Logan, Rufus *see The Professional World*
Logny 127, 129
Loving, Maj. Walter H. 104–105
Loving vs. Virginia 140
lynching 145, 149, 160, 164, 186*ch*11*n*1

USS *Madawaska* (*Koenig Wilhelm II*) 113–115, 185*n*28
Mangin, Gen. Charles 124
McCord, Charles Harvey *see The American Negro as a Defendant, Defective, and Delinquent*
Merrill, Col. 35.
The Messenger 102, 184*n*13
Meuse-Argonne Offensive 124
Military Intelligence Branch (MIB) 103–105
Militia Act of 1862 37
miscegenation 139–140
Misselwitz, Francis 165–166, 170
Missouri Compromise 29–31
Missouri Statesman 23, 28–29, 32, 46, 48–49, 182*ch*3*n*1, 182*ch*4*n*8, 182*ch*4*n*9, 182*ch*4*n*14, 182*ch*4*n*15
Mont des Signes 108, 125
Monument for James Scott 108, 177

National Association for the Advancement of Colored People (NAACP) 95–99, 103, 105, 148, 155, 160–161, 168, 178, 186*ch*11*n*2; *see also* Vaughn, George
Nutter, Charles 157–158, 166, 168, 178

Owen, Chandler 102

Pershing, John J. (Black Jack) 117
Pontanezen Barracks 115, 128
Post Office of the U.S.A. 105–106
Price, Sterling, Sr. (Confederate general) 33, 35–37
The Professional World 56, 71–73, 86, 88, 183*ch*5*n*3, 183*ch*6*n*1
public transportation 58, 70

Race riots: Brownsville 100, 184*n*10; Chicago 58, 64, 132–136, 156, 183*ch*5*n*5, 183*ch*5*n*7, 185*ch*9*n*4, 185*ch*9*n*5, 185*ch*9*n*6, 185*ch*9*n*7, 184*n*8; East St. Louis 100–102, 104; Houston 111–113, 185*ch*7*n*26; Springfield 98–100, 184*n*8
racial equality (inequality) 6, 39, 44, 61, 71, 81–82, 86, 90, 98, 103, 106, 110, 118, 130–132, 135, 139, 173, 180
racism 4, 39, 71, 73–86, 90, 98, 100, 103–104, 112, 140, 179
Randolph, A. Philip 102
riot control 98–99, 101
Roberts, Col. T.A. 122–124, 126, 131, 153

Index

Rowland, Police Chief Ernest 145, 153, 167
Ruffin, the Rev. Clyde 2, 108, 177–178

St. Louis 4, 6, 13, 37, 45, 49–50, 56, 67, 72, 74–75, 82, 93, 109, 138–139, 148, 160, 165, 168, 170, 174, 181*intro.n*2, 181*ch*1*n*3, 182*ch*4*n*4, 184*n*2, 184*n*12, 186*ch*10*n*5, 186*ch*11*n*2
St. Louis Argus 96, 170, 181, 184*n*2, 186*ch*11*n*2
St. Louis Post Dispatch 139, 165, 170, 181*intro,n*2
Sandburg, Carl *see The Chicago Race Riots*
Sapp, David 108, 178, 182
Scott, Akers (brother of James T. Scott, Jr.) 12, 19, 56–57, 59, 61, 69. 78, 92, 141, 168–169, 172–175
Scott, Emmett J. 69, 105, 169, 183, 185*ch* 8 *n*3)
Scott (née Carter), Gertrude (3rd wife of James T. Scott, Jr.) 11, 140–141, 171–172
Scott (née Williams), Grace (1st wife of James T. Scott, Jr.) 59–60, 62, 65–67, 169, 175, 177
Scott, James T., Sr. (father of James T. Scott, Jr.) 11, 13, 15, 52, 138
Scott (née Smith), Lucille (2nd wife of James T. Scott, Jr.) 12, 62, 65–66, 135–136, 138, 141, 175–176
Scott (née Brown), Sarah (Sally; mother of James T. Scott, Jr.) 11, 13, 15, 18–19, 39, 51–52, 54–60, 66–69, 138, 168–169, 172–174; *see also* Akers, Gilbert
Second (Missionary) Baptist Church 2, 44, 48, 52, 77, 108–109, 140, 148, 177
Secret Information memo *see* Linard
Sedition Act 104
segregation 4, 6, 17, 38–39, 41, 43–44, 61, 64–65, 71, 81–82, 90–94, 98–99, 100, 103–104, 106, 110, 112–113, 117–118, 128–132, 135, 139, 155, 170, 184*n*37
Shelley vs. Kraemer 148
slavery 21–31, 39–46
Social Darwinism 73–86
Spingarn, Joel E. 95–96, 99, 103, 105
Stephens College 28–29, 93, 171
Stewart Bridge 156, 164
Switzler, William F. *see History of Boone County Missouri*

Thompson, Big Bill 131, 132, 134, 135
trench and gas warfare 119–121, 125–126

Universal Negro Improvement Association 102
University of Missouri 28, 73, 85, 90, 177, 184*ch*3*n*37, 184*ch*3*n*39

Vaughn, George 96, 148, 152–153, 155, 159, 161, 168, 178, 181*intro.n*2, 183*ch*6*n*4, 186*ch*10*n*2, 186*ch*10*n*4
Vincendon, Gen. *see* General Orders No. 4785

Washington, Booker T. 6, 8, 68–69, 71, 96, 135, 173, 179
Watson, Ollie 3, 145, 147, 149, 166, 169–170
Wells-Barnett, Ida B. 58, 67, 79, 95, 144, 183*ch*5*n*6, 185*ch*10*n*1
The Whip 68, 134, 185*ch*9*n*4
Wright, Marie T. *see The Childhood of Famous Americans*
Wright, Richard 7, 54, 182*ch*5*n*1

www.ingramcontent.com/pod-product-compliance
Ingram Content Group UK Ltd.
Pitfield, Milton Keynes, MK11 3LW, UK
UKHW042011140426
5217IPUK00015B/1108

9 781476 674926